Bible Study Textbook Series

The Social Institutions and Ideals of the Bible

A STUDY OF THE ELEMENTS OF HEBREW LIFE IN THEIR DEVELOPMENT FROM THE BEGINNINGS TO THE TIME OF CHRIST, AND OF THE SOCIAL TEACHINGS OF THE PROPHETS, OF THE SAGES, AND OF JESUS

BY

THEODORE GERALD SOARES, PH.D., D.D.

Head of the Department of Practical Theology, The University of Chicago

THE ABINGDON PRESS

NEW YORK CINCINNATI

TO
MY WIFE
COMPANION AND COLLABORATOR

CONTENTS

PUBLISHERS' ANNOUNCEMENT

For some time past there has been a growing conviction of the need of a more complete and comprehensive study of the Bible in all the colleges. Quite recently the matter has received new emphasis and practical direction. A complete course of Bible study has been outlined by a joint committee representing the Eastern and Western sections of the Association of College Instructors in the Bible, the departments of colleges and universities and of teacher training of the Religious Education Association, the Student Y. M. C. A. and Y. W. C. A., and Sunday School Council.

In harmony with the action just noted The Abingdon Press has arranged for the prompt publication of a series of Bible study texts. The complete course will include the following books: Old Testament History, by Prof. Ismar J. Peritz, of Syracuse University; New Testament History, by Dr. Harris Franklin Rall, President of Iliff School of Theology; The Bible as Literature, by Prof. Irving F. Wood and Prof. Elihu Grant, of Smith College; Social Institutions and Ideals of the Bible, by Prof. Theodore G. Soares, University of Chicago; and The History and Principles of Religious Education, by Prof. F. H. Swift, University of Minnesota.

The volumes on New Testament History and The Bible as Literature have been in use during the college year 1914-1915. Professor Peritz's volume on Old Testament History and Professor Soares' Social Institutions and Ideals of the Bible are now published. The last book in the series, The History and Principles of Religious Education by Professor Swift, is in preparation and will be ready for use in the second semester of 1915-1916. These books have been prepared with a view to the requirements of the college course and the needs of the students. The authors are acknowledged experts in their respective fields—scholars and teachers of wide repute. The publishers cordially commend this course to the attention of Bible students and teachers everywhere.

THE ABINGDON PRESS.

PREFACE

THE title of this volume is somewhat more extensive than the contents would strictly warrant. A full discussion of the institutions and ideals of the Bible should include those of the apostolic age, particularly the life and organization of the Christian community and the social teachings of the apostles. It is with no sense of the unimportance of these subjects that they have been omitted, but solely in order to meet the conditions of a suitable textbook for two semesters of college work. In the practical study of the subject one semester may well be devoted to a consideration of the development of social institutions in Israel up to the time of Christ, and a second semester to the social teachings of the prophets, of the sages, and of Jesus. The study of the apostolic age as a whole would naturally be a separate subject.

There is a decided advantage in devoting considerable time to the study of the actual social life of Israel. As a matter of fact, this is one of the best means of introducing the student to the study of human society, for in the fascinating biblical stories he has actually in his hands the original source material on the basis of which the social study must be made. He is able to secure a comprehension of the social process as he sees the development of the fundamental institutions of society passing before his eyes in the unfolding biblical narrative. Here is the opportunity to secure the social imagination and the social sympathy which are essential to any significant attempt to understand the problems of modern life.

Furthermore, the only way to appreciate the development of religion is to realize how it enters into the social life of a people and relates itself to their institutions. As one follows the process of the developing Hebrew life, he can see the unfolding of that religion which began as a tribal cult and reached its culmination in the experience of Jesus.

But the chief reason for the study of Hebrew society is that it affords the absolutely necessary background for an understanding of the prophets and of Jesus. The study of the social teachings of the Bible may easily be misleading. If we simply search the prophetic books and the Gospels for passages which have some connection with the various social problems of to-day we shall quite likely be led astray. There is no such thing as absolute social teaching. Morals are not static to be delivered by accredited teachers once and for all. Any social teaching involves adaptation to a specific social situation. The prophets can be understood only against the background of the actual living conditions of their time. We must have the patience to reconstruct that old life—a most fascinating and fruitful study—in order that the glowing words of those great tribunes of the people may yield their inspiration for our own tasks. And the teaching of Jesus especially requires for its comprehension an appreciation of the whole social development that preceded him, and a careful understanding of the various currents of thought in the complex times in which he lived.

The method employed in the presentation of the various social institutions involves a certain amount of repetition. We start again and again from the nomadic stage and work onward. We start very often from the exile and note the influence of that critical experience upon the various phases of Hebrew social life. But the very repetition may be advantageous, as it compels the student repeatedly to see that social institutions can be studied only genetically, and thus habituates him to seek always the history of any social problem with which he has to deal.

The endeavor has been made to send the student constantly to the sources. The text abounds in biblical references. These are not offered so much as authorities for the statements of the author, as guides to the student to seek the actual source of information which he should interpret for himself. The first of the directions for study might well have been in every chapter: Look up all the references in the text and construct your conception on the basis of a careful examination of the source material. The "Directions for Study" themselves are additional suggestions to help the student first to an appreciation of the social process as it was in Israel and as it is to-day, then to an appreciation of the ideals that stirred the souls of prophets, of sages, and of Jesus in their situations, and finally to an evaluation of those ideals for our modern social life.

The principal books in English that deal with the various phases of the subject are noted in the Appendix. The chief emphasis would best be laid, however, on a thorough study of the biblical material itself. The use of the American Revised Version is strongly recommended.

THE AUTHOR.

The University of Chicago, Midsummer, 1915.

PART I

HEBREW SOCIAL INSTITUTIONS

CHAPTER I

THE EVOLUTION OF HEBREW SOCIAL INSTITUTIONS

When one undertakes the study of Hebrew social institutions, he is concerned with a development that stretches over more than a thousand years. From the period when we first have knowledge of the Hebrews as a nomad race on the borders of Palestine to the life of the Jews in the days of Christ there is a stretch of time about equal to that which separates the Anglo-Saxon conquest of Britain from the present day. We recognize a long development in social institutions from the primitive conditions of the pagan Angles and Saxons to those of the complex civilization of the twentieth century. If, for example, we should undertake to study the family in English and American life, it is evident that we should have to consider the many modifications which that institution has undergone through the centuries as a result of the changing conditions of society. A treatment of the subject in a static fashion would be wholly misleading. We must take the same point of view in the study of the social life of Israel.

In the case of the Hebrews there are certain very marked epochs in each of which there were peculiar influences operating. Some of the most original of the social institutions suffered significant changes in the progress of the national life. Some of them died out altogether. Some of the most important of them were either nonexistent or merely embryonic in the earlier stages of Hebrew culture, and only gradually attained the important place which they hold in the complete perspective of Hebrew history.

It is necessary, therefore, to consider the five great stages of the history and the major influences that were in control in each of them. Then the various social elements may be studied genetically as they developed in the historic process.

§ 1. Social Institutions of Primitive Israel

We know the Hebrews, first of all, as a group of loosely united clans of the Arabian desert. Their social institutions were determined by nomadism. They were dwellers in the rude tents of the Bedouin. Their organization was patriarchal, families naturally living together, recognizing the ties of kinship, and accepting the government of the Clan-Father. Their wealth was that which could be conveyed from oasis to oasis in the desert—flocks, herds, asses, camels, the furniture of tents, perhaps some gems and costly garments. They were fighters, and by the conquest of other tribes secured captives to be their servants. So a patriarchal form of slavery existed in which the children of the slaves were the hereditary property of the children of their masters. Social duties and obligations were simple in such primitive life. There were rights of property that must be observed. There were certain great needs, such as water and pasturage, concerning which a very definite sense of right came to exist. And there was a body of custom regulating marriage, child life, inheritance, and other personal relations.

The religion of the Hebrews in the nomadic stage was also very simple. There was the recognition of the tribal God, Jehovah, from whom protection and benefit were expected. There were certain animal sacrifices offered by the Clan-Father, and certain ceremonials to be observed at stated periods of the year and of human life. And there was a body of custom, consisting largely of taboos, which regulated the relation of the people with the Deity.

Of course in later times this desert stage of Israel's history was idealized. Many of the institutions of the more developed culture were supposed by subsequent generations to have existed in the desert days in the same form in which they were afterward known. We shall, therefore, gain a correct view of the evolution of Hebrew life and religion only if we carefully estimate the real attainment of this primitive epoch.

§ 2. Social Institutions Before the Exile

It was a great advance in the life of the Hebrews when they moved from the desert into Canaan. There they came into contact with a people further developed in civilization than themselves. They learned from the Canaanites more of the arts of war, for the older inhabitants were skilled warriors, trained in the school of the Egyptians. More important still, they learned the arts of the agricultural life, for the Canaanites had already developed the fertility of Canaan, and produced the grape, the fig, the olive, and the various grains. Moreover, Palestine was a land of cities, where permanent houses, some provision for the storage of water, and walls of defense made life more regular and secure. And as the trade routes between the East and West passed through Canaan there was opportunity for obtaining the produce of the most civilized lands. Into all this the nomad Hebrews came, and their social institutions developed into the higher agricultural stage. New obligations of property arose. The possession of the land involved problems of measurement, landmarks, trespass, inheritance, purchase and sale, simple forms of mortgage.

The patriarchal organization of society was modified by the closer neighborhood of different families involved in the residence for protection in walled cities. The principal wealth being in the land, those who were landless and yet freemen, together with the orphans, the widows, the debtors, formed a poor population for whom no clan leader was responsible. Problems of justice and of charity arose in connection with these.

With the advent of the kingship the social order developed into more coherence. The rule of the court brought its culture and its luxury. Taxation was regulated, the administration of justice was to some degree organized, and trade was developed. It would be too much to say that the Hebrews passed from the agricultural to the commercial stage, but under Solomon, Jehoshaphat, Omri, Ahab, and particularly under Jeroboam II and the later Judæan kings, there was considerable trade with Arabia and with the Syrian peoples.

The terrible wars to which the Hebrews were subject brought into prominence the military chieftain. It would seem that a military and court aristocracy replaced the old tribal leadership, and serious problems of wealth and social justice arose in consequence.

The religion of this period was determined partly by the presence of the numerous Canaanitish shrines at which the Hebrews worshiped Jehovah under the forms, often cruel and sensual, of the local Baals. This resulted in the development of a class of professional priests. With the building of the Solomonic temple a more elaborate cultus became possible, and this undoubtedly developed in the hands of the Jerusalem priesthood during the four hundred years that the temple stood. The great attempt made in the reign of Josiah to confine the sacrifices to the temple was a potent force in the evolution of Hebrew religious life.

But altogether the most significant religious influence of this period was that supreme product of the Hebrew genius, the line of men of profound religious experience and of passionate interest in social justice, who, against the religious formalism and the cynical selfishness of their times, preached the immortal sermons that we call prophecy.

§ 3. Social Institutions as Affected by the Exile

The social life of all later Judaism was profoundly modified by the extraordinary experience of the deportation of a considerable part of the ablest citizens from Jerusalem to Babylonia. If these exiles had simply disappeared from the Hebrew life, as was usual in such cases, they would have left their fellow countrymen impoverished, but that would have been all. But very many of the exiles retained the liveliest interest in the destiny of their people as inhabitants of the sacred land. They utterly refused to become a part of the Babylonian life. They set themselves to a preparation for the rehabilitation, improvement, and particularly for the religious reformation of their race. Even though there may not have been so general a return from the exile as the Jewish traditions would indicate, there was a very intimate relationship between the Jews of Babylon and those of Palestine, and the influence of the stronger Eastern element was very marked.

While the purpose of Nebuchadrezzar in deporting the Hebrews may have been partly that he might have an agricultural population to supply his own cities with food, it is certain from the numerous Jewish names that appear in the documents of the period that the Jews became apt pupils in the school of Babylonian commerce. There they received the impulse toward trading that was so important a factor in their later development.

But the most significant change produced by the exile arose from the fact that the people, being obliged to give up the performance of their ceremonies and customs, were constrained to preserve them for future generations in literary form. In the process of describing their ancient usages, they interpreted and rationalized them. The agricultural festivals were given a national and historical significance. The cultus of the temple, which had been observed by the initiated priesthood as a technique of worship, was now elaborated, reinterpreted, given a new theological significance. And the whole body of ancient law was codified and reorganized with reference to the establishment of a religious community in Palestine when the exiles should be able to return.

The legislation thus produced in Babylon was a theoretical legislation. There was no opportunity of putting it into immediate practice. It gathered an authority, not of successful experience, but of religious explanation and constant repetition. There is difficulty even now in determining how much of that legislation was ever actually operative in Palestine itself. Great care must be taken, therefore, in estimating the conditions of Jewish life solely on the basis of the exilic prescriptions.

Side by side with this elaboration of the law continued the free spontaneous voice of prophecy. Some of the profoundest views of the meaning of life uttered by the prophets were born of the strange conditions of the Babylonian exile.

§ 4. Social Institutions in the Theocratic Community

The organization of Jewish society after the exile was largely ecclesiastical. Independent national existence was impossible under the dominance of the Persian rule. The limits of the Jewish community were restricted to Jerusalem and its environs, a district about the size of an ordinary American county. The kingship had disappeared, the court and military aristocracy, always more important in the North than in the South, had likewise gone, the trading Jews remained in Babylon where their fortunes were much brighter; naturally, therefore, the priests were the organizers of rehabilitated Judaism.

It was not a large or generous life. There were petty questions of the ownership of the restricted land area that remained to them. There were burdens of taxation to their Persian masters. There were jealousies with their neighbors, particularly those to the north, and there was a thoroughgoing endeavor to realize an ecclesiastical ideal of social organization.

The important religious institutions that have been so

determinative of Jewish life developed in this period. The law acquired its authority. The synagogue became the center of the community interests. The scribe became the teacher. The Sabbath was recognized as the fundamental religious observance. The Jews began to be the separate people and to take the attitude toward the world which made their history so tragic.

This all-pervasive ecclesiasticism was not congenial to the prophetic spirit, and it is probable that very little prophecy may be dated in the Persian period. It is a great mistake, however, to assume that the religion of the Second Temple was all external and conventional. The triumphant refutation of such a view and a noble testimony to the possibility of profound religious experience in connection with elaborate and prescriptive ritual is afforded by the fact that very many of the psalms, those lyrics of the religious soul, were written at this time and adapted to the service of the temple choirs.

§ 5. The Social Life of the Hebrews in the Græco-Roman World

Alexander the Great changed the face of the Eastern world. The life of every nation that he touched must be dated anew from his day. And neither the obscurity nor the seclusion of the Jew exempted him from the universal influence of the Greek thought, culture, language, and life. Paganism presented itself to the Jewish youth with a beauty and persuasiveness, and with a summons to freedom and to fortune such as had never been before. It accorded little with the rigid requirements and prescriptions of the law, but the law was already felt by many to be a burden grievous to be borne.

It might have been that Israel would have been swept into the current of the pervasive Hellenism and have lost its distinctive place in the world, but there was a repulsion as well as an attraction in the new influence. The noblest spirits among the Jews were constrained to put an added emphasis upon all that had come down to them from their fathers. Hebrew religion found little help from the Greek, and it was religion that saved the Jew from extinction. Two forces were thus working to modify the social life of Israel. The pressure of Hellenism was molding it to its own model, and the strictness of the "Pious" was leading them to accentuate their separateness from the world.

The continuance of this antagonism through several centuries gave a peculiar intensity to Jewish life. And this became the more extreme as the antagonism became a struggle for existence against the Syrian tyrants, then an internal conflict under the secular rule of the later Maccabees, and then a bitter resentment against the iron domination of Rome. This was relieved only by the hope that the antagonism was to be resolved by the *tour de force* of the miraculous advent of the Messiah. Religion became largely the passionate expectancy of the ardent apocalyptic writings.

To this social situation Jesus came. He resolved the antagonism for himself in terms of a spiritual religion and a perfectly simple social program. His disciples followed him as far as they could understand him, and the Christian Church was the result.

CHAPTER II

THE DEVELOPMENT OF HEBREW SOCIAL LEGISLATION

§ 1. The Growth of Law

"The memory of man runneth not backward to the contrary"—so Blackstone, the great English jurist, explains the common law which is the basis of the administration of justice wherever the English language is known. It is the consensus of public opinion as to what is right. In this way law has grown up among all peoples. A primitive man is able to say only, "It is the custom."

Two examples of such custom, whose origin is lost in remote antiquity, and both of which found their place in Hebrew life, were blood revenge and the *lex talionis*. If a man were slain, it was felt that his kinsfolk had the right and duty to avenge his death. So fundamental was this right that public justice never supplanted private vengeance (2 Sam 3. 30), and the utmost that the law could do was to provide places of asylum for the unwitting man-slayer (Exod 21. 13). Blood revenge still exists among the Arab tribes to-day.

The *lex talionis*—eye for eye, tooth for tooth (Exod 21. 23ff.)—springs from an elemental sense of equity. At first the retaliation was effected by the injured party or by his friends, but with the development of social life some central authority undertook the responsibility. Thus also the amount of punishment would be more fairly assessed, as public sentiment took the place of private anger.

But while primitive people generally think of their customs as of great antiquity, in point of fact they are constantly undergoing modification under the stress of new conditions. The decision in any disputed matter would always be made in accordance with precedent, and with a general sense of fitness. But new situations might cause a marked change of attitude. With the acquisition of private property it would be necessary to safeguard it from theft. Manifestly, restitution would be the equitable requirement together with some added penalty (Exod 22. 1).

Precedent arose in simple societies much as it exists among ourselves. Cases of dispute would be referred to the chief or headman, or perhaps, inasmuch as justice was always intimately associated with religion, to the priest of the tribe. Decisions would be rendered in accordance with acknowledged customs (compare Exod 18. 13-27). The remembrance of such decisions would persist and become determinative of future decisions; thus a body of precedent would grow up which would have the force of law.

Still another element in the growth of law was the presence of great personalities who would see confusion in the body of precedents, and would see opportunities of reform and improvement in the customs of the people. Such men would codify the existing law, simplifying, modifying, expanding it, removing the abuses which inevitably develop in any institution, and would then rightly present this new code of laws as the ancient and acknowledged principles of justice of the nation. We are familiar with such developments in the codes of Draco, Solon, Lycurgus in Greece, of Justinian in Rome, and of Edward I in England. And, indeed, there is practically the same process in operation in the great Code Napoléon in modern times.

There can be no better approach to the study of Hebrew legislation than an appreciation of the significance of the Code of Hammurabi, which was discovered in 1901, four thousand years after its promulgation by the great Babylonian king. The student of Hebrew social institutions should become familiar with the general outlines of this code, which dates back far beyond Moses. A very good account, by C. F. Kent, with a consideration of parallels between the Babylonian and Mosaic legislation, was published in the Biblical World, March, 1903, and a full discussion will be found in Hastings's Dictionary, Extra Volume, pp. 584ff.

Three important characteristics of this code aid us in an understanding of the Hebrew law: (1) it is essentially the great common law of Babylon developed through many centuries, so that the people recognized it as their ancient law; (2) it is founded in religion, the laws are given by the gods; (3) it is the great king's attempt to bring the law up to the level of the best public sentiment. So the Hebrew codes were never entirely new legislation, but were always founded on the accepted practice of the past; they derived their highest sanction from Jehovah, who is supremely concerned with justice; they were always the work of commanding personalities from Moses to Ezra, who sought to advance the morality and religion of the people. Whatever is most significant and permanent in Hebrew legislation arises from the nature of the religious experience of those great men whose religion was ever deeply concerned with human justice and love—an experience which the church has fittingly termed *inspiration*.

§ 2. The Early Common Law of Israel

The earliest life of the Hebrews of which we have knowledge was of that simple kind in which custom was the social regulator. In the nomadic life agreements were necessary with regard to pasturage (Gen 13. 2-9); certain rights existed in wells (Gen 21. 25-30); the custom of the purchased wife which continued far into organized society was already developed (Gen. 24; 29. 13-20); slavery existed so that a man might have a great company of hereditary slaves (Gen 14. 14); and the right of the wife over her own slave girl, even though she had been given to the husband, was recognized (Gen 16. 6). The nomad must at last have a permanent resting place, so custom regulated the purchase of the sepulcher (Gen 23. 3-16).

If the Decalogue (Exod 20. 2-17) in its original simpler form (that is, without the expansions in the second, third, fourth, fifth, and tenth commandments) was proclaimed by Moses, we may see in it the summary of the great religious and moral obligations which were recognized in those early times. It must not be read from our modern point of view as if it included all righteousness. It is concerned simply with rights. One must not wrong God in his worship, his spirituality, his name, his day, his representatives; one must not wrong man in his possessions, his life, his wife, his goods, his honor, nor even desire to wrong him.

With the advancement to the agricultural stage the obligations of social justice developed. This gradually produced a body of social law which doubtless took its rise in the decisions of Moses and his representatives (Exod 18. 13-26), and finally acquired written form so that it was accessible to the E writer for inclusion in his narrative.

This code, which is generally known as the Book of the Covenant (Exod 20 to 23), is concerned with a simple society. The right of property in slaves held an important place, and while some provisions seem very harsh, as that a man may beat his slave *almost* to death (21. 20f.), it is an advance upon the time when the slave had no rights whatever. And in many respects the rights of the slave were carefully guarded, indicating an advance of humaneness. (See the discussion of slavery, Chapter IV.)

Other topics of the code are kidnaping of a free person, various kinds of assault, trespass, theft, carelessness, slander; and there are simple religious requirements, chiefly ritualistic.

Justice, especially for the poor and the alien (23. 6, 9), was vigorously required, and the common iniquity of bribery was sternly denounced (23. 8). Kindly provisions regulated the lending of money (22. 25-27) and conduct toward an enemy's property (23. 4f.).

§ 3. The Deuteronomic Legislation

Law is always progressive. It never remains stationary so long as the people is living a vigorous life. The appreciation of this fact in the history of the Hebrews is essential to an understanding of their social institutions. As new occasions arose, new laws were developed. Such for example was the law of booty, that the fighting men and the guards of the camp should share alike in the spoil (1 Sam 30. 21-25). When some one fell from the housetop of his neighbor it came to be felt that it was a man's duty to provide a battlement about the roof (Deut 22. 8). In the absence of title deeds to property, and when metes and bounds were indicated by heaps of stones, the removal of the landmark was an easy matter; it was therefore recognized as a criminal act of great gravity (Deut 19. 14).

The advancing humaneness of the people under the influence of their religious leaders resulted in modifications of the harsher customs of earlier days. Originally, when a man committed a crime his entire family was involved in the penalty (Josh 7. 24, 25). The time came, however, when this was felt to be unjust (Deut 24. 16). As commercial life developed the inevitable difficulties of unfortunate business arose. The sense of kindness, which was an important element in the Hebrew law, led to the custom of canceling the debts of the poor at the end of the seventh year (15. 1-3). These are a few of the examples of the advance of social custom during the period of the kings.

Thus the Book of the Covenant did not remain the fixed law of Israel. The elders and priests continued to render decisions on disputed matters, and a developed sense of right modified previous custom. From time to time brief written records of the precedents that had been established were made. But no great development of the Book of the

Covenant was prepared until the work of the great reformers of the seventh century.

In the period of reaction from the influence of the prophets, when Manasseh led the people in idolatry and evil life, the successors of Amos, Hosea, Isaiah, and Micah were unable to preach publicly in Jerusalem. They betook themselves, therefore, to writing, and in cooperation with certain earnest-minded priests undertook the preparation of a new codification of the law. This was to have the following characteristics: (1) it was to reiterate the provisions of the old law with new appeals to religious motives, and with earnest exhortations; (2) the modifications that had taken place in the old customs were to be definitely recognized, and the ideals of right and justice which the prophets had preached were to be put as far as possible in legislative enactment (Deut 16. 18-20; 24. 14, 15, 17); (3) kindness, benevolence, humanity were to be emphasized (14. 29; 15. 7-18; 23. 24, 25; 24. 6, 19-21); (4) a great religious reform was to be inaugurated in the abolition of the numerous local sanctuaries which had become centers of idolatry, superstition, and even of immorality, and Jerusalem was to become the only legal place of sacrifice (12. 2-14); (5) recognition was to be given to the elaboration of the sacrificial and festival system which had greatly developed since the institution of the temple and the adoption of the agricultural festivals.

This law book which was accepted and promulgated by king Josiah (2 Kings 22. 3-20) is the second great stratum of Hebrew legislation. It comprises the greater part of the book of Deuteronomy. It was so clearly and designedly a development of the ancient law of Israel that it was fittingly published in the name of Moses, the great lawgiver. (See Wood and Grant, The Bible as Literature, Chapter XV.)

§ 4. Later Development of the Written Law

While the headmen of the cities and villages were intrusted with the execution of justice, and the king was the supreme judge, the decision of numerous matters of conduct, including all questions of ceremonialism, such as cleanness and uncleanness, payment of vows, duties of sacrifice, were relegated to the priests. They formed a distinct guild and were in a position to develop a hereditary class of students of the law. Thus a very considerable body of Hebrew legislation was derived from the priests.

Two codes are especially noted as coming from this source. The first is known as the Holiness Code (Lev 17 to 26). It represents a somewhat further elaboration of legislation than Deuteronomy, with the great religious motive that the people are to be holy, that is, separated from all that is displeasing to God. It is in this code that the great statement of social relation occurs which Jesus made the second element in his summary of the law—"Thou shalt love thy neighbor as thyself" (Lev 19. 18).

As an example of the development of legislation in these codes may be noted the endeavor to meet the failures of previous legislation. It had been the ancient theory that a Hebrew unable to pay his debts was sold as a slave, but could be retained in servitude only six years. In the seventh year he was to be freed. This provision appears both in the Book of the Covenant (Exod 21. 2) and in Deuteronomy (15. 12). But in practice people found it convenient to keep their slaves, and the aggrieved man was powerless to protect himself (Jer 34. 6-16). In the face of this failure of a good law the Holiness Code made a provision that a man who was sold for debt should be treated as a hired servant, and that every fiftieth year should be a jubilee at which all Hebrew slaves should be freed (Lev 25. 35-41). There were other provisions for this great semicentennial period, but it is probable that it was altogether theoretical and was never carried out in practice.

The social legislation of the Holiness Code relates to

chastity (ch. 18), provision for the poor (19. 9f.), honesty and fair dealing (19. 11-13), justice in judgment (19. 15), freedom from malice (19. 17f.), respect for elders (19. 32), justice to foreigners (19. 33f.), fairness in trade (19. 35f.). The major part of the Holiness Code, however, is concerned with the ceremonial law.

The other and great code of the priests was fully developed in the Babylonian exile. Deprived of the temple and removed from their functions, the priests naturally sought to preserve for the future the elaborate technique, which it had been unnecessary to commit to writing so long as every priest learned it in his apprenticeship. Moreover, the far-seeing members of the Jerusalem priesthood who were living in Babylon looked forward to the reestablishment of the Hebrew life in Palestine, and wished that it should be safeguarded by a ritualistic system which would give a quality of holiness to all its details. On the basis, therefore, of the old temple technique there was developed a great body of ceremonial enactment, which is now contained in Exodus, chs. 24 to 31, Leviticus, and Numbers.

§ 5. The Oral Law

The process of bringing together the various strata of the law codes, editing and harmonizing them, was carried on in Babylon, and was practically in the complete form of our present Pentateuch by the time of Nehemiah and Ezra. The law of Moses, properly so called because it was all ultimately derived from that great beginning, was presented to the people of Jerusalem in 444 B. C. (Neh 8. 1), and from that time was the settled direction of Jewish life. The Book of the Law was canonized and regarded with a peculiar sanctity as the divine constitution of Judaism.

But even a law thus sacredly canonized could not remain stationary. To be sure, no addition was ever made to it from that day forward, nor ever could be. But there was necessity to apply its provisions to new situations, and to interpret them as occasion might require. Just as most of our modern law is made, not by the legislatures which enact laws, but by the courts which construe them, giving rise to that mass of precedent which the lawyers call "case law," so the decisions of the Jewish courts and the opinions of the great students of the law resulted in a great body of interpretations that not only extended the old law but practically replaced it.

A new class of professional teachers arose, the scribes, whose special duty was the study and interpretation of the law. The great scribes formed schools and delivered to their disciples opinions which were treasured and handed down as having peculiar authority. In process of time there came to be a mass of such revered opinion, significant either because of the name of the distinguished rabbi who had rendered it, or as representing the consensus of view of the learned for many generations. These interpretations were not committed to writing, but remained an oral tradition, and became known as "the tradition of the elders" (Mark 7. 3).

The scribes were more concerned with ceremonial matters on which they could exercise their ingenuity than with plain moral and social obligations—so much so that not infrequently great human duties were subordinated to pedantic theological considerations (Mark 7. 8-13). Thus it was that Jesus, with his clear and simple demand for social justice and love, came into constant clash with these men, who tithed mint and anise and cummin and neglected the weightier matters of the law, justice, and mercy, and faith (Matt 23. 23).

DIRECTIONS FOR STUDY

1. Read Exod 20 to 23, and note the principal subjects dealt with by these laws. Consider what stage of culture such legislation indicates.
2. Read 1 Sam 14. 24-45. Note the custom of the vow, and the instance of public sentiment abrogating an ancient custom.

3. Read Deut 17. 8-13, and consider what this implies as to the administration of justice.
4. Read Deut 17. 14-20. What was there in the conduct of the kings of Judah, especially of Solomon, which would give rise to these provisions?
5. Note the special ideals of the Holiness Code as indicated in Lev 18. 1-5; 20. 22-26.
6. Compare Lev 23 and 24 with Exod 23. 14-19. Note how greatly the interest in this ceremonial had developed.
7. Read Jer 34. 6-16. Why did the people retain their slaves beyond the six years allowed by law? Why did they suddenly liberate them? Why did they take them back in bondage again? What did Jeremiah say about the matter? What does this incident indicate regarding the enforcement of the law of release? How far would the provision in Lev 25. 39-41 have improved the condition of the debtor slave?
8. Glance hastily through Exod 24 to 31, Lev 1 to 16, and Num. What are the general subjects of these regulations? To what stage in the development of Hebrew life would they be most appropriate?

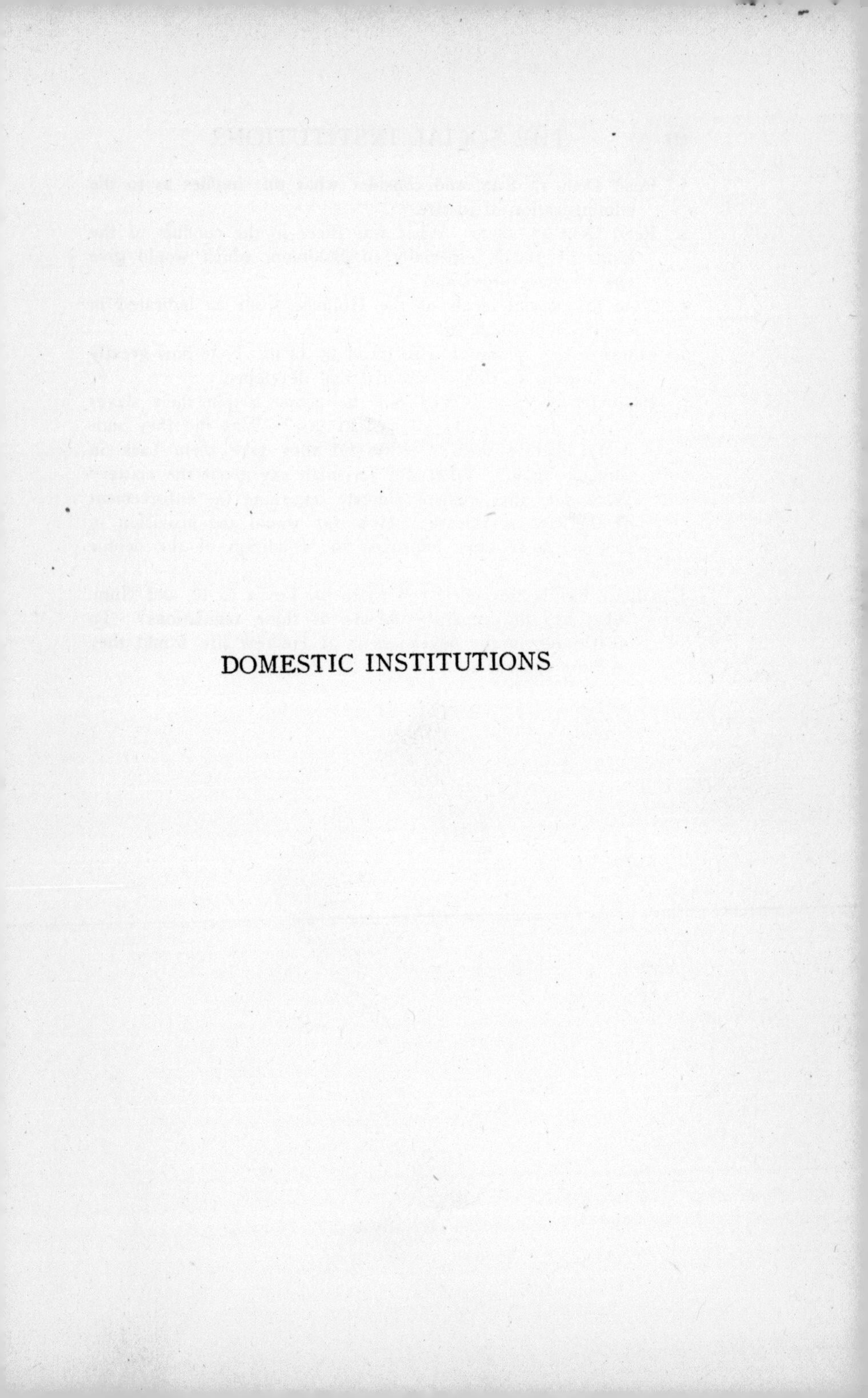

DOMESTIC INSTITUTIONS

CHAPTER III

THE FAMILY

THE gravest misconceptions have arisen from the idea that Moses enacted a great body of laws which were designed to constitute an ideal social organization. Such a fundamental institution as the family is not the product of any single piece of legislation, but of the operation of many social forces over a long period of time. Among the social forces are to be included personalities of great moral and religious power, and these were, of course, extraordinarily effective in Israel and in Christianity.

Anthropologists are not agreed as to the origin of the family and its earliest forms; but, while there are some indications in the Old Testament of an earlier stage of organization, the first family life of the Hebrews that is there presented has definitely reached the patriarchal form.

Naturally, the literature of a people is concerned with its prominent personages. We learn of the common folk and their life only incidentally. The Old Testament is no exception to this rule, and the histories there recorded are for the most part those of chieftains, kings, and nobles. This must be borne in mind in estimating the character of the family organization. To a degree what was true of the family of the great men was true also of that of the poorer classes, but, in the nature of the case, there must have been some marked differences.

§ 1. The Patriarchal Headship

As the name implies, the characteristic of the patriarchal stage in the development of the family was the importance of the Clan-Father. In order to understand this it is only necessary to remember that such a family, in the larger sense of the term, was not only the most important social unit but was practically the whole of social organization.

The protection of one's rights against enemies could be achieved only through the family when as yet there was no tribe or nation (compare Gen 14 and 34). And in like manner the only possibility of government was within the family group (Gen 37). The patriarchal family is evidently looked at in the light of a monarchical state. Some authority is necessary if society is to exist at all, and custom had naturally placed that authority in the hands of the father. If it seems strange for sightless old men like Isaac and Jacob to be exercising supreme rule over sons grown to middle life, we need only remember the reverence and obedience given in our own time to sovereigns whose great age has carried them far beyond the time of their best power.

The authority of the father, therefore, as of the later king in the state was practically supreme, limited by certain well-recognized customs, and exercised always in the case of good men with moderation and kindness. When the social organization grew more complex and many kindred families lived together as tribes, and later still when the state was developed, some of the rights of the father passed over to the elders and the king. But still government was exercised largely within the family, and patriarchal headship continued.

The position of the wife in such a family was naturally entirely subordinate. She was purchased by the husband with money (Gen 34. 12; Ruth 4. 10); she became his property (Exod 20. 17), and his rights over her were those which he had over a slave. Of course this was modified by the husband's love, the woman's influence, the respect and fear for her family, sometimes by the marriage contract (Gen 31. 50), and gradually by certain limiting customs which came to be embodied in law. But even in the early days of Christianity Paul, while exhorting the husbands to love their wives, felt the obligation to command wives to be in subjection to their husbands (Eph 5. 22-24; Col 3. 18). It is to be noted that he told the husbands to manifest their headship of the family as Christ manifested his headship of the church by supreme sacrifice. Little question of superior rights could arise on such a basis.

The power of the father over his children extended even to life and death. Thus Abraham could offer Isaac as a sacrifice (Gen 22), Jephthah was free to fulfill his awful vow (Judg 11. 29-40), and even in the times of the kings fathers actually sacrificed their children to Molech (Lev 18. 21; 20. 2-5; 2 Kings 23. 10; Jer 32. 35). However, while the child that struck or cursed father or mother was to be put to death (Exod 21. 15, 17; Lev 20. 9), it would seem that the punishment was to be inflicted by the community after due evidence had been given before the elders. This was specifically required by Deuteronomy (21. 18-21) in the case of the stubborn or rebellious son, the glutton, and the drunkard. Such a requirement was high exaltation of the parental dignity (it is to be noted that the mother is included with the father), yet was at the same time a limitation of the paternal authority in the execution of the punishment.

The rights of the father over his children extended to selling them as slaves (Exod 21. 7), though this seems to have been done only in the case of severe poverty (Neh 5. 5)). But a phase of this authority which was universally exercised was the sale of daughters in marriage. This was no fiction of law. A man's children were his wealth (Psa 127. 4). His sons remained with him and built up his house. His daughters, whose labor in the household was valuable, were lost to him when they became married and thus entered other families, for the woman left her father's house and entered that of her father-in-law.[1] The father,

[1] Such cases as Jacob and Moses, where the husband entered the family of his father-in-law, were exceptional on account of these men being fugitives.

therefore, was indemnified for his loss by the payment of money. The value of a girl depended upon the dignity of the father, and upon her own beauty, while the matter was arranged as a bargain with which she had very little to do (Gen 24. 50, 51; 29. 18-20; 1 Sam 17. 25. It is worthy of note that all of these were love marriages nevertheless). The dowry, which in our time has come to be a marriage portion provided by the father, was in Israel a price paid by the husband or by his family for the bride (Gen 34. 12; 1 Sam 18. 25).

How definite this attitude was is evident from the fact that a man guilty of wrongdoing toward a maiden was considered to have injured her father, and was required to pay to him the amount of the dowry whether he married the girl or not (Exod 22. 16, 17).

§ 2. Polygamy

While there is a very marked tendency throughout the Old Testament narratives in the direction of monogamy, the custom of the Hebrews, and the law in all its codes, definitely sanctioned polygamy. There was no limit set to the number of wives that a man might acquire by the regular procedure of purchase in marriage, or by purchase of slaves, or by capture in war. There was a distinction between the regular married wives and those of subordinate rank, who were generally slaves. No reproach attached to a man, however, for the possession of concubines, nor to the women themselves, who occupied a recognized position in the patriarchal household. The children of such unions were legitimate and might share in the inheritance with the children of the wedded wives.

The original privilege of a man to acquire as many wives as he pleased and to treat them as his property was, however, definitely modified in the various legislative codes. The slave girl who became one of the lesser wives of her master could not thereafter be sold. She might be redeemed by her kinsfolk. If she had been espoused to the son of her master she was to be treated as one of his own daughters (Exod 21. 7-9). In the Deuteronomic Code (21. 10ff.) the same privilege was accorded the maiden captured in war (compare 20. 14), who became one of the lesser wives of her captor. She could not thereafter be sold as a common slave. Moreover, the rude passions of war were mitigated by the provision that the woman should be allowed a month after being torn from her own people before her master could espouse her. A further provision for the slave wives was that they could not even be neglected. If the master took an additional slave wife, he must either continue the first in the position and privileges of wifehood or allow her to go free; she could not be sold (Exod 21. 10f.).

Naturally, polygamy was too expensive to be common among the people generally, and the relative equality in the number of the sexes would make it impossible. The slaughter of the men and capture of the women in warfare doubtless provided a large number of female slaves. Among the middle classes bigamy was probably the most usual form of the practice, and that would often result from a man's dissatisfaction with his first wife. Thus the two wives, the one loved and the other hated, must often have caused domestic tragedy in Israel. So we have Leah and Rachel (Gen 29. 30), Hannah and Peninnah (1 Sam 1. 1-6). In all polygamous households the different mothers plot and scheme for their own children and the inheritance is often secured by the favorite for her sons. But the Deuteronomic law made special provision that where there were two wives, the one loved and the other hated, the law of primogeniture should rigorously obtain (21. 15-17). A particularly offensive form of polygamy, the marriage of two sisters, as in the case of Jacob, was forbidden in the later law (Lev 18. 18). Of course this had nothing to do with the marriage of a deceased wife's sister, which has often even in modern times been a most gracious arrangement for the care of the dead sister's children.

While polygamy was thus recognized by law and practiced by the noble characters in Israel, there was a marked tendency among religious leaders toward monogamy. This is seen in the story of Adam (Gen 2. 18-25), in the examples of Noah, Isaac, Joseph, Moses, the high priest (Lev 21. 14), Job, and, so far as we know, of the prophets. It is seen also in the apology for Abraham on account of the childlessness of Sarah (Gen 16. 2), and of Jacob on account of the deception of Laban (Gen 29. 21-30), also in the disapproval of the harem of the king (Deut 17. 17). Polygamy was not absolutely forbidden in the Christian Church, but was incompatible with the spirit of Christianity and soon entirely ceased.

§ 3. Divorce

There is no more vital question with regard to the family than that of its possible dissolution by causes other than death. Naturally, if the woman is the property of her husband, he may send her away as he would dismiss a slave. This was actually done by Abraham (Gen 21. 14), and must have been done very often with less reason than that which actuated the patriarch.

The Deuteronomic law endeavored to mitigate the evil of divorce. In the case of a woman who had been wronged and subsequently married, she could not be put away (22. 13, 19, 28, 29). And it was not expected that a man should exercise his rights of divorce unless some unseemly thing were found in the wife. In this case it was provided that he should give her "a bill of divorcement" as an indication that she was free to contract another marriage (24. 1, 2). The limitation was so vaguely expressed that it cannot be regarded as statutory, but must be considered, rather, as a prophetic injunction to husbands to realize that only conduct unbecoming a wife could justify divorce. It still remained for the husband to decide the matter as he pleased. But in later Judaism, when the endeavor was made to enforce every detail of the law, this became a subject of grave dispute, and most diverse interpretations of the requirement were made.

It is clear that divorce was increasingly common after the exile and particularly called for the denunciation of Malachi. It was declared that Jehovah hated "putting away" and treacherous dealing with the wife of one's youth (2. 13-16).

It must be noted that the supreme crime which is the breaking of marriage did not enter into the question of divorce in Old Testament times. A woman guilty of unfaithfulness was not divorced but was put to death (Deut 22. 22; Lev 20. 10). A man guilty of unchastity was regarded as criminal only in so far as he invaded the rights of another man. His conduct could not constitute grounds for the woman to secure a divorce, for, in the nature of the case, the woman could not under any circumstances divorce her husband. This practice only came in with the Græco-Roman customs of the later times.

§ 4. Family Ideals

The provisions of law are generally directed against the harsher phases of life. But much higher conduct than can be required by statute may often be secured by a summons to ideals.

In spite of the subordinate legal position of a woman, the place of a mother was very high in Israel (Psa 45. 16f.). Her name is always given in connection with the accession of her son as king. The mother stands with the father as the recipient of the pious honor of her children (Exod 20. 12; Lev 19. 3; Deut 5. 16). The proverbial advice indicates the importance of the mother's teaching (Prov 1. 8; 6. 20; 23. 22; 31. 1), and the description of the worthy woman (Prov 31. 10ff.) shows her influence in the household and the community. The gracious influence of Mary of Nazareth is clearly written in the gospel story, and we know that the Jews down to the present day have given beautiful honor to the mother of the family.

There were bonds of love uniting the members of the Hebrew family, which appears among much that is sordid in the patriarchal history, and in much that is unwise in David's conduct toward his children. This element of affection is particularly clear in the beautiful story of Ruth and Naomi, and is wonderfully revealed in the devotion of Hosea to his unfaithful wife. This is evident also from the use which the prophets and the psalmists make of family relations to symbolize the relations of Jehovah with his people (Psa 68. 5; 103. 13; Isa 49. 15; 54. 5-7; Jer 3. 14; 19-22; 31. 32; Hos 2. 19, 20; Mal 2. 10). And Jesus must have had a noble experience of the paternal regard of Joseph as a basis of his selection of the name of father as his supreme expression for God.

Family religion in Israel and the home as an educational institution may be considered in connection with the general subject of education.

DIRECTIONS FOR STUDY

1. What reasons existed for the supreme authority of the father in ancient times which do not have force to-day?
2. What are some of the limitations which modern law places upon paternal authority, and what is their justification?
3. Compare the practice of the marriage of daughters in Israel with that existing to-day in China and Japan, and until recently in European countries. In a wisely organized society what responsibility should rest with parents in controlling the marriage of their children?
4. Why would it be very difficult to limit the man's right of divorce in a patriarchal society? What evidence is there that the lawgivers and prophets sought to do so in the later social development of the Hebrews?
5. Read Gen 46. 5-27. Note the description of an ancient Israelitish family. How many names of sons are given? How many of daughters? What does this indicate as to the

comparative estimate in which they were held? How would you explain this? To what extent does the same idea hold in any modern society, and to what extent has it disappeared? How do you account for these facts?

6. Note the stories of Deborah (Judg 4 and 5), Ruth, Hannah (1 Sam 1 and 2), Abigail (1 Sam 25), "the great woman" of Shunem (2 Kings 4. 8-37), Esther, Judith, the Marys of the Gospels, Dorcas (Acts 9. 36ff.), Priscilla (Acts 18. 26). Consider what these imply as to the position of woman among the Hebrews.
7. What are the excellencies of the worthy woman? (Prov 31. 10-31.) What does this imply as to the estimate in which the wife was held?
8. In an ideal family how far does the question of authority arise? Where does authority properly reside?
9. What is involved in the equality of the sexes economically, morally, socially, politically? Have we reached a state of social organization in which this equality is possible?
10. What were the social values of the patriarchal organization of the family? Consider the subject from the standpoint of Hebrew life, using the historical imagination to put yourself into that social process.
11. What are the social values of the democratic organization of the family? Upon what conditions do they depend?
12. What are the dangers of a transition from the patriarchal organization of the family to the democratic organization? Consider how far such a change is taking place to-day in Japan, among the immigrants in America, and even among Americans themselves.

CHAPTER IV

SLAVERY AND HIRED SERVICE

§ 1. The Origin and Character of Ancient Slavery

Slavery has played a most important part in the development of civilization. Man has to learn very gradually the value of work. The modern self-discipline by which we keep ourselves to difficult tasks because we believe that the results will justify our efforts was slowly acquired by the race. And the value of work was learned first by making others work and entering into the result of their labors. Modern civilization is possible because men are willing to serve the community in various capacities in return for financial recompense. This represents a highly complex stage of culture. Ancient civilization had no such basis upon which to rest, and Egypt, Greece, Rome were possible because of the great slave populations that performed the mechanical tasks.

The origin of slavery was doubtless in the restraint of the barbarian to spare the life of his beaten enemy, and compel him to carry wood, draw water, and perform the disagreeable tasks of the camp. Ingenuity soon devised additional duties which could thus easily be performed, and a desire for additional captives who could be so employed was stimulated. Ancient warfare was often little more than robber raiding for the capture of the wealth of the stranger, and a considerable part of the booty was the strong young men and women who could be employed in the service of the conquerors. To our modern thought slavery is the most degrading position conceivable, degrading alike to the master and to the slave. Our high ideas of the rights of personality, of the dignity of the individual, give us this feeling, but in the ancient world men were not so thought of and did not so think of themselves. They were accustomed to submission to many authorities, and slavery seemed as natural to them as hired service seems to us. Doubtless many phases of our modern industrial system will seem utterly barbarous to our posterity.

Several considerations, therefore, should be borne in mind in the endeavor to enter with sympathy into a state of culture in which slavery was fostered: (1) In the case of the captive a grace had been extended to him. His life was forfeit, and it had been spared. The very picturesque account of the Gibeonites (Josh 9. 3ff.) indicates this attitude on the part of the conquered race. (2) Distinction must be made between two kinds of slavery. There was the bitter unrequited toil which the great kings and nobles exacted from their hordes of captives, where no personal relations between master and slave existed, and where the only purpose was to construct gigantic works regardless of the cost of human suffering. Thus the Pharaohs built pyramids and tombs, and the Assyrian kings their splendid palaces and temples. This type of slavery was not common in Israel, though it doubtless existed at various times (1 Kings 5. 13-17; 9. 15-23). The more common slavery was agricultural and domestic, where the servants as members of the patriarchal household carried on the duties of the house and farm, and were comfortably cared for and generally kindly treated. There were many free dependents attached to large families, who would share such labor, thus mitigating the difference between the slave and the free. Hebrew slaves for the most part were of this latter kind, and had come into their condition through poverty or debt. Their lot was the lot of the poor in any civilization. (3) The entire absence of a wage-earning class in the earlier times, and the comparative unimportance of that class until very much later times, made slave labor not only inevitable but natural. (4) Much of ancient life was organized on this basis. As we have noted, every woman was the property of somebody—father, or husband, or brother. Only a widow living in the house of her son could really be regarded as a free woman.

But, however inevitable slavery may have been, and however natural it may have seemed, it was always a condition in which there were great possibilities of hardship. We know from the Roman satirists how terrible slavery might be. And while we are glad to believe that their pictures did not represent Roman life in its general aspects, it is certain that where such tyrannies are possible they will often occur, and lesser tyrannies will be far from uncommon. In Israel's greatest poem, one of the benefits of Sheol, that shadowy land to which the dead go, is thought of as the freedom of the slave from his master (Job 3. 19).

The legislation of Israel made a very marked distinction between Hebrew slaves and foreigners. The former generally came into bondage through debt or poverty. And they were the subjects of increasing consideration in the various codes of law. The foreigners were naturally not so much regarded, although they were not without certain rights under the law.

§ 2. Alien Slaves

The Deuteronomic law definitely permits what must have been the long custom of Israel as of all other peoples, the enslavement of the captives of war (20. 10-14); and it is explicitly stated that this is a privilege which is not to be granted to the males who give trouble to the Hebrew army by refusing to surrender their cities.

These captives male and female became perpetual bond servants, and their children after them. There is no provision for redemption or release. The Levitical Code, which is peculiarly considerate to Hebrew servants, makes provision for a permanent traffic in alien slaves, whether of the surrounding peoples or of the foreigners within the Hebrew community (Lev 25. 44-46). Thus the Canaanitish population seems to have been reduced to bondage (Deut 29. 11; Judg 1. 28, 30, 33, 35). To these slaves, however, certain important privileges were accorded. They were included in the covenant of Israel by the rite of circumcision (Gen 17. 12); they were allowed to participate in the Passover (Exod 12. 44), and in all the festivals which were joyously celebrated by the Hebrew family (Deut 12. 12, 18; 16. 11-14). It was especially provided that they should have the Sabbath rest from toil (Exod 20. 10).

It is probable also that the provisions in the Covenant Code regarding the maltreatment of slaves apply to aliens as well as to Hebrews. The provision that a man may beat his male or female slave almost but not quite to death, the survival of a day or two being judged sufficient to exculpate him (Exod 21. 20f.), seems barbarous. But it is to be remembered that this was an advance upon the practice of unlimited rights of life or death over slaves. It is not to be understood as advocating severe punishments, but as limiting them. The further provision that mutilation by the destruction of the eye or the tooth should operate for the manumission of the slave (Exod 21. 26f.) is also an advance in the same direction. But at the best, legislation can never limit very much the control of a man over his absolute property. It was not through legislation, but through the growing humanity of the better men in Israel, that the slaves owed whatever comforts and kindness they enjoyed.

We have already noted the special provision which the Deuteronomic law humanely made in the case of the female captive whom the warrior desired to espouse. She was permitted a month of mourning as a transition from the home of her own people to the home of her master (21. 10ff.).

§ 3. Hebrew Slaves

If a Hebrew could not pay his debt in money, he was

expected to work it out in service either by himself or by his children. In theory this might not seem a very harsh requirement, but practically it meant slavery.

There does not seem to have been any gradation in the amount of service to be given in discharge of debt. But the earliest legislation contemplates a six-year period (Exod 21. 2). At the end of that time the bondman was to be released. This release did not, however, in the earlier time extend to female slaves (Exod 21. 7). They were generally sold to become the lesser wives of their masters, and their case was treated under the more permanent institution of marriage rather than under that of slavery.

If a male slave were married when he entered service, he was to take his wife with him at his release, but if he had married one of his master's slave women, he could not take her. She and her children belonged to the master (Exod 21. 3f.). Evidently, the union was not looked upon as very sacred, for, as far as the bare statements are concerned, it would seem that either party might form another union. But it might be that the conditions of service were kindly. The man was poor, and would give up home, food, clothing, and, moreover, he would give up wife and children whom he loved. Provision was therefore made that he might elect to become the permanent property of his master (Exod 21. 5f.). Many slaves must have taken advantage of this provision.

The Deuteronomic Code was much fairer than the earlier law, showing a greatly developed sense of justice. The man had served for six years, and when he went forth free he was to be started again in independent living. The master was to furnish him liberally (15. 12ff.). The same privileges were also extended to the woman (15. 17f.). Nothing is said about marriage, but it would follow that, at the worst, the wife could remain in bondage only a few years after the release of her husband, that is, until her six-year term expired. The family would not therefore be broken. There is some indefiniteness, however, at this point.

Provision for electing perpetual slavery because the slave loved his master and his house, and because it was well with him, was specifically repeated, indicating that the service was often a happy one in a good Hebrew household. The picture in the book of Ruth indicates that the lot of the family slaves might be envied by a poor foreigner (2. 4-13).

But significant as these provisions were, it is by no means certain that they were carried out. After six years a servant would become very useful, and it might not be convenient to let him go. In the time of Jeremiah (34. 8-16) it would seem that the law had become a dead letter. Probably the Deuteronomic reformers had tried to make the old law effective and more generous, but in the general social injustice which increasing luxury had brought the slave had no rights that could not easily be ignored.

The law of debt could be rigidly enforced, so that almost any poor man might be enslaved. After his death his children might be sold to meet his obligations (2 Kings 4. 1). Among the bitter denunciations of Amos was the charge that the poor were sold for their inability to pay for a pair of sandals (2. 6).[1]

Increasing taxes levied to meet the tributes that had to be paid to the Assyrian conquerors often caused the poor to sell their children. And Nehemiah found this same state of affairs when he entered on the governorship of Judah (Neh 5. 5).

The Levitical Code endeavored to meet these harsh conditions by the abolition of Hebrew slavery altogether. The seventh-year system had broken down, and the endeavor was made to substitute a fiftieth year, when all Hebrew slaves should become free at the same time (Lev 25. 39-46). It was stipulated that even though a Hebrew were in com-

[1] The regular price of a slave was thirty shekels of silver (Exod 21. 32), somewhat less than eighteen dollars; the purchasing power of money, however, was very much greater than in modern times.

pulsory service until the Jubilee it was not to be rigorous, but was to be of the nature of hired service. The people were exhorted to confine themselves to aliens for their slaves. However, this was rather hortatory than legislative. The language is susceptible of different meanings, and it is doubtful whether it had any marked effect on social conditions. It is practically certain that the Jubilee scheme never came into actual operation.

A further provision in the Levitical law for the benefit of the Hebrew slaves was concerned with the contingency of a Hebrew having come into bondage to a resident foreigner. In the postexilic period the foreigner was not necessarily so poor an individual as in the earlier history; he might, therefore, become the owner of a Hebrew debtor. In that case he must hold his slave subject to redemption by any Hebrew kinsman, and subject, of course, to the manumission at the Jubilee (Lev 25. 47-55).

One of the evils of slavery is the ease with which a man may be stolen and held in bondage. Such kidnaping of Hebrews was naturally regarded as a capital crime, and even in the earliest code was punishable by death (Exod 21. 16). The reaffirmation of the law in the Deuteronomic Code (24. 7) would indicate that the practice was not uncommon.

One very interesting, and at first sight peculiar mitigation of Hebrew slavery, was the provision that a fugitive slave was not to be returned to his master (Deut 23. 15f.). It seems to have been an extension of the rights of hospitality, and he probably became the slave of the man who received him.

§ 4. Hired Service

It was unusual for a free man to be unattached to some family in whose service he would naturally have a part. As we have noted the patriarchal family included "the poor relations," who were provided for out of the bounty of the chief. If for any reason a free man found himself without such family ties, he might offer his service for wages. Such was the case of Jacob, who worked for Laban, first in return for his wives (Gen 29. 15, 18-27) and afterward for wages (30. 28-30). There is also the interesting case of the young Levite who was engaged as priest or private chaplain by Micah, receiving an annual stipend of ten pieces of silver, a suit of clothes, and his board (Judg 17. 7-10).

Hired service was not sufficiently important to receive any mention in the Covenant Code. We may, therefore, conclude that there were very few wage-earners during the early period of the monarchy. As the great estates increased and the small landholder was unable to maintain himself, he may have sought opportunity to hire himself to a master. But as the hireling is generally coupled with the foreigner, and was specifically forbidden to eat of the Passover (Exod 12. 45), it is likely that most of this class were poor non-Israelites, who, being landless and having no attachment to any family, were glad to take what wages were given them in order to secure subsistence.

The lot of the hireling was a hard one. He was practically at the mercy of his employer, for he had little opportunity to appeal to the courts of justice. In both the Deuteronomic and Levitical Codes it was found necessary to require that the laborer should receive his wages at the end of the day (Deut 24. 15; Lev 19. 13). And the stern words of Jeremiah (22. 13) and of Malachi (3. 5) suggest that frequently he was cheated of his wretched pay. The Hebrew poet laments the condition of the working classes:

> They cut his provender in the field;
> And they glean the vintage of the wicked.
> They lie all night naked without clothing,
> And have no covering in the cold.
> They are wet with the showers of the mountains,
> And embrace the rock for want of a shelter.
>
> . . . .

> They go about naked without clothing,
> And being hungry they carry the sheaves.
> They make oil within the walls of these men;
> They tread their winepresses and suffer thirst.
> From out of the populous city men groan
> And the soul of the wounded crieth out (Job 24. 6-12).

There is no information as to the amount of a day's wage. In the time of Jesus a denarius (nineteen cents) was considered fair pay (Matt 20. 2ff.). It is difficult to know how much that represented in purchasing power, perhaps half a dollar in modern conditions, less than anything paid in America, but not less than the wage in some European countries. Thus treated, the hireling worked grudgingly (Job 7. 2). His labor was considered only half as good as that of a slave (Deut 15. 18), and little confidence was placed in his loyalty (John 10. 12f.). It is abundantly clear from all the history of the ancient world that slave and free labor cannot be satisfactorily maintained side by side.

DIRECTIONS FOR STUDY

1. Read the book of Genesis and note all references to servants (slaves), considering what these indicate as to their treatment.
2. Read the stories of Eliezer (Gen 24), Joseph (Gen 39), Samson (Judg 16. 18-21), Saul and his servant (1 Sam 9. 1-10), Naaman's slave (2 Kings 5. 1-4). Consider what these imply regarding the conditions of Hebrew slavery.
3. Note the references to slaves in the Gospels (Matt 8. 5-13; 18. 23-34; Luke 12. 42-48; 17. 7-9; 19. 11-26). What do these indicate about the conditions of the slaves in the time of Christ? Remember that Jesus is referring to common customs by way of illustration, but is passing no judgment upon them.
4. Compare the legislation regarding slaves in the three codes. What specific social advance does this indicate?
5. Compare the serfdom of feudal Europe with Hebrew slavery.
6. Compare the system of imprisonment for debt as it existed a century ago in England with the Hebrew custom of working out a debt in bondage.
7. Consider in what respects the life of a slave under the best

conditions in a godly Hebrew family might have been more comfortable than that of a wage-earner under modern industrial conditions. What does that suggest as to the various directions in which amelioration under modern conditions must proceed?

8. How far has all civilization from ancient times to the present been built upon compulsory labor, whether called slave or free, of those who perform its mechanical tasks? What would be involved in a civilization that was really democratic? Are we moving in that direction to-day?
9. Compare the evolution of the family with the evolution of industry. Note that both were originally autocratic in organization. Which has proceeded furthest toward democratization?
10. If slavery is wrong, why did not the Hebrew law forbid it altogether? Consider all that is involved in your answer regarding the evolution of morality and religion.

CHAPTER V

EDUCATION

Education is technically the conscious effort of the mature mind to help the immature toward the appreciation of the experiences which the race has gained. Education may be thought of as a result as well as a process, in which case it is simply the enrichment of experience. We are so accustomed to think of education in intellectualistic terms and as mediated through books that we narrow its meaning to the exercises of the schoolroom. But the varied experiences of our social life are always potent educators. Therefore in considering the subject of Hebrew education we must recognize that while the school probably appeared late in the development of Israel, there was a very significant education long before.

§ 1. Education in the Family

In simply organized societies education is largely imitative. The children learn by practice the arts of the tribal life. So the girls learn to do the work of the women, and the boys become hunters, archers, shepherds, warriors by the inevitable apprenticeship of youth. History among such people is preserved in the tales of the heroes, or the songs of the great past, which the elders tell in the evening or before the campfire, and which children learn by constant hearing or by repetition. Morality is the permitted. Certain conduct is expected of every one, certain other conduct is reprobated. Punishment bears its swift disciplinary part for any violation of convention. Religion is participation in the ritual acts of the social group, and this in the same way is learned by imitation.

The patriarchal family of early Israel and the clan or tribal life down to the exile afforded just such a social education to the Hebrew children. Jacob's sons were shepherds, who had doubtless shared with him the hard experiences of the faithful tender of a flock, responsible for their well-being night and day (Gen 31. 38-40). So Rebecca (Gen 24. 15-20) and the daughters of Jethro (Exod 2. 16) had learned to carry their pitchers to the well and water the flocks. This practical education formed a large part of the training of the Hebrew youth.

The early religion of Israel centered in the family. The Sabbath rest (Exod 20. 8-10) was distinctly a family regulation. In early times there was no worship provided for this day, but its religious character arose from the fact that it was the Lord's day, which could not be profaned by work. It had none of the legal exactness of observance which made it a burden in later Judaism and in later Puritanism, but was a joyous release from labor as a gift from Israel's God.

The Passover was doubtless a family sacrifice in its beginning, as it continued to be till the end. It may have been connected with the offering of the firstlings of the flock and of the herd (Exod 13. 12ff.; Deut 15. 19ff.; 16. 1f.; passages which belong to the later legislation, but reflect earlier customs). This springtime recognition of the gift of Jehovah would powerfully affect the youthful mind. The earliest record of it provides that the children shall be instructed as to its meaning (Exod 12. 26f.). This was later elaborated into a regular formal explanation to be given every year in answer to a question from the youngest child.

Before the nationalizing of religion the sacrificial feasts and offerings were family matters. So the patriarchs had to sacrifice wherever they might be (Gen 12. 7f.; 35. 1; Job. 1. 5); the family of David might have their own clan sacrifice (1 Sam 20. 29). The children were witnesses or partakers of these ritual acts, which were picturesque presentations of religion and therefore far more effective in the education of youth than intellectual ideas conveyed by words.

The three annual festivals which were enjoined in the early legislation upon all males (Exod 23. 14-17), were agricultural feasts, suggestive of thanksgiving to the God of the harvest, and must have been impressive object lessons for the boys who were especially commanded to go with their fathers. It is noticeable that women also attended the feasts, which were in reality family celebrations (1 Sam 1. 7).

The collection of incomparable stories that comprise so large a part of the first ten books of our Bible were folk tales repeated from father to son long before they were committed to writing by the prophets. It was by this means rather than by catechetical instruction that parents told their children what Jehovah had done for Israel in the past (Psa 44. 1).

As the great religious leaders sought to lift religion from ritualism to spiritual fellowship with God, and to lift morality above conventional customs, they sought to make education more definite. Thus the prophets in the great exhortation to Israel which is the purpose of the Deuteronomic legislation, laid special emphasis on the parental training of children. The great commandments against evil and idolatry, the whole-hearted love of Jehovah the one God, the joyous religion of justice, humanity, and faith—all these "thou shalt teach thy children, talking also when thou sittest in thy house, and when thou walkest by the way, and when thou liest down, and when thou risest up" (Deut 4. 9; 6. 4-9, 20-25; 11. 18-19; 32. 46). Thus religious education in the family became, as it has continued, a special mark of Judaism.

But the exile was the great seedtime of Hebrew education. With the complete cessation of the national worship the priests were freed from their customary duties and were confronted with the danger that the manner of the ritual would be forgotten. They set themselves therefore to put into definite statutory form every requirement which the sacrificial system could lay upon the Hebrew. A special religious significance, intended to be educational in its character, was given to the old customs that had hitherto held only a conventional significance. Circumcision was traced back to the covenant of God with Abraham (Gen 17). The elaborated ceremonial of the Passover and of the feast of unleavened bread were described as part of the Egyptian experience (Exod 12. 1-20). Detailed sacrifices were provided for the Sabbath and for each of the festivals (Num 28 and 29). Even symbolic meaning was attached to articles of common dress (Num 15. 37-41).

It was the priestly purpose that the whole of life should be sanctified by a significant ritual which should be an object lesson of holiness to every Israelite. This developed Jewish system was solemnly presented to the reconstituted community in Jerusalem by Ezra the scribe (Neh 8. 2, 3). All the people—men, women, and "all that could hear with understanding"—were present. From thence forward it was the solemn duty of every father and mother in Israel to make known the commandments of Jehovah to their children, and to explain to them the religious observances that held so large a place in their lives. The wise men added to the requirements of the law their own exhortation to parents to train their children in the way which they should go (Prov 22. 6).

How thoroughly this was done by the earnest parents of the Hebrews is attested by the references of godly men to the instructions which they received (Psa 78. 3-6), by the confidence with which the later religious teachers felt that they could exhort young people to abide by their parental instruction (Prov 1. 8; 4. 3, 4; 6. 20; 13. 1; 23. 22-25), and in many evidences of the faithfulness of parents (Tobit 4. 14; 2 Tim 1. 5; 3. 15).

It is this religious education in the family which is responsible more than anything else for the permanence of the Jew in history. A most vivid account of its present character may be read in The Promised Land, by Mary Antin.

It should be noted that it was considered essential, because of "the natural foolishness" of the child, that he should receive freely the rod of correction (Prov 13. 24; 19. 18; 22. 15; 23. 13-14; 29. 15-17; Sirach 30. 1-13), and this passed over from the discipline of the home to that of the school.

§ 2. Hebrew Schools

We know nothing of schools before the exile. The term "schools of the prophets," which has often been used, does not appear in the Bible, and the description of such schools as if they were theological seminaries has no basis in the biblical narrative. The expression used is "sons of the prophets," which means simply disciples of the prophets. They evidently lived a common life in guilds where the technique of prophesying was learned by serving an apprenticeship (1 Kings 20. 35; 2 Kings 2. 15ff.; 4. 38ff.; 6. 1ff.; Amos 7. 14). In the same way there was no school for the priests, but the young priests learned the technique of their duties by actual service in the sanctuary.

There must have been some method of teaching reading, writing, and arithmetic, for while knowledge was not common it was always possible that the records of the kingdom should be written and the prophetic stories compiled. Isaiah could write a placard in Jerusalem which he expected the people to read (Isa 8. 1). Moreover, such men as Amos and Micah, who were not of the upper classes, could secure the necessary training to make them able writers. But there is no information that warrants any statement as to what methods of instruction were employed.

After the exile two great classes of scholars (unless,

indeed, as some think, they are identical) developed in Israel, the scribes and the sages. The scribes gave themselves to the study and exposition of the law, the sages to the principles of practical ethics. The product of the former was the mass of oral tradition which was handed down by the laborious method of memorizing until it was committed to writing long after the time of Christ. The product of the latter was the great wisdom books of Proverbs and Sirach and Wisdom, besides Job and Ecclesiastes, which deal with individual problems. With the noble foundation principle that "the fear of Jehovah is the beginning of wisdom" (Prov 9. 10; Sirach 1. 14), these books deal with the practical problems of human life.

The scribes and the sages formed guilds, to which young disciples might attach themselves and thus secure the learning of the masters. But this represented, as it were, the college education of later Judaism. We do not know how children, who were thus to become disciples of the wise, were given elementary instruction. Every father or mother who could read and write would inevitably instruct the children. Literacy is always self-perpetuating. Learning was evidently regarded as the privilege of the leisure classes, for the sage very definitely declares that workingmen, while valuable to the state, have no time for wisdom (Sirach 30. 24; 31. 12). This was the distinction between Jesus, who had not attended the rabbinical schools (John 7. 14f.), and Paul, who had been the disciple of the most distinguished rabbi (Acts 22. 3).

The Greek influence which was so potent in Jerusalem from the time of Alexander must have resulted in the establishment of schools for the well-to-do, and Josephus refers to the existence of such in the third century B. C. (Josephus, Antiquities, XII, iv, 6). It is evident that there was some general culture, for there was great multiplication of books (Eccl 12. 12), and in the Maccabean times many people had copies of the law (1 Macc 1. 57).

While Josephus insists that the Jews took most pains of all with the instruction of children (c. Apion, I. 12), there is no evidence that the Jewish elementary school system was established until shortly before or after the time of Christ. In the pre-Christian centuries the great educational institution was the synagogue. Here the scribes and wise men expounded the law and the sacred history and discussed the ethical problems of common life. Moreover, the ritual of the synagogue was impressively educational (see page 191). It was not primarily intended for children, but they were present and received the indelible impress of its religious character, while the parents were stimulated by the instruction there received in the performance of their parental obligations.

When the Jewish elementary school came to be established it was connected with the synagogue, and it grew out of the conviction that every Jew should be able to read the law. To the minister of the synagogue belonged the duty of teaching all the boys who were brought to him at the age of six years. The Book of the Law was the textbook by which the alphabet and reading were learned. The writing was subordinate, but was taught in order to assist in the mastery of the Hebrew tongue. So definitely was the school intended for religious education that it was called "the house of the book."

The teacher was seated on a stool while his scholars sat before him on the ground (Luke 2. 46; Matt 26. 55; Acts 22. 3). The method of instruction was by memorizing, every student repeating his texts aloud. The monotonous drone of the learners may be heard to-day in any Jewish or Mohammedan school. For other details of the methods employed the reader may be referred to Edersheim's brilliant account of Hebrew education in the time of Christ. (Life and Times of Jesus the Messiah, Bk. II, Chap. ix.)

The injunction in Deuteronomy (11. 19) was interpreted as referring only to sons, and so the girls were not sent to the synagogue schools. They were, however, doubtless taught at home by their mothers.

It should be noted as an educational element of some value that the people of Palestine in later times were practically bilingual. They would learn Aramaic in the home, and probably pick up Greek early in life as the common medium of intercourse with the Gentiles.

The rabbis had the healthy idea that every boy should learn a trade. Naturally, the son of a mechanic would follow his father's calling, as in the case of Jesus (Mark 6. 3), but even the sons of the well-to-do were instructed in manual labor as Paul learned the coarse trade of a tent maker (Acts 18. 2, 3).

DIRECTIONS FOR STUDY

1. Read 1 Sam 16 to 2 Sam 21. Note every point that throws light upon David's education. Upon the basis of this narrative alone what would you know of education in his day?
2. What would be the education of a Hebrew boy in the time of Josiah, if his parents followed diligently the directions of Deuteronomy? Consider especially the effect of the festivals (Deut 16. 1-17).
3. What are the values of family ceremonial in the education of children? How far does our modern life make use of this opportunity? How far can home, school, church, and state employ ceremonial effectively for educational purposes to-day?
4. Read 1 Sam 3. 1-18; 1 Kings 19. 19-21; Isa 8. 16; Jer 36. 1-8. What do these passages imply as to the education of the prophets?
5. Name some educational values of the book of Proverbs.
6. What was the educational value to the Jewish youth of learning the psalms by heart? What parallel values are possible in modern education?
7. Read Josephus, Antiquities, XX, xii, 2. Consider what this implies as to the education of an orthodox Jewish gentleman in the first century A. D.
8. Make a list of the quotations of Jesus from the Old Testament. From how many books does he quote? What does this imply as to his education?

9. Read Matt 21. 23; 26. 55; Mark 14. 49; Luke 2. 46; 20. 1; 21. 37; John 18. 20. What do these passages suggest as to method of teaching?
10. In the light of this study, what distinction would you make for our modern life between general education, moral education, and religious education? What are the respective duties of the modern home, school, and church?

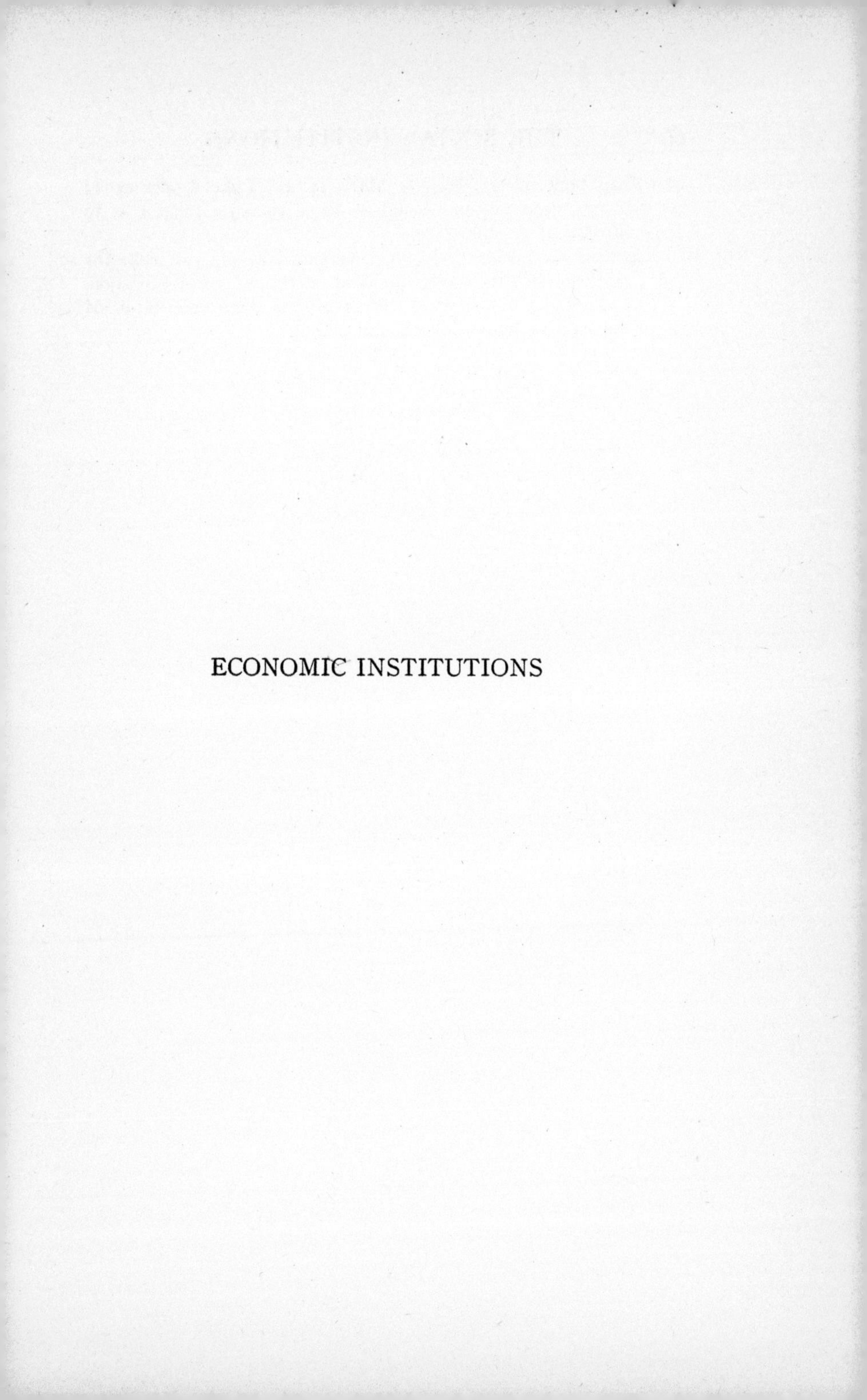

ECONOMIC INSTITUTIONS

CHAPTER VI

THE PRIMITIVE PASTORAL LIFE

§ 1. The Characteristics of the Nomadic Stage

The earliest records show the Hebrews in the pastoral stage of culture. Abraham and Lot, who moved from pasture to pasture in Palestine and the southern wilderness, were rich in flocks, herds, asses and camels, tents and slaves, and in silver and gold ornaments and costly garments (Gen 13. 2-5; 24. 22, 35, 53). Abraham's family was really a clan, for he had three hundred and eighteen young slaves fit for warfare who had been "born in his own house" (14. 14).

Jacob, when he fled from home as a fugitive, found refuge with his uncle, who was also a pastoral chief. In his service he acquired the wealth of a nomad (32. 5, 13-15) and then returned to Palestine, where he found pasturage for his flocks and herds (37. 12).

The sojourn of the Hebrews in Egypt was one of those temporary residences of the nomad in a settled community, brought about in this case through famine (47. 3, 4); and, in spite of the bondage into which they were brought by the Egyptians, when they went out from their land it was still as shepherds (Exod 12. 32-38).

Moses fleeing from Egypt had gone back to the nomad life as son-in-law of Jethro, whose flocks he tended (Exod 3. 1). When he assumed the leadership of Israel it was to lead them as a pastoral chief through the wilderness from oasis to oasis. And even the land of Canaan to which they were journeying is pictured as a rich pastoral land, for the familiar phrase "flowing with milk and honey" (Num 13.

27; Deut 6. 3) is not the description of a land of agriculture, still less of cities, but of pasturage for cattle and of flowers for wild bees.

The uplands of Gilead east of the Jordan offered especially rich pasture land, and the Hebrews who settled on that side of the river continued to be essentially a pastoral people (Num 32. 1-5; Judg 5. 16). Sleek sheep and cattle were called after this region (Deut 32. 14; Amos 4. 1).

The Hebrews of western Palestine continued after they became agriculturists to give large attention to the raising of cattle, sheep, and goats. Pasturage was excellent in the more fertile parts of the land, and even on the rocky hills of Judah the skillful shepherd could find good grazing for his sheep (Psa 23). Flocks and herds were always very important to the Hebrews for purposes of food (Judg 6. 19; 13. 15; 1 Sam 9. 24; 14. 32; 2 Sam 12. 4; 1 Kings 4. 23; Prov 15. 17; Luke 15. 29, 30), as offerings for sacrifice (Num 28; 1 Kings 8. 63), and for their products, milk, butter, and wool (Deut 32. 14; 1 Sam 17. 18; 2 Sam 17. 29; Prov 27. 26f.; 30. 33; Isa 7. 15; 53. 7; 55. 1).

During the pastoral stage of Hebrew life there were some beginnings of a more settled state. A certain amount of grain was probably raised for the needs of the households (Gen 30. 14; 37. 7), and simple trade transactions took place, as we see from the purchase of the burial ground at Machpelah (23. 17f.), the sale of Joseph into slavery (37. 25-28), and the journey of the Hebrews to buy grain in Egypt (42. 2).

The social life of the pastoral stage was very simple. Government was patriarchal, the Clan-Father exercising authority according to the recognized customs that had grown up through the centuries (38. 24). There would not be many sources of friction, though troubles might arise about pasturage (13. 7) and wells (26. 12-22), and, of course, on personal matters (27. 41; 31. 1f.; 34. 7; 37. 18f.). There would be no real poverty, as the clan has a solidarity: no one starves unless they all starve (42. 1f.). Thus the great class of problems which arise in more complex life had no existence. And the institution of slavery with its good and bad phases very simply provided for all the enrichment of life that depends on labor. The pastoral stage is a rude and even a harsh condition of society, but with certain fine magnanimities and hospitalities (13. 8; 14. 22f.; 18. 1-8; 20. 14-16; 24; 44. 18-34; 45. 1-15).

§ 2. The Influence of the Nomadic Stage

The Hebrews never quite forgot that they belonged to the desert. Indeed, they might well remember it, for every height in the land affords a view of the deep gorge of the Jordan beyond which stretch the uplands whose hinder side is the great wilderness from which they came. And from the Mount of Olives opposite Jerusalem the desert of the Dead Sea looks as if it were just beneath one's feet.

A result of this remembrance was a restiveness under restraint. They could not endure the highly organized government which the long-settled peoples were willing to accept; and this was particularly true of the northern tribes. Thus Solomon's imperialism, to which later Jews looked back as a time of glory, chafed the freedom-loving children of the desert, who at the first opportunity threw off the yoke of his successor.

> What portion have we in David?
> Neither have we inheritance in the son of Jesse:
> To your tents, O Israel:
> Now see to thine own house, David (1 Kings 12. 16).

The monarchy was always elective in the north, though with a general acceptance of the principle of inheritance. The frequent changes of dynasty indicate how easily the people were moved to enforce their independence.

Attractive as the new life in Canaan was in comparison with the hard conditions of the desert, there were always those who felt that it was a luxury too dearly bought. Civilization then, as now, was full of corruptions. The religious festivals themselves were times of self-indulgence and debauchery. The life of the city tended to the accentuation of wealth and poverty, and promoted injustice and fraud. To many an earnest soul the nobler times of Israel's life seemed to be in the past, when men lived in tents and had never learned the soft arts of the agricultural and commercial life.

The most outstanding instance of this protest was the group of Rechabites, a sect of nomads who took a perpetual vow that they and their descendants would not plant seed nor live in houses nor in cities, and particularly would eschew the vine, which was esteemed the richest product of the soil (Jer 35. 5-11). They lived among their fellow citizens as an example of the simple life of the desert.

The prophetic protest had in it certain elements of this stern contempt for luxury with its dangerous seductions. Thus Elijah came from that Gilead east of the Jordan, where the pastoral tribes had settled (1 Kings 17. 1). In striking contrast with the luxurious Ahab, he was clad in a rough garment woven of hair, with a leather belt (2 Kings 1. 8), and with a sheepskin for a cloak. Against the king, whose covetousness to enlarge his royal gardens had caused the infamous murder of a just citizen, and against the heathen princess who had instigated the deed, this stern man announced the wrath of God (1 Kings 21).

It would not be correct to say that the prophets were opposed to the agricultural and commercial life that had developed. On the contrary, their brightest pictures are of a future righteous society where the people are to be settled in the good land that God has given them (Jer 31. 1-14; Amos 9. 11-15; Micah 4. 1-4). And yet the ascetic note of the prophets, as when Amos denounces the revelers (6. 1ff.), and Isaiah makes his contemptuous enumeration of the finery of the women (3. 16ff.), and Micah sees reformation only in the destruction of the cities (5. 10ff.), until John the Baptist comes out of the desert itself a second Elijah (Mark 1. 1-8), may well have had its origin in the remembrance of the days of the fathers in the wilderness when they were near to God, and when man had not learned to be covetous of luxury and to oppress his neighbor to secure unrighteous ends.

DIRECTIONS FOR STUDY

1. Read Genesis and enumerate the elements of wealth possessed by the various patriarchs.
2. Read Gen 23, and note the characteristics of an ancient bargain.
3. What does Gen 43. 11 indicate as to the acquisition of the fruits of the soil by the nomad?
4. Read Genesis again carefully and, bearing in mind that these narratives are the product of a much later time, consider what social virtues the pastoral stage of life may develop.
5. In what respects is the pastoral stage morally inferior to more developed culture?
6. What contribution does the rough life such as that depicted in Ralph Connor's stories of the western plains make to our modern civilization?
7. How far is the modern reformer justified in holding up for our emulation the simpler and cruder life of earlier days in our history?
8. Is there any prospect of American life growing less complex? If not, what is to be learned from the virtues of simpler social organizations?
9. By what means can the softness which is the product of enervating luxury be offset in a highly civilized society?
10. Is a thoroughly virile civilization compatible with great wealth?

CHAPTER VII

AGRICULTURE

§ 1. The Hebrews as Agriculturalists

The nomad loves the freedom of the desert, but he feels its hardships and limitations. He looks with longing eyes to the settled lands where men dwell in houses, with water, the life-giver, ever at hand in wells or cisterns or in exhaustless springs, and where the harvest brings food and oil and wine in abundance to the happy possessor (Gen 27. 28; Deut 6. 10, 11).

The earliest traditions of the Hebrews show them looking for a home and believing themselves destined, in the good providence of God, to be the possessors of Canaan, where their fathers had sojourned and wandered as strangers (Gen 12. 1-3; 13. 14-18; 26. 2; 28. 13; Exod 3. 7f.). It was not a very rich land as we should think, comparing its small size with our great corn and wheat and grazing areas, or comparing it with the marvelous fertility of Egypt or of the irrigated lands of the Tigris-Euphrates valley in ancient times. But Palestine was a good land, capable of sustaining a large population, and to the eyes of the desert wanderer it seemed marvelously rich (Deut 8. 7-9).

The Canaanites, who were already in possession, were agriculturalists. With them the nomad stage had entirely passed. They were settled in towns, many of which were fortified for protection against just such invaders from the desert as the Hebrews (Num 13. 28); and they had achieved a considerable culture. Egypt had held sway over Palestine for a long period and had exercised her civilizing influence. The correspondence between the Egyptian officials and the Pharaoh, which is preserved in the Tel-el-Amarna tablets, reveals a condition of culture at least as advanced as that attained by Israel in the time of David.

The Hebrews with vigorous onslaught secured a footing in Palestine, as is recorded in the later traditions preserved in the book of Joshua, and then for a long period, as the book of Judges indicates, they lived side by side with the Canaanites, now increasing their territory and now yielding it in a struggle that lasted for many generations. The pastoral Hebrews, while continuing their interest in flocks and herds, learned the agricultural arts from their new neighbors. They adopted the agricultural festivals, especially those belonging to the harvests and vintage (Deut 16. 9-17). Depending largely upon other peoples for the artistic elements of life, they devoted themselves to the soil and exchanged its products for the wares of the trader. It is typical of the wealth of the land when the master is exhorted to furnish his departing slave out of the flock, the threshing floor, and the winepress (Deut 15. 14). And Jeremiah, describing the gifts of Jehovah, refers to the grain, the new wine, and the oil, and the young of the flocks and of the herd (Jer 31. 12).

We naturally think of the Hebrew as a man of business, because the harsh laws of the peoples that have ruled over him for two thousand years have forbidden him to be a possessor of the land. But during the whole period of his national history he was predominantly an agriculturalist. It is a significant fact that the great body of legislation which developed up to the middle of the fifth century B. C., and which is embodied in the Pentateuch, is entirely concerned with a people in the agricultural stage of development. They did become in the Greek times a commercial people to a limited extent, but even in the days of Christ the Jews were largely inhabitants of villages and tillers of the soil.

§ 2. The Products of Palestine

The little country of Palestine is singularly diversified

in climate and soil. It would be difficult to find another territory no larger in extent in which such a variety of agricultural operations could be carried on. The deep gorge of the Jordan leading into the plains about Jericho provides an almost tropical region where the date palm flourishes. The great fertile plains of Sharon and Esdraelon will produce all the grains, vegetables, and herbs of temperate climes. The rich uplands of Gilead are particularly well adapted to the pasturage of cattle. The hill country of Judæa, while sterile, and yielding only a fair pasturage to flocks, was readily adapted to the culture of the vine by the simple process of terracing, which conserved the soil. The lake of Galilee and the Jordan River yielded a goodly variety of fish.

Wheat was one of the most important crops and was grown extensively throughout Palestine (Isa 28. 25), the varying climate giving different periods of harvest from April to August. Numerous references to the "fat of the wheat" indicate that some excellent qualities of the grain were produced (Deut 32. 14; Psa 81. 16; 147. 14; compare Matt 13. 8).

While still green the wheat was often cooked in the ear before the fire. This is the parched grain that is often mentioned as an article of food (Lev 2. 14; 1 Sam 17. 17; 25. 18; 2 Sam 17. 28). When ground into meal (Exod 11. 5; Matt 24. 41) it made the best bread either as flat leavened cakes or as raised bread (Judg 6. 19; 1 Kings 4. 22). The wheat crop was sufficiently large for this grain to become an article of export (1 Kings 5. 11; Ezek 27. 17).

Barley was also an important crop (Isa 28. 25; Ruth 2. 23) which could be grown in all parts of the land. The harvest was earlier than that of wheat (Ruth 1. 22; 2. 23). The grain was used for the horse (1 Kings 4. 28), but was also the food of the poor (Judg 7. 13; 2 Kings 4. 42; Ezek 4. 12; John 6. 9, 13).

Ezekiel mentions two grains which are translated with some uncertainty—*millet* and *spelt* (4. 9). The latter seems to have been sown on the corner of the barley field, its toughness making perhaps a kind of hedge for the field. Modern writers speak of several coarse grains which are grown in Palestine to-day as food for the poor. The prophet may have referred to some of these.

Beans and *lentils,* still important articles of diet in Palestine, were also ancient crops (Gen 25. 34; 2 Sam 17. 28; 23. 11; Ezek 4. 9). Mention is likewise made of *cucumbers* as growing in Palestine (Isa 1. 8; Baruch 6. 70), and of the Hebrew fondness for the *melons, leeks, onions,* and *garlic* of Egypt (Num 11. 5), vegetables which are cultivated at the present time throughout Syria.

In the picturesque story of the spies, who went up to report upon the country which the Hebrews were planning to invade, it is significant that they brought back as evidence of the goodness of the land a branch with a cluster of *grapes* requiring two men to bear it (Num 13. 23). The vine became so valuable in Israel that the prophet could poetically identify the destruction of the land with the ruin of the grape industry (Isa 7. 23), and it is always associated with prosperity and wealth (Gen 49. 11; 1 Kings 4. 25; Sol. Song 8. 11; Jer 31. 5; Micah 4. 4.

The grapes were so valuable that towers were built in which watchmen guarded the fruit from marauders (Isa 5. 2; Matt 21. 33).

The value of the vine was enhanced by the fact that it grows best on mountains which are so numerous in Palestine and that it can flourish in locations and in soil that are not favorable for other crops. By the simple system of terracing the rocky slope and removing the stones (Isa 5. 2) the hills were converted into fruitful vineyards (Isa 5. 1; Jer 31. 5). It is the neglect of this terracing, with the consequent washing away of the soil, that has made Judæa so poor a land to-day.

The grapes were eaten ripe (Mic 7. 1) or were dried in the sun into raisins (1 Sam 25. 18; 30. 12; 2 Sam 16. 1). But it was the blood of the grape which was most desired (Deut 32. 14). The fruit having been carried to the winepress was there trodden by the feet of the young men and maidens (Isa 63. 3) as they sang,

> "Destroy it not,
> For a blessing is in it" (Isa 65. 8)

and the vintage season was a time of great rejoicing (Judg 9. 27; Isa 16. 10; Jer 48. 33).

The expressed juice was allowed to ferment and was then put into skins (Mark 2. 22). Wine drinking was practically universal and was taken as a matter of course (Gen 49. 11f.; Deut 32. 14; Judg 9. 13; Psa 104. 15; Eccl 9. 7; Joel 3. 18; Amos 9. 13f.; Luke 22. 17f.; John 2. 3). However, the danger of its intoxicating effects was clearly recognized (Prov 20. 1; Isa 5. 11; 28. 1, 7; Jer 23. 9; Hosea 4. 11; 7. 5), as also the economic danger of its excessive use (Prov 21. 17). There were, of course, different kinds of wine, some more intoxicating than others, and probably that used as a common beverage was very slightly alcoholic, but the attempt that has been made to show that only unfermented wine is approved in the Bible is not successful.

The social problem of drunkenness is far more acute in our day than was the case in the very much simpler life of Israel. There was a feeling, however, that the wine-drinking that was associated with the more luxurious life of the Canaanites was a departure from the conditions of the more abstemious days of the desert; and this protest is seen in the asceticism of the Nazirites (Num 6; Judg 13. 4f.) and of the Rechabites (Jer 35. 1-11). The prohibition of wine to the priests while performing their sacred rites was probably only to secure perfect fitness of administration (Lev 10. 8ff.).

Scarcely less in importance than the grape was the *olive,* which grew abundantly all over Palestine. It was used as a food, either green or ripe, much more commonly than with us. The rich oil which was obtained by pressing the berries was also a very valuable commodity for food (2 Chron 2. 10) and was used in cooking (Lev 2. 4) and as a kind of butter with bread (Exod 29. 23). It was also employed as an ointment for wounds and in sickness (Luke 10. 34; James 5. 14) and for ceremonial purposes (1 Sam 10. 1; 16. 1; Psa 23. 5). Placed in small vessels in which a wick was floated the olive oil was a valuable illuminant (Exod 25. 6; 27. 20; Zech 4. 3, 11-14; Matt 25. 3). The use of oil was regarded as a luxury which might be too freely enjoyed (Prov 21. 17). The abundance of the yield of oil is evident from its appearance as an export from Judah to Tyre (2 Chron 2. 10; Ezek 27. 17).

The *fig* is constantly mentioned as a valuable tree in Palestine (Num 13. 23). It is coupled with the olive and the vine (Jer 5. 17; 8. 13; Joel 1. 7-12; Hab 3. 17f.). To dwell under one's own vine and fig tree was the expression of peace and prosperity (1 Kings 4. 25; Mic 4. 4; Zech 3. 10; 1 Macc 14. 12). The figs were eaten fresh, of which the early ones were best (Isa 28. 4; Jer 24. 2; Mic 7. 1), or dried and pressed into a kind of cake (1 Sam 25. 18; 30. 12).

Palm trees flourished in the neighborhood of Jericho (Judg 1. 16; 3. 13; Deut 34. 3; 2 Chron 28. 15) yielding the *dates,* which were much esteemed. *Pomegranates* were freely used as food (Num 13. 23) and the juice as a wine (Sol Song 8. 2).

Honey, while very plentiful, so that it was included among the exports (Ezek 27. 17), seems to have been the product of wild bees (1 Sam 14. 25; Deut 32. 13; Psa 81. 16; Matt 3. 4). It was a valued article of food (Judg 14. 9; 2 Sam 17. 29; Psa 19. 10; Luke 24. 42 marg.), but the wise men knew that so rich a sweet was to be enjoyed with moderation (Prov 25. 16).

Linen garments were extensively used by the Hebrews (Lev 13. 47, 59) and were doubtless made from their own *flax,* for this plant was produced by the Canaanites (Josh 2. 6) and continued to be a staple crop (Hosea 2. 9).

§ 3. The Tenure of Land

Certain grazing, and even arable lands, were probably held in common by the people of the community. But other property was definitely owned and inherited. We have no means of knowing how the individual Hebrew families acquired title to such possessions. The idealistic division of the land by lot, which the priestly writers sketched many centuries later (Josh 18 and 19), could not have taken place while the Canaanites were still so largely in possession; and in any case this refers only to the division among the tribes and not to individuals.

The earliest legislation contains no reference to land tenure. In the Deuteronomic Code is the provision, "Thou shalt not remove thy neighbor's landmark, which they of old time have set" (19. 14; 27. 17), indicating that land was definitely delimited and owned. The incident of Naboth shows that land was held as an inheritance which it was considered improper to alienate (1 Kings 21. 3). When anyone was obliged to sell his land for any reason there seems to have been some right of the near of kin to redeem it, that it might not be permanently lost to the family (Jer 32. 6-10; Ruth 4. 1-6). However, Isaiah's denunciation of those "that join house to house, that lay field to field" (5. 8) shows that the loss of the patrimony was by no means uncommon, and that the great estates were built up by such means.

We have noted the provision for the liberation of the Hebrew slaves in the seventh year both in the Book of the Covenant and in the Deuteronomic Code. A like provision for the land to lie fallow during the seventh year appears in the Book of the Covenant (Exod 23. 10f.). This was probably the result of the experience of the needs of the soil which many peoples have discovered, but there was added in the Hebrew legislation the beneficent provision that the crops of the fallow year should be for the poor of the land. It is not implied that the whole land should lie fallow at the same time, but that each field should have its regular sabbatic rest. In the Deuteronomic Code, as we shall note, there was a seventh-year provision for the release of debt (15. 1f.). This latter was probably a common year for the whole nation.

The Levitical Code (Lev 25) endeavored to bring these earlier requirements into consistency by the establishment of a regular seventh year in which all the land should lie fallow at the same time, "a sabbath of solemn rest for the land, a sabbath unto Jehovah" (v. 4). Seven such periods of seven were then to be crowned by the fiftieth year, the Jubilee, in which also the land was to lie fallow (v. 11). Moreover, in this Jubilee year every man who had sold his ancestral estate was to receive it back without payment (vv. 13ff.). At any earlier time land which had been alienated could be redeemed by purchase (vv. 24ff.), but in any case all titles were to revert to the original owners at the Jubilee. This, of course, would be tantamount to an inalienable title to land, so that the owner could only sell the use of the land until the next Jubilee; that is to say, there could be a maximum lease of forty-nine years. This applied to farms and houses in villages, but not to city houses which could be sold in perpetuity (vv. 29-31).

The sabbatical year seems to have been observed in the postexilic times (1 Macc 6. 49, 53; Josephus, Antiquities, XIII, viii, 1; XIV, x, 6; xvi, 2; XV, i, 2. B. J., I, iv, 4), but there is no evidence that the Jubilee was ever more than an ideal. The reversion of all property to the families of the original owners every half a century would be an interesting social experiment, but we have no means of judging from Jewish history how it would work.

DIRECTIONS FOR STUDY

1. Read the book of Judges and note (1) the characteristics of various invaders from the desert, (2) the agricultural character of the inhabitants, (3) the Hebrew development to the agricultural stage.
2. Read the Book of the Covenant (Exod 20 to 23) and note its agricultural provisions.
3. Read Deut 15 to 26 and note its agricultural provisions.
4. What do Deut 8. 7-9 and 1 Kings 4. 23-28 indicate regarding the products of Palestine?
5. The Israelites in Hosea's time were worshiping the Canaanitish Baals who, as they believed, had given them the agricultural gifts. The prophet insists that all the gifts are from Jehovah. Read ch. 2 and note the information conveyed regarding the products of Canaan.
6. What are the main social problems when man is in the agricultural stage?
7. Compare the joy of the vintage in Israel with that in Greece. What does this indicate regarding the attitude of men toward wine?
8. What differences do you see between the use of wine in ancient Palestine and modern social drinking?
9. An ardent temperance advocate once said that if Jesus ever drank fermented wine, he could not be his Saviour: What was the error in that man's point of view?
10. What are the social reasons for the modern total abstinence and prohibition movements? What is the relation of the principle laid down in Rom 14 to those movements?

CHAPTER VIII

INDUSTRY, TRADE, AND COMMERCE

§ 1. Artisans

The Hebrews were not conspicuous for their ability as craftsmen. When David wanted a palace he had recourse to Phœnician workmen (2 Sam 5. 11). Solomon's temple and magnificent structures owed their beauty to the same skilled people (1 Kings 5. 6; 7. 13f.). It is significant that the Hebrew tradition of the origin of metal-working ascribed the art to Tubal-Cain (Gen 4. 22), and not to the line of Shem.

However, the Hebrews were not entirely without artisans. The simple tools of agricultural life would need some rude fashioning. It is especially noted that during the Philistine oppression no smiths were allowed in the land, indicating that they were usually available (1 Sam 13. 19). They were probably workers in copper, a metal from which most tools were then made (Deut 8. 9; 2 Sam 8. 8). The smiths were sufficiently numerous at the time of the captivity to be especially mentioned as carried away with the principal part of the population (2 Kings 24. 14-16).

The smiths of Babylonia are noted by the exile prophet (Isa 44. 12; 54. 16), and it is probable that the craft was somewhat developed in Judæa in postexilic times, for Sirach gives a very lively description of the smith at his work (38. 28).

The potter appears very early in most civilizations. Indeed, one of the methods of tracing the history of peoples is by the pottery remains in the buried cities. The pottery of the Canaanitish times has been found in many of the mounds of Palestine. "Earthen vessels" are mentioned in the time of David (2 Sam 17. 28), and the art of the potter is very vividly described by Jeremiah, who went down to the house of the potter and found him "making a work on the wheels" (18. 1-4). There are numerous other references to this interesting craft by the prophets and wise men (Isa 29. 16; 45. 9; 64. 8; Wis. 15. 7ff.), and Sirach in the famous passage before quoted, includes a description of the various operations of the potter (38. 29f.). In the book of Chronicles the potters appear as one of the Jerusalem guilds (4. 23).

The Hebrews depended for their carpentry and mason work, as for other skilled labor, upon the Phœnicians (2 Sam 5. 11; 1 Kings 5. 6), and this was the case even as late as the building of the second temple (Ezra 3. 7). Whether the carpenters and masons who repaired the temple under the kings were Hebrews is not stated (2 Kings 12. 11; 22. 6), nor whether there were carpenters among the "craftsmen" carried into captivity (Jer 24. 1; 29. 2). However, there must have been some simple carpentry done in early Israel (2 Kings 6. 2) and by the time of Sirach there were skilled Hebrews in the trade (38. 27). Amos was familiar with the plumb line which is the builder's tool (7. 7). Joseph of Nazareth was a village carpenter (Matt 13. 55) probably engaged in very simple work, and Jesus followed him, as was customary for a son to follow a father (Mark 6. 3).

§ 2. Trade in Early Israel

A glance at the map of the ancient East shows that Palestine lay in the line of a great commerce. Two caravan roads from Damascus, the one running north and the other south of the Sea of Galilee, led through the passes of the mountains to the plain of Sharon, and thence down the coast to Egypt. A most vigorous trade was carried on between Babylonia and Egypt through Damascus. This must have been in existence when the ancestors of the

Hebrews first made their appearance in Palestine, and the Tel-el-Amarna tablets indicate that it had reached large proportions in the later Canaanitish times.

The Hebrews in their nomadic period were more or less in contact with this commercial civilization into which they had not as yet entered. Simple barter and trading transactions must have taken place between them and their neighbors. If the patriarchs had gold, silver, jewels, and costly garments, they must have purchased them from traders. That they were accustomed to use "the current money of the merchant," and weigh it out according to custom, is evident from Abraham's transactions with Ephron (Gen 23. 1-16).

The story of the sale of Joseph affords a typical picture of the trading caravan, the laden camels bearing goods to Egypt, and the shrewd merchants ready to strike a bargain for the handsome young slave. The sale of slaves, while not a regular practice with the Hebrews, was always a possibility (Exod 21. 8); and the satisfaction of the sons of Jacob in the possession of the silver indicates that they knew how it could be put to good purpose. The later incidents in the story, where money is taken to Egypt to purchase food and valuable articles are carried down as presents (Gen 43. 11f.), show the part that the nomads might naturally take in the trade of the times.

When the Hebrews entered Canaan they found a people who had been accustomed to the conditions of a commercial civilization. Not only the good things of the vintage and the harvests were the rewards of their toil, but the luxuries which the merchants carried from the more highly civilized lands were available for purchase.

We have no definite statements that indicate the extent to which the Hebrews before the monarchy entered into commercial life. One of the difficulties of which the Song of Deborah speaks is the interruption of caravans by the oppression of Sisera (Judg 5. 6, marg.). The Phœnician commerce, which, as we shall presently note, played so large a part in the development of Israel under the monarchy, must have already been influential in the unsettled times of the Judges. We may think of the Hebrews, therefore, as visited occasionally by the trafficker from Tyre, who would sell to these newcomers into the civilization of the world some of the articles of convenience and beauty that were manufactured so extensively by those peoples who had already made great advance in commerce and the arts.

§ 3. The Development of Commerce Under the Monarchy

It was the task of David to unite the scattered and jealous tribes under one government, and to subdue the surrounding peoples so that Israel could be free to live an unmolested life. Solomon inherited a kingdom already established, and the opportunity was his to undertake its thorough organization. At his accession the Hebrews were little more than farmers and vinedressers, the few cities that existed being only large villages fortified for defense. The tribute which was exacted of the subject peoples (1 Kings 4. 21; 10. 25) and the large areas which the Hebrews were free to cultivate without disturbance (4. 25) brought a greatly augmented wealth into the country. The development of commerce was natural and inevitable.

The caravan routes already described were, of course, available for trade with Egypt, Damascus, and the East. Solomon kept these open and protected (10. 15). The alliance with Phœnicia which resulted in the exchange of the timber of Lebanon for the wheat and oil of Israel (5. 6-12) doubtless included also a much more extensive exchange of products. The brass work of the temple was specifically ascribed to the Tyrian artificer (7. 14, 16, 23, 27, 38, 40-46), and King Solomon was not the man to allow any of the costly luxuries of the Phœnicians to be wanting in his splendid court.

The coming of the Queen of Sheba "*with a very great train, with camels that bare spices, and very much gold, and precious stones*" (10. 2), and the regal present which the great king gave her in return (10. 13), indicate an exchange of commodities which marked a new era in Israel. The great trade with Egypt in horses, an animal not previously used by the Hebrews, is noteworthy in the same direction (10. 26-29).

As regards sea commerce, it is to be borne in mind that Palestine has no natural harbor. There is not a part of that coast to-day at which anything but a small boat can land. The Phœnicians had possession of the best harbors, which by great moles they had made available for their extensive commerce. The Philistines had the only other port, Joppa, but it was then, as it is to-day, nothing but an anchorage from which ships could be loaded by lighters. Solomon was therefore dependent for his access to the Mediterranean upon his Phœnician allies.

The Red Sea trade, however, was open to Israel. David having subdued the Edomites (2 Sam 8. 14) was able to take possession of their port of Ezion-Geber. Here Solomon built a fleet which he manned with Phœnician sailors and with Hebrews as deck hands, carrying on a vigorous trade with Ophir (probably southeastern Arabia), whence they brought ivory, apes, peacocks, and great quantities of gold and silver (1 Kings 9. 26-28; 10. 22).

Solomon's organization was too elaborate for Israel to bear. His reign closed in trouble, and the kingdom was divided under his son. Much of the tribute ceased to be paid, and much of the wealth which the magnificent king had gathered was quickly lost (14. 26; 15. 18f.). There seems to have been difficulty about continuing the seaport trade at Ezion-Geber (22. 48). But during the periods when the two Hebrew monarchies were prosperous the trade which Solomon had established was evidently still carried on.

Jerusalem and Samaria were to some extent commercial cities. Ahab was so much concerned about trade that in making peace with Benhadad he stipulated for the privilege of a district in Damascus for Hebrew bazaars (20. 34). That a very lively traffic was carried on is evident from the luxury which the prophets so vigorously denounced (Isa 2. 6, 7, 16; Hos 2. 8; 12. 1, 7, 8; Amos 6. 3-6; 8. 5; Zeph 1. 8). If the extraordinary description of female finery attributed to Isaiah (3. 18-23) is really from his pen, the caravans must have brought to Jerusalem costly wares from all the lands of the East.

But the trade was largely in the hands of the Phœnicians. Even in later times the merchant who came to buy the work of the thrifty housewife was from these same people (Prov 31. 24, marg., where Canaanite stands for Phœnician). The agricultural products of Palestine were exchanged with the Phœnicians for manufactured wares (Ezek 27. 17). One may realize the impression made by these remarkable traders upon the Hebrews by the language of the exile prophets when disaster finally overtook Tyre. There is scorn and exultation, but there is admiration also: *"Tyre the bestower of crowns, whose merchants are princes, whose traffickers are the honorable of the earth"* (Isa 23. 8); Tyre that had said, "I am perfect in beauty" (Ezek 27. 3).

The troublous times that closed the two monarchies doubtless interfered seriously with trade, and the heavy tributes which the Assyrians and Babylonians laid upon the land left less surplus wealth for foreign luxuries.

§ 4. The Economic Influence of the Exile

The Jews were carried by Nebuchadrezzar in considerable numbers to Babylon (2 Kings 24. 14-16; 25. 11), where they were allowed to carry on their own life and to pursue the occupations for which they were fitted. It is probable that the conqueror thought that it would be convenient to have a considerable body of agriculturalists who would minister to the needs of his great and growing population. Evidently, the captivity was not considered harsh by many of the exiles, for when permission was given in the Persian period for the Jews to return to Palestine very few took advantage of the opportunity. Babylon was a richer land, and from every point of view a more comfortable place to live. As the modern Jew looks with a wistful longing to the ancestral land and is ever mindful of its interests, but prefers for himself to remain where the great business opportunities exist, so it was that the Babylonian Jews, while loyal to their religion and deeply concerned for the welfare of Palestine, preferred to remain in the wealthy Tigris-Euphrates valley, where they became a more and more important part of the population.

It is probable that the Jew learned business in Babylon. The code of Hammurabi, which represents the conditions of a millennium and a half before the exile, reveals a developed commercialism as already existing in that remote time. The Babylonians continued to be a commercial people with an extensive trade, reaching every country of the known world. And this was elaborated to the point of the organization of credits and the institution of banks. In the fifth century Jewish names appear in the contracts of Babylonia, and we are able to understand that the allurements of business kept many of these ambitious people from returning to the meager life of Palestine.

The Jewish territory was restricted to the city of Jerusalem and a limited district about it. How poor was the condition of the people is attested by the prophets Haggai (1. 7-11; 2. 16f.), Zechariah (7. 7), Malachi (3. 14), and by Nehemiah (1. 3; 2. 17; 4. 2; 5. 1-5). We know that the simple business life of Jerusalem had been restored to a degree, for the goldsmiths and the merchants were there (Neh 3. 31f.), and the necessaries of life were brought to the city for sale (13. 15-18). But even so, the Phœnician trader was doing the business. And in the story of Jonah, which belongs to this period, it is significant that he is dependent upon Gentile sailors to give him passage from the port of Joppa (Jonah I. 5).

How far the commercialism of the Babylonian Jews may have affected their brethren in Palestine it is impossible to say, for we have little knowledge of exact conditions in Jerusalem from the time of Nehemiah until the Greek period.

§ 5. The Influence of Greek Commercialism

It was the Greek who brought the Jew into the currents of the world's life. Alexander conquered the East with the great ambition of universalizing the Greek language and the Greek culture. The story of the Hellenization of the Jews, and of the great protests which brought about the Maccabean revolt, and of the continued potent influence of Greek life that in turn Hellenized the Maccabeans, and of the further protest that produced Pharisaism, is one of the most interesting chapters in the history of civilization. We are concerned here with only a single phase of that complicated process, namely, the development of the Jewish trader and man of affairs.

The policy of Alexander resulted in the establishment of Greek cities all over the eastern Mediterranean world, of which Alexandria and Antioch were the most conspicuous examples. Jews were eagerly sought as colonists for these new cities, and were accorded special privileges. While Jerusalem, therefore, did not greatly increase in wealth and dignity, the Jews spread over all the Greek world, learned the methods of commerce, and took their place in the extensive trade that covered the Mediterranean with shipping and kept all the roads of the Levant busy with merchandise. While the Jews, therefore, took some part in the maritime trade, the life of the seafarer was never a familiar one to them. "They that go down to the sea in ships, that do business in great waters" were regarded with a certain wonder, and their adventures as full of peril (Psa 107. 23-30; Sirach 43. 24f.).

The Jews of the Dispersion maintained intimate relations with Jerusalem, to which they returned from time to time in pilgrimages, and they must have exerted some influence on the commerce of the land. Commercialism must have been increasing when Sirach wrote his treatise, for he had some fear that business involved moral dangers: "A merchant shall hardly keep himself from wrongdoing, and a huckster shall not be free from sin" (26. 29); "sin will thrust itself in between buying and selling" (27. 2); and a warning is found necessary against the abandonment of agriculture for the ways of commerce (7. 15).

The freedom from foreign oppression which the Maccabean rule secured was favorable to commercial development. It is specially mentioned that Simon captured the port of Joppa and "made an entrance to the isles of the sea" (1 Macc 14. 5). This wise ruler, who was much concerned to build up Judæa, must have used every opportunity to advance its trade and agriculture. The extending territory and increasing wealth of the later Asmoneans are evidences that the country was taking its independent place in the great Greek world.

The Roman influence and the reigns of the Herods were altogether favorable to the extension of commerce. Josephus has many references to the prosperity and business activity of his countrymen (Antiquities, XII, iv, 10; B. J., II, xxi, 2). The Gospels, though altogether incidentally, reflect busy commercial conditions. The market place is prominent in the people's life (Matt 20. 3; 23. 7; Mark 6. 56; 7. 4). Food is offered for sale in the villages and towns (Matt 14. 15; John 4. 8). Oil (Matt 25. 9), clothing (Mark 15. 46), cattle (Luke 14. 19), weapons (Luke 22. 36) are articles of purchase, as also costly ointments and spices (Mark 14. 5; 16. 1; John 19. 39). The trader journeys from place to place with his wares (Luke 10. 30-37), not only with common articles, but the jewel merchant carries on his costly business (Matt 13. 45f.). Men of wealth, and even noblemen, engage in trade through the medium of their servants (Matt 25. 14-30; Luke 19. 12-27), banks are in operation at which money may be placed at interest (Matt 25. 27; Luke 19. 23). Men may be so engrossed in business as to be careless of spiritual values (Matt 22. 5), and what we should call "graft" is not unknown, for trading is permitted in the temple precincts by the permission and for the advantage of the priests (Matt 21. 12f.).

DIRECTIONS FOR STUDY

1. Read Josh 7. 21; 1 Sam 13. 19-21; 14. 3; 17. 38f.; 18. 6, 11; 26. 5, and consider carefully how the Hebrews could have obtained the various articles referred to.
2. Read 1 Kings 4. 20 to 7. 50; 9. 15 to 10. 29, and note every item of Solomon's commerce and manufacture. What were the good and the bad results of this development in the life of the people?
3. Read Lev 19. 35f.; Prov 11. 1; 16. 11; 20. 10; Amos 8. 5; Mic 6. 10f.; Sirach 42. 4. What type of business do these injunctions particularly relate to? How far are such laws important to-day? Is obedience to these laws sufficient to make modern business satisfactory?
4. Read Ezek 26 and 27, and note the great impression made by Tyre upon the Hebrew mind. Note carefully the fine allegory of Tyre as a beautiful vessel that suffers shipwreck (ch. 27).
5. Make a list of the articles of the Tyrian commerce in Ezek 27 and identify as far as possible the various countries mentioned. Consider the effect upon Israel of having such a people as her near neighbor.
6. Read the book of Acts, and note (1) the indications of the presence of Jews throughout the Roman empire, (2) the different means of communication available in the empire, (3) the evidence of the commerce of Paul's day.
7. Rev 18 represents the feeling of satisfaction in the destruction of Rome, the tyrannical city. Note the description there given of Roman commerce. Consider that the Jews were living in that Roman empire.

8. What are the social problems that arise in a commercial society as distinguished from an agricultural society?
9. What causes have contributed to make the modern Jew a man of business? Does this represent an advance in his culture? What kind of civilization would be possible in Palestine to-day if political conditions were satisfactory?
10. What is the best balance between a people's commercial and industrial activities, on the one hand, and their agricultural activities on the other? What are the tendencies of our American life in this particular? Do you regard them as healthy?

CHAPTER IX

WEALTH AND POVERTY

§ 1. The Conditions of the Problem

We have seen that Palestine was a good agricultural land, productive, watered, with extensive pasturage, that it had some mineral wealth, and that it developed a simple commerce. In comparison with Phœnicia, Egypt, Babylon, it was not a wealthy country, and, of course, according to modern standards its riches were quite insignificant. Yet all judgments must be relative, and Palestine afforded an opportunity for a considerable population to develop a high degree of civilization. How large that population was it is impossible to compute with any accuracy. The present population west of the Jordan is estimated to be upward of half a million. In the times of prosperity under the Kings and in the time of Christ the land must have been able to sustain a very much larger number of people. Most of the cities mentioned in the Bible and on the monuments are to-day ruins or wretched villages. We may well believe, therefore, that at different times the little country was quite populous.

There was wealth enough in Palestine, and there were people enough, for the social problem of wealth and poverty to become very definitely manifest. It is an interesting and suggestive study to trace the course of the history from the simple beginnings when there was little contrast in the conditions of men to those later developments when the contrasts became so bitter. We may be able to see more clearly on that smaller stage the true character of the tragedy, whose outlines are obscured to us by the vastness and complexity of our modern life.

The primitive pastoral life, while already involving the great distinction between the freeman and the slave, was yet simple in its social structure. The wealth of the clan was practically held in common, although the head would determine the proportions in which it should be enjoyed by the various members. Jacob with his wives, and his sons with their wives and children, and his slaves with their wives and children, constituted a unified clan to which everyone belonged. There was no beggar nor pauper: all shared the fortunes of all.

The early agricultural life in Palestine was not markedly different. The clans settled on the land. Much of it was held in common, but every family probably had its own inheritance. Distinctions soon doubtless appeared. Some had better land than others, some suffered less from the depredations of the common enemies, some were more industrious, some escaped the misfortunes that destroy crops and flocks and herds. In the settled life of the agricultural state the family ties were not quite so strong as in the nomad camp. The fatherless and the widow with no protector did not always receive the due consideration that the family solidarity implied. The frequent reference to these dependents indicates how surely this was the case (Deut 10. 18; 24. 17; 27. 19; Job 31. 21; Isa 1. 17). Moreover, another element existed in society. Not only were there the freeman and the slave, but there was now the stranger (Deut 1. 16; 24. 17; 27. 19), the man who belonged to no Hebrew family, but had come into the country from abroad. Some misfortune or danger had driven him from his own land, and he was therefore poor. He must either work as a hireling—an unsatisfactory condition at this time in Israel (see pages 55f.)—or he must be dependent on charity (Exod 22. 21; 23. 9; Deut 10. 18f.; 26. 12). He could, indeed, sell himself into slavery, in which case he was on much the same footing as the Hebrew slave, except that there was no opportunity of redemption.

From many causes, therefore, there were soon the wealthier and the poorer among the Hebrews. Gideon says his family was the "poorest in Manasseh" (Judg 6. 15). Nabal was a great man with three thousand sheep and a thousand goats (1 Sam 25. 2). The distinction was well known in David's time, or Nathan's parable of the poor man would have had no point (2 Sam 12. 1ff.). And when David fled from Saul he was able to gather four hundred men about him who were "in distress, in debt, or discontented" (1 Sam 22. 2).

§ 2. Debt and Interest

Evidently, one of the earliest causes of the inequality of wealth arose from debt. We are so accustomed to debt as an important element in business that it is necessary for us carefully to remember that there was no system of commercial credits in Israel until probably the Greek period. Debt, therefore, was always of the personal kind, and arose out of the difficulty of the borrower. A man's crop would fail and he must needs have recourse to some one more able than himself to tide him over until the next harvest. Carelessness or extravagance might reduce one to poverty and compel him to borrow of his neighbor. The case is recorded of a widow whose husband owed a small debt, and upon his death the creditors were about to sell his sons as slaves (2 Kings 4. 1-7).

During the governorship of Nehemiah (ch. 5) a condition of distress occurred which was probably not uncommon during all the Hebrew history. Taxes were heavy and must, of course, be paid; in order to raise the money the people had been obliged to mortgage their lands; the interest exacted was one per cent per month (v. 11); when the mortgages were foreclosed and the people still were obliged to pay taxes and to live they had no recourse but to sell their children into slavery.

The religious leaders from the beginning protested against

the rich taking advantage of the troubles of the poor to exact interest from them for loans. Although the custom of lending upon interest and receiving pledges was common (Isa 24. 2), the law codes protested against it. They insisted that the loan was a temporary help given by brother to brother (Exod 22. 25; Lev 25. 36f.; Deut 23. 19). The well to do was to lend to the poor according to his need, and the heart of the lender was not to be grieved in doing it (Deut 15. 7-15). The psalmists, the wise men, and the prophets all objected to the putting of money to interest (Psa 15. 5; Prov 28. 8; Ezek 18. 8, 17; 22. 12), while the man who lent graciously was commended (Psa 37. 26; 112. 5). It is an interesting indication of how easily evil customs may be accepted without thought that the good Nehemiah did not realize till it was called to his attention that a shameful condition prevailed as a result of debt and usury. But when he understood it he passionately called upon the nobles to remit the loans, and was successful in his appeal (Neh 5. 9-12).

Lending to the foreigner was always put upon a different basis, and interest from him might be exacted (Deut 23. 20).

The taking of pledges for a loan was permitted, but under restraints. Clothing might not be kept overnight (Exod 22. 26f.), nor taken forcibly (Deut 24. 10-13), nor taken at all from a widow (24. 17). The millstone could not be taken because it was necessary for subsistence (24. 6). The hardships caused by the taking of pledges and the refusal to restore them was one of the evils denounced by the prophets and the sages (Job 22. 6; 24. 3, 9; Amos 2. 8; Ezek 18. 7-16; 33. 15).

The attempt was made in the Deuteronomic Code to meet the serious problem of debt by the device of the year of release (15. 1-6), which was a development of the sabbatical year of the Covenant Code. It was in reality a simple bankruptcy law. Every seven years a clean sheet was to be opened and the embarrassed man given a new chance.

It was especially urged that the near approach of the year of release was not to operate against the granting of loans (15. 9). From the provisions of this humane law the foreigner was also to be exempted (15. 3), apparently on the ground that lending to a Hebrew was a brotherly help, while lending to a foreigner was business (15. 6). There is no evidence that this year of release ever came into general use, and Nehemiah does not seem to know anything about it.

Provisions regarding loans and interest manifestly belonged to the noncommercial stage of Hebrew life. The laws were never very much observed, and as business developed they were not observed at all. The books of Wisdom indicate the hardships of debt, and the danger of going surety for another (Prov 6. 1-5; 11. 15; 20. 16; 22. 7, 26; 27. 13; Sirach 18. 33). In later times the rabbis cleverly avoided the letter of the law, as was their wont when hard pressed with troublesome requirements, so that loans, pledges, and interests became a recognized part of Hebrew economic life (Matt 18. 23-35; 25. 27; Luke 7. 41f.). Josephus states that the bonds of the debtors were kept in the public archives (B. J., II, xvii, 6).

§ 3. The Development of Great Estates

With the development of a more complex social organization opportunity arises for the strong to make themselves wealthy at the expense of the poor. In the times of the Hebrew monarchy conditions were favorable for the privileged classes to get the land into their own hands. First there was the poverty which was produced by the wars. When the foreigner ravaged the land the farms of the poor would be overrun, and they would be forced to borrow from their wealthier neighbors for food and seed. When the Hebrews went out themselves to battle, the farmers would be forced to serve as soldiers with little or no remuneration, and their own interests would necessarily be neglected. If the foreigner were conqueror and exacted tribute, taxes would fall heavily upon the poor. If the kingdom was prosperous, the court would become luxurious and taxes would still be heavy.

An oppressive form of taxation was the *corvée,* that is, the requirement of labor for the service of the king. Solomon built his palace and the temple by this obnoxious means (1 Kings 5. 13; 12. 4). When Jeremiah denounces him "*that buildeth his house by unrighteousness . . . that useth his neighbor's service without wages*" (22. 13) he may be referring to this unrequited toil. We have no means of saying how extensively this was employed by the later kings, or how far the nobles may have been able to require it for their own service.

We have noted above how conditions which brought the people into poverty made them debtors to the rich with the result that their lands were mortgaged and by reason of the usurious interest were often lost. Thus more and more as time went on it was possible for the rich to secure the small ancestral estates of the poor, adding them to their own domains. Ahab's dispossession of Naboth from his vineyard (1 Kings 21) is suggestive of the kind of conduct that was sometimes pursued. The Shunammite woman's loss of her land is another case in point (2 Kings 8. 1-6); and the evil had become so serious in the time of Isaiah that he could utter a bitter woe against those that "*join house to house, that lay field to field, till there be no room*" (5. 8).

The prophets felt heavily the oppression of the poor and spoke scathing words against those who were exploiting them (Isa 3. 14f.; 10. 2; 32. 7; Ezek 18. 12; 22. 29; Amos 8. 4). The wronging of the poor was an evil also deplored by the wise men (Job 24. 4-14; Prov 22. 22; 30. 14). The great hopes of a reconstructed social state that was to come in the future included justice for the poor (Psa 72. 2, 4, 12; Isa 11. 4), and the promise that the poor should be the first to enjoy the new prosperity (Isa 14. 30; 25. 4; 29. 19).

In postexilic times the opportunities of wealth were so often connected with unpatriotic relations to the heathen oppressors that the godly were generally poor. It is doubtless because these conditions existed that the later psalms seem almost to identify the poor with the godly. Moreover, the enemy who is so often denounced in the so-called imprecatory psalms was often the social enemy, the oppressor, the tyrant. The psalmist is not speaking forth his personal hatred, but is uttering the passionate protest against those who use their power and opportunity to wrong the weak. The awful prayer, "Break thou the arm of the wicked" (Psa 10. 15), appears in the light of the whole psalm as a noble longing for the helpless to be saved from the heavy arm of his destroyer.

The development of commercialism in the Greek age and the freedom from foreign taxation for a period under the Maccabees doubtless brought added prosperity to Palestine generally. The reigns of the Herods were also, on the whole, productive of prosperity. The Galilee of the time of Jesus was a region whose people were generally in simple but comfortable circumstances. There was not wanting, however, the harsh distinction between the rich and the poor, and wealth appears generally in the New Testament as a spiritual danger. This phase of the subject may be more conveniently discussed in connection with the teaching of Jesus.

§ 4. Philanthropy

The book of Deuteronomy, speaking out of the bitter experience of the centuries, states that "the poor will never cease out of the land" (15. 11). In view of this condition, Hebrew religion laid great stress upon philanthropy. The provisions above noted for loans without interest were in reality not economic laws but injunctions to generous brotherly assistance to the unfortunate. Indeed, in Deuteronomy the loan scarcely differs from the gift. It is the opening of the hand to the poor.

In the earliest legislation there is a specific provision that the yield of the fallow lands in the seventh year is to be for the poor (Exod 23. 11). Presumably, any one might gather what grew in those untilled fields. A gracious custom that developed and that was particularly fostered in the Deuteronomic legislation was that of gleaning. The reapers were not to go back to the forgotten sheaf. The olive beaters were not to go over the trees the second time, and the gleanings of the vineyard were not to be taken by the owner. All these belonged to the poor, especially to those three classes of the poor, "the sojourner, the fatherless, and the widow" (Deut 24. 19-21). The later legislation insisted that the corners of the fields should not be reaped but should be left for the poor (Lev 19. 9f.; 23. 22). The book of Ruth presents in vivid form the practice of the gleaning.

A somewhat similar kindly provision was that one might eat his fill of grapes as he passed through his neighbor's vineyard and might eat of the standing grain, but, of course, could not carry anything away with him (Deut 23. 24f.; compare Mark 2. 23).

A kind of tax for the poor was the tithe of the produce of every third year (Deut 14. 28f.; 26. 12). Two years this tenth was to be used for the family festival (14. 22-27), but the third year it was to belong to "the Levite, the sojourner, the fatherless, and the widow." And to the regular festivals of the harvest the poor were to be invited, that they might rejoice with those who had plenty (16. 11-14).

In addition to these provisions for the poor generosity was always to be emphasized. The prophet declares that it is more pleasing to Jehovah than ritual observance (Isa 58. 7). The virtue of charity is frequently commended

(Prov 3. 3; 19. 17; Ezek 18. 17; Dan 4. 27; Mic 6. 8; Tobit 1. 3, 16, 17; Sirach 4. 5; 16. 14; 35. 2), and it is included among the characteristics of the worthy woman that "she stretcheth out her hand to the poor" (Prov 31. 20).

Of course there was danger that as almsgiving came to be regarded as well pleasing to God it should become itself ritualistic and be done for the reward. Prov 19. 17 might look in that direction, and the references to almsgiving in the Apocrypha show such a tendency. (In addition to those just quoted note Tobit 14. 10f.; Sirach 3. 14; 29. 12; 31. 11; 40. 17, 24.) In considering the teaching of Jesus upon this subject we shall note the later Jewish developments.

DIRECTIONS FOR STUDY

1. Read 1 Sam 8 and 9. What is suggested in the speech of Samuel and in the conditions of Saul's family as to the change which the monarchy brought in Israel?
2. Read 1 Sam 25; 2 Sam 17. 27-29. What do these indicate as to riches in ancient Israel?
3. Enumerate the provisions for the protection of the poor that are contained in the Book of the Covenant.
4. Note the provisions for the poor in Deuteronomy 14 to 16. How satisfactory do these seem to be for such a social situation as that in Judah?
5. Read the book of Ruth, and, while remembering that it is a later idealization, consider what it implies regarding the condition and treatment of the poor.
6. Read Job 21. 6-33, which is a description of the strange fact of the prosperity of the wicked. Consider what it implies as to social conditions.
7. Divide the references given on the subject of wealth and poverty into two classes—those that deal with justice and those that deal with charity (kindness). Note how the splendid statement of Mic 6. 8 includes both of these as fundamental in religion.
8. Which is the more important for our modern life, justice or charity? To what extent can they be separated in any scheme of social regeneration?
9. Read Psalms 10, 37, 58. Considering that these are utterances of men deeply troubled by the oppressions of the great,

what would you say were the social conditions that called them forth? Note in Psa 58. 6 the comparison of the oppressor with a raging beast. Can you think of any modern oppressors of the weak concerning whom it would be suitable to pray such a prayer?

10. What are the fundamental social problems in connection with wealth and poverty? What help does our study of Hebrew legislation give us in understanding these problems?

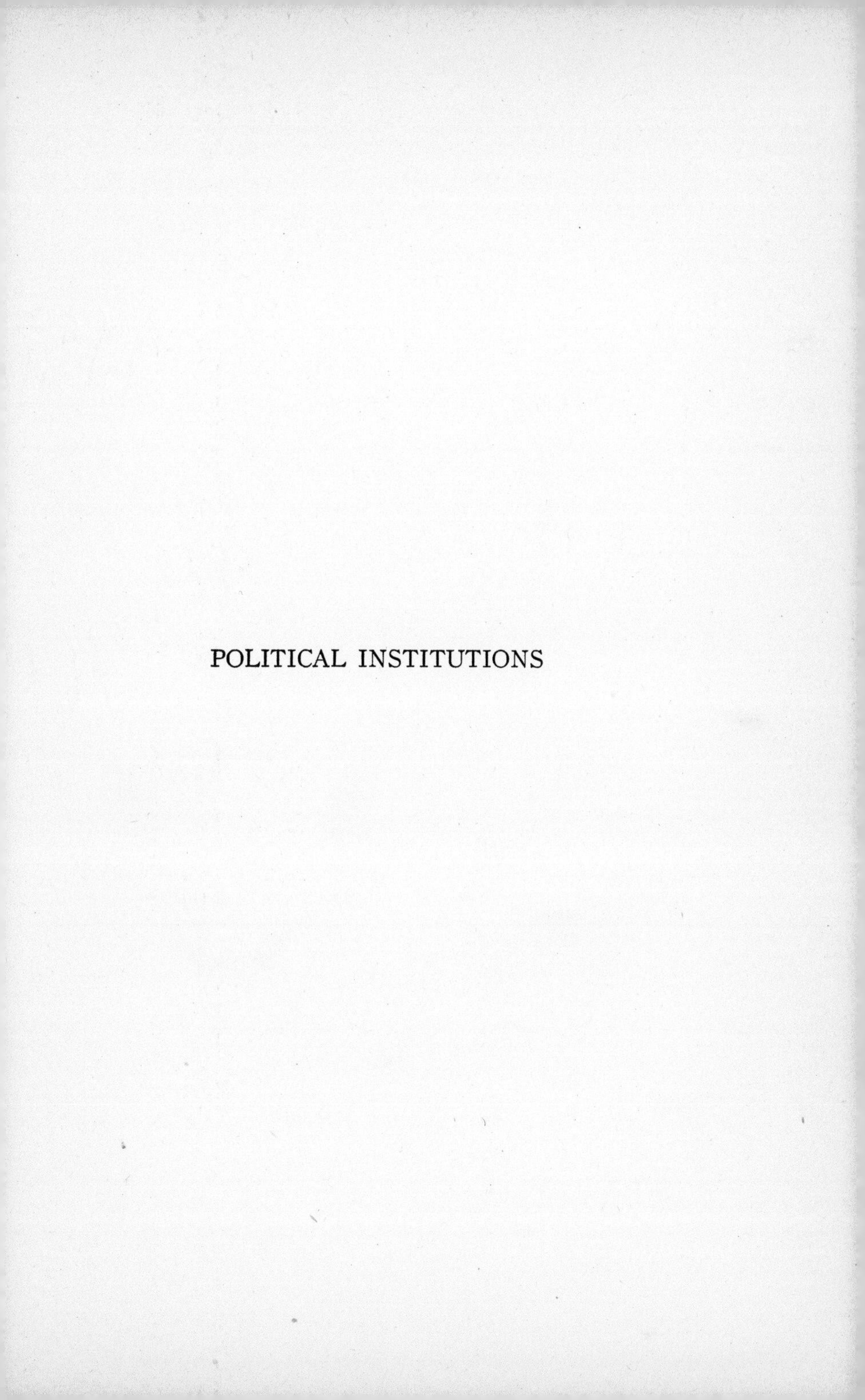

POLITICAL INSTITUTIONS

CHAPTER X

CLAN AND TRIBAL ORGANIZATION

Ancient peoples generally supposed themselves to be descendants of some single great ancestor. Thus the Greeks regarded themselves as the children of Hellen. The Romans traced their descent from Romulus and Remus, and the Hebrews, when they began to write the story of their past, found a mass of folk tradition which carried their lineage back to the sons of Jacob.

Of course national development is not quite so simple as that. Many elements combine to form the complex totality that thinks of itself as a single people. Every modern nation is such a complex, and so was every ancient nation. The Hebrews were no exception to this rule. It may well be that Abraham, Isaac, Esau, Jacob, and the twelve patriarchs were historical characters, whose fortunes have been correctly brought down in those epic stories that are part of our literary and religious inheritance. But there have doubtless gathered about their names some of the characteristics that later belonged to the peoples who were reputed to be their descendants. And some incidents in the lives of the patriarchs may in reality represent movements of peoples rather than of individuals. The patriarchal stories, therefore, are full of suggestions as to the origins of the Hebrews.

§ 1. The Nomad Clan

The family was the unit of organization. As we have seen, the family was a more complex body than that which bears the name among ourselves. It included the patriarch and his wives of full and secondary rank, his sons and their wives and their children, his daughters until they were married, and his slaves with their wives and children. If we should take the story of the family of Jacob literally, it might present a typical family, the old man being head and judge of the entire group. But suppose that Jacob's family had remained in Canaan, what would have happened after his death? There would have been twelve families each composed of father, mothers, children, and slaves. It would not be one family, and yet the family ties would still remain, a sense of kinship would be there, and, above all, the blood-bond requiring every member of the group to avenge the death of any member would be recognized. Moreover, the family religion would be common to all, including certain ceremonies peculiar to that particular group. Such were the festivals in David's family (1 Sam 20. 29).

This group of families would constitute the clan. The largest or the oldest or the strongest of the families would have a kind of preëminence, and the head of this family would be the chieftain of the clan. Such is the organization of a modern Arab clan to-day with its sheikh, or elder, the familiar word which meets us so often in the Hebrew political organization. The patriarchal authority which existed in each separate family was transferred to the group of families, and the elder was a kind of umpire to whom disputed questions could be referred, and who had authority in matters relating to the group as a whole.

But the clan would scarcely ever be so homogeneous as this illustration would indicate. A stranger might easily be assimilated, as Moses entered the family of Jethro (Exod 2. 16-22). The clan settling down for a time in one place might enter into such relations with the inhabitants that a coalescence would be effected. The acceptance by one of the religious ceremonies of the other would cement the union and soon they would be regarded as of common blood. Such a fusion was contemplated between the clan of Jacob and the Shechemites (Gen 34), but a feud prevented its success.

§ 2. The Development of the Tribe

As the clan was the enlarged family and included various heterogeneous elements, so the tribe was a group of clans. The process by which any tribe attained its full development cannot be followed exactly, for such origins are always lost in prehistoric social relationships. Actual blood kinship was always doubtless a considerable factor. Geographical propinquity was almost equally important. Indeed, such was the condition of ancient life that neighbor clans must either fight or fuse (compare Gen 26). If they were of about equal strength, it doubtless often happened that there began to be mutual concessions of pasturage and wells; intermarriage followed, and common action against enemies; at last their diverse origin was forgotten, and they were the clans of the common tribe.

An interesting illustration of the process is seen in the Calebite clan which became a part of the tribe of Judah. The Hebrew word *Keleb* means "dog," so that we have here also possibly an illustration of totemism, this group having originally had the dog as its totem. Caleb in the fine story of the spies (Num 13f.) appears as an individual hero, and there may well have been such a noble incident in the journey toward Canaan. But in the story of the conquest of the south country (Judg 1. 8-15) we must regard Caleb as a clan securing its possession in the highlands of Hebron. Now, Caleb was not a Hebrew, for it is distinctly stated that he was a son of Kenaz (Judg 1. 13), a Kenizzite (Num 32. 12); and the Kenizzites were an Edomite clan, for Kenaz appears as one of the sheikhs descended from Esau (Gen 36. 11). We are to understand, therefore, that the Calebite clan separated from the Edomites, to whom they belonged, and settled in the hill country of southern Canaan, a region which continued to bear their name in the later history (1 Sam 25. 3; 30. 14). The tribe of Judah found them hospitable instead of antagonistic, entered into friendly relations with them, and ultimately the Calebites became members of the tribe of Judah. In the genealogies which were formed many centuries later with the design of tracing the lineage of every family in Palestine back to the single ancestor, Caleb appears as the great-grandson of Judah (1 Chron 2. 3-5, 18). The Jerahmeelites were another such foreign clan also living in the extreme south (1 Sam 27. 10; 30. 29).

By such means the various tribes gradually formed. That the process was not complete when they entered Canaan the above noted accretions to the tribe of Judah sufficiently indicate. It is probable that other tribes also coalesced with certain of the peoples among whom they settled, and, as we shall see, the tribe gradually became practically a geographical rather than an ethnographical term.

The force which brought together the scattered elements which later formed the Hebrew nation was their common devotion to Jehovah. Religion was at the heart of the social organization in ancient times, and those people were of common blood who acknowledged the same God. It is probable that each tribe had its own special religious observances, as Laban had his household gods (Gen 31. 19, 30). After the tribes settled in Canaan they appear to have had their own individual sanctuaries (Deut 33. 18f.; Judg 18). But the worship of Jehovah was that which cemented them together in the wilderness, and it was the bond of union in the great emergencies of the conquest of the land (Judg 1. 1f.; 5. 2; 7. 18; 1 Sam 4. 3-6). Instead of saying, therefore, that the Hebrew people at the close of the period of the Judges were all those who had descended from Abraham, the common ancestor, it would be historically correct to say that they were all the people who through kinship or by assimilation had come to be worshipers of Jehovah.

The *elders* of the clans collectively formed the governing body of the tribe. When the district of Gilead was in danger "the elders of Gilead" sent for Jephthah to help them (Judg 11. 5). When David hoped to secure the kingship he sent presents to "the elders of Judah" (1 Sam 30. 26), and to these same elders he appealed after the conspiracy of Absalom (2 Sam 19. 11). Only in special emergencies when a chieftain came to the front was there a single governor of the tribe. The Song of Deborah (Judg 5), which is one of the oldest pieces of Hebrew literature, refers to the tribal leaders always in the plural, "the governors of Machir," "the marshals of Zebulun" (v. 14), "the princes of Issachar" (v. 15). There was no great need of a central government, as the patriarchal organization sufficed for all ordinary purposes, and the group of elders were the umpires or arbitrators in cases of dispute. The single governor, whose authority was supreme and to whom recourse could be had in cases of difficulty, was the God of the tribe. This was, of course, in its beginning a very crude idea, as in the ritual for jealousy (Num 5. 11-28), but there was in it the possibility of that fine conception of the relation of God to Israel which appears in the prophets and the psalmists, and which attains its fullest expression in Jesus's teaching of the kingdom of God.

§ 3. The Rise of the City

The earlier organization of Hebrew life was naturally modified by the change from the nomadic to the settled condition. We have seen that the Hebrews in Palestine became agriculturalists, but this does not mean that, like our farmers, they lived far apart from one another on their own farms. Such a condition would have been quite impossible in those lawless times. As one travels to-day over the great plain of Esdraelon, which is well cultivated, he does not find a single house; the people live together in villages and come out by day to their farms (compare Ruth 2. 4). Two necessities were sought in the village—the well or spring which could supply water, and the mutual protection which was essential to preserve life and property. Naturally, the families and clans settled in the same district, and the clans which had formed the tribe occupied contiguous tracts of country.

But the village itself was not security enough. The Canaanites dwelt in fortified cities (Judg 1), and the Hebrews found that they could preserve themselves only by adopting the same means. The city was only an enlarged village with a wall around it (Lev 25. 30f.). It was still the place from which men would "sow fields and plant vineyards" (Psa 107. 35ff.). It was often built upon a hill and always with the water supply within the walls. The city did not supplant the village but afforded protection to it. In the list of cities in Joshua (chs. 15 and 19) there is always the addition "with their villages," and sometimes the picturesque expression is used "the city with its daughters" (Num 21. 25; 32. 42, marg.). Thus the town of Laish dwelt "quiet and secure," depending for protection upon the powerful city of Sidon, of which it was a dependency (Judg 18. 27f.).

The development of the city modified the ancient clan and tribal government. A clan would occupy a city, but other elements would necessarily be included. The new body thus formed would not have as definite a relationship to the former tribe which had now become scattered over a considerable territory. The city was sufficient in itself and recognized the authority of its own elders, who would constitute a kind of senate. We know, for example, that in Succoth there were seventy-seven elders (Judg 8. 14). So it came about that the elders of the city largely took the place of "the elders of the tribe" (Deut 19. 12; Judg 8. 16; Ruth 4. 2; 1 Sam 11. 3). Jehu wrote to the "rulers of Jezreel, even the elders" (2 Kings 10. 1). The authority of the city elders was so well recognized that Jezebel had to make use of them to secure the condemnation of Naboth (1 Kings 21. 5-14).

It had been considered that the clan numbered about a thousand souls, and the term "thousand" was used to designate it. So Gideon objects that his "thousand" is the least in Manasseh (Judg 6. 15). Samuel calls upon the people to present themselves by their tribes and by their thousands (1 Sam 10. 19). The term was transferred to the city with its dependent villages, and it is in this sense that Bethlehem is called little among the "thousands of Judah" (Mic 5. 2).

The tribes conquered their territory in Canaan as they could, sometimes together, sometimes separately. There was no rigid preservation of tribal lines in the distribution of the people through the country, and within the territory occupied by a given tribe there might be many alien elements. These gradually coalesced with their neighbors, and the term "tribe" came to designate the district rather than the racial group. During the period of the monarchy the tribe greatly declined in importance, but when the northern tribes lost their identity in the Assyrian deportation there came to be a longing for the reestablishment of ancient Israel. The particular references to the tribal boundaries in the Hexateuch belong to this later time and represent an idealization of the history of the past.

DIRECTIONS FOR STUDY

1. Review the chapter on the family, and consider the political significance of the early Hebrew family.
2. Read Gen 14 and 46. Note that clan movements are there described.
3. Read Judg 5. Note the references to the clans and tribes and to the Jehovah religion as the unifying bond.
4. Note similar facts in Judg 6 to 8.
5. By the use of the historical imagination reconstruct the tribal movement with its possibility of amalgamating alien elements indicated in Judg 18.

6. Work out a parallel between the English and Hebrew nations, as developing from various constituent elements and gradually losing the sense of those differences.
7. Compare the Hebrew tribal organization with that of the American Indians.
8. Compare Hebrew city organization with that of Greece.
9. By what steps does the patriarchal form of government pass into the aristocratic form?
10. Consider the development of the self-governing city. How far did it exist in Israel? What is the genetic relation between our aldermen and the Hebrew elders?

CHAPTER XI

THE KINGSHIP AND THE COURT NOBILITY

§ 1. The Development of the Kingship

The first unified leadership of the tribes of Israel was effected by Moses. He held no official position. Appearing in a time of stress, he was accepted as the messenger of Jehovah, led the people out of Egypt and through the wilderness, and was accorded the authority which belongs to a great personality. The emergency of the conquest required a continuance of such leadership, and the authority of Moses was great enough for him to appoint his own successor. Joshua, therefore, became the war chief whom the people followed.

Once a settlement had been made in Canaan, and the tribes had become scattered each to its own region, the federation ceased, and there was no central authority. This condition was most unfavorable to national defense, and again and again it was necessary for conspicuous military leaders to marshal the tribes, or at least some of them, for battle. A man who had behind him the prestige of military success was naturally looked upon as fit arbiter in matters of dispute. These occasional leaders, therefore, became known as judges. It is unlikely that any of them had any definitely constituted authority other than his personal influence, and it is probable that the authority and influence were always local rather than national. The absence of any central government is indicated in the expressive statement that in those days "every man did that which was right in his own eyes" (Judg 21. 25).

When the people said, "*We will have a king over us* . . .

that . . . he may judge us, and go out before us and fight our battles" (1 Sam 8. 19f.), they expressed the need of a permanent political organization for the scattered population of Israel. Samuel, while, according to the later version, protesting against the kingship, according to the earlier story, actually selected the king by divine direction. The form employed was that of anointing (1 Sam 10. 1), which was the ancient usage among many peoples, probably symbolic of a divine enduement of power and authority (Judg 9. 8). The practice seems to have been followed throughout the kingship (1 Sam 16. 13; 2 Sam 2. 4; 5. 3; 1 Kings 1. 39; 2 Kings 11. 12; 23. 30). Thus the king was known as "the Messiah of Jehovah" (the Lord's anointed, 1 Sam 26. 11; Psa 2. 2).

Saul, the first king, came to his office much as the judges had come to the front—through a heroic act of martial leadership (1 Sam 11), and his conduct of the office differed little from that of the judges. He remained in his ancestral city of Gibeah (1 Sam 14. 16), where he kept a simple state, sitting among his servants and attended by a guard (1 Sam 22. 6, 17), ready to hear cases that might come before him. At the beginning of each month at the new moon he held a feast at which his officers were expected to be present (1 Sam 20. 24f.). In time of war he was commander in chief, and the record of his reign shows that he was considerably engaged in campaigns against Israel's enemies.

Under David and Solomon with the increase of territory and of wealth there was a marked development of the kingship. The institution of the harem (2 Sam 3. 3-5; 1 Kings 11. 1-3) was an assimilation to the customs of the eastern emperors. David captured Jerusalem and made it the capital of the land (2 Sam 5. 6-10). Solomon built there a magnificent palace and a temple for royal worship (1 Kings 6. 37 to 7. 1). When the kingdom was divided Jeroboam set up his own capital (1 Kings 12. 25), but it remained for Omri and Ahab to extend the institutions of the South to the Northern Kingdom. A new capital strongly fortified was built in Samaria (1 Kings 16. 24), and splendid palaces gave dignity to the king's court (1 Kings 21. 1; 22. 39).

§ 2. THE FUNCTIONS OF THE KING

The first duty of the king continued to be that of leading his people in war. Already under Saul the nucleus of a standing army was formed (1 Sam 14. 52) and the "captain of the host" was appointed (1 Sam 17. 55). David during his outlaw life had gathered around him a picked band, and these continued during his reign to be his bodyguard. The exploits of the great first three heroes and of those next in valor, and then of the thirty mighty men were considered worthy of special mention in the chronicles of the king's reign (2 Sam 23. 8-39). At the time of the conspiracy of Absalom David had a guard of Philistine mercenaries of six hundred men who remained true to him through all the crisis (2 Sam 15. 18-22). The same regiment of household troops again served the king's need in the last conspiracy of his reign (1 Kings 1. 8, 10, 38), and at a later time was available to restore the Davidic line to the throne (2 Kings 11. 4). These faithful Philistine mercenaries have been compared to the famous Swiss guard who have been so conspicuous in European warfare.

In addition to the foot soldiers David kept a hundred chariots of those which he captured from his enemies (2 Sam 8. 4). This arm of the service was greatly increased by Solomon, who is said to have had fourteen hundred chariots (1 Kings 10. 26), and four thousand horses (1 Kings 4. 26; 2 Chron 9. 25). Twelve thousand horsemen are also mentioned as on his establishment, but it is never safe to give too much weight to the round numbers of ancient documents.

Besides the regular troops, the armies consisted of the

male population summoned from their homes for the emergencies of battle (1 Kings 22. 36). There was no regular system of training these men, but they were skilled in the use of the weapons of their day. At one time Benjamin could furnish *"seven hundred chosen men left-handed; every one could sling stones at a hairbreadth and not miss"* (Judg 20. 16).

The northern army at one time at least was organized with two commanders under the king, "the captain of half the chariots" (1 Kings 16. 9) and "the captain of the host" (v. 16). This latter title seems to have belonged to one man in preeminence, but it was also applied to all generals (2 Kings 9. 5). Of the minor officers, we know particularly captains of thousands (1 Sam 8. 12), captains of hundreds (2 Kings 11. 4), and captains of fifties (1 Sam 8. 12; 2 Kings 1. 9-13; Isa 3. 3).

The king held an important place in the administration of justice which may be left for discussion in connection with the treatment of that topic. (See Chapter XIII.) As regards legislation, it is particularly to be noted that there was no idea of a legislative authority in ancient times. Law was not thought of as the result of enactment, but as the time-honored custom of the tribe or nation. It was God who gave laws. As we have noted, the prophets who produced the Book of the Covenant and the Deuteronomic Code did not think of themselves as innovators, but as expressing, in the name of Jehovah, the great duties and prohibitions, most of which had existed from time immemorial, but some of which were particularly required by the entrance into the land of Canaan. The province, then, of elders, judges, and king was to administer justice in accordance with these time-honored prescriptions.

§ 3. The Royal Revenue

The royal revenue was not divided into personal and state expenditures. Indeed, there was no distinction between the king's household and the government. In addition to the maintenance of his army and provision for the national defense, such as the building of fortifications (1 Kings 15. 22; 2 Chron 14. 6; 26. 9), the king undertook little government that required expenditure, except that it is likely that he maintained the royal sanctuary.

One tenth of the produce of agriculture seems to have been regarded as the king's tax (1 Sam 8. 15, 17). He had also the right to the first mowing of the grazing land for his horses (Amos 7. 1; 1 Kings 18. 5). In addition to these, it was expected that he should be given presents (1 Sam 10. 27; 16. 20), and he doubtless had the lion's share in the spoils of war (2 Sam 8. 11; 12. 30). When the king was exercising suzerainty over foreign nations tribute from these peoples came in to increase his revenues (2 Sam 8. 10; 1 Kings 4. 21-23; 10. 14-25; 2 Kings 3. 4; Psa 72. 10; Isa 16. 1).

Solomon divided his kingdom into twelve districts for the purpose of securing supplies for his great court. The record of his splendid state gives the food requirements for a single day (1 Kings 4. 22f.). If this was the basis upon which the levy was made upon each of the taxation districts for a month, it must have been a considerable burden upon the people. It is a fact worthy of note that these districts did not correspond with the boundaries of the tribes, showing partly that the old tribal divisions had ceased to be important, and also that Solomon was desirous of minimizing the old social organization which might interfere with his imperial designs.

In addition to these ordinary taxes the king could impose special burdens in times of emergency, such as the payment of tribute to a foreign conqueror. Menahem laid such assessments on the men of wealth (2 Kings 15. 20), while Jehoiakim exacted the payment of the common people (23. 35). That such taxes generally fell heavily upon the poor is evident from the conditions in Nehemiah's day (Neh 5).

The use of the temple treasure on occasion to pay these foreign exactions (2 Kings 15 and 18) was justified by the fact that the sanctuary was largely sustained at the king's expense.

A strong king with an army behind him could, of course, exercise almost despotic power, and the speech that is attributed to Samuel (1 Sam 8. 11-18) doubtless expresses the views of later years when the kingship was found to be rather a burden than a blessing to Israel (Ezek 46. 18).

The brief Asmonean kingship was much like that of the preexilic time, except that it was united with the priesthood and was modified by the thoroughly organized priestly institutions and by the influence of the parties which developed in later Judaism.

§ 4. The Court Nobility

The military establishment which the kings developed, the great royal household which was especially marked in the reign of Solomon, but was approximated always both in the north and the south so far as the prosperity of the country permitted, and the magnificent royal worship, all combined to create a court nobility which was distinct from the old leadership of the tribes. These nobles are referred to collectively as the princes (1 Kings 4. 2; Jer 26. 10, 21; 32. 32; 34. 10, 19; 36. 12; 38. 4; 52. 10), and very significantly also as those "that saw the king's face" (2 Kings 25. 19), an indication of the withdrawal of the Oriental sovereign from his people.

Of first importance among these were probably the military nobles. Thus in Solomon's day there are mentioned prominently his *"men of war, and his servants, and his princes, and his captains, and the rulers of his chariots and of his horsemen"* (1 Kings 9. 22). The captain of the host who "mustered the people of the land" (2 Kings 25. 19) was the commander in chief of the entire army, except the royal bodyguard, which had a captain, or as we should say, a colonel of its own (2 Sam 8. 18; 20. 23; and perhaps 2 Kings 25. 19). Either one of these or another prominent general was "the captain on whose hand the king leaned" (2 Kings 7. 2). The frequency of warfare throughout the kingly period and the opportunities of spoil in times of success must have given the military leaders a great position in the land. In the Northern Kingdom one of the generals again and again usurped the kingship (1 Kings 16. 9, 16; 2 Kings 9. 5; 15. 25).

The civil officials were very numerous. The "remembrancer" was probably the prime minister (2 Sam 8. 16; 20. 24; 1 Kings 4. 3; 2 Kings 18. 18, 37; 2 Chron 34. 8), though he may have been only the recorder or chronicler. The scribe was the secretary of state (2 Sam 8. 17; 20. 25; 1 Kings 4. 3; 2 Kings 12. 10; 18. 18, 37; 22. 3-9), and it is to be noted that Solomon had two of these officials.

We have an interesting insight into the great office of major domo of the palace, "the officer over the household" (1 Kings 4. 6; 18. 3; 2 Kings 18. 18, 37; 19. 2), from the fact that Shebna, who held the position in the reign of Hezekiah, was the subject of denunciation by the prophet Isaiah (22. 15-25). The authority of this official in the palace was so great that he was said to hold "the key of the house of David." But the power of the office had come to extend beyond the palace to the city of Jerusalem and even to the kingdom itself (v. 21). The emoluments of the position were such that Shebna lived in princely state with splendid chariots, and was engaged in building a magnificent sepulcher to give himself an enduring name (v. 16).

Three officers are mentioned whose functions it is difficult to describe: the king's friend (1 Kings 4. 5; so also perhaps 2 Sam 15. 37; 16. 16), the king's servant (2 Kings 22. 12), the king's counselor (2 Sam 15. 12; 16. 20, 23; 17. 1, 7, 14; Isa 3. 3). There were evidently from time to time distinguished officers of state about the king's person.

The *corvée* (see p. 99) required a superintendent during

the reigns of David and Solomon (2 Sam 20. 24; 1 Kings 4. 6; 5. 14; 12. 18) besides numerous chief officers whose positions would be influential (5. 16). There is some evidence of the continuance of this forced labor after Solomon's days.

The commissary-general had charge of the collection of the supplies for the royal household from the twelve divisions into which the kingdom was divided for this purpose (4. 5). Under him were twelve district superintendents each responsible for one month's supplies (4. 7-19).

As the population of the two capitals increased the police authority became a matter of importance. It is natural, therefore, to find that there was a "governor of the city" both in Samaria (22. 26) and in Jerusalem (2 Kings 23. 8).

A dignitary who had charge of the royal and probably also of the priestly robes was called "the keeper of the wardrobe" (2 Kings 22. 14).

Other officials are mentioned as having charge of the various properties of the king (1 Chron 27. 25-31). There were certain "officers" who made proclamations to the people when they were assembled for military purposes, and who probably organized the mobilization (Deut 20. 5, 8, 9; Josh 1. 10; 3. 2). And there were always ready at the king's bidding officials without specific designation (1 Kings 22. 9; 2 Kings 8. 6), who were perhaps chamberlains, and possibly eunuchs, introduced in connection with the institution of the harem.

The ecclesiastical dignitaries are properly included among the court nobility, for they were specially concerned with the royal worship. It is to be remembered that the temple was not the central sanctuary for the whole people until the time of Josiah, and, indeed, until after the exile. It was built by Solomon for his own worship, which, however, was, of course, representative in character. The priests are named as ministers of the king (2 Sam 8. 17f.; 1 Kings 4. 4). They received their appointment from the king

(2. 35) and a considerable part of their emoluments came from the royal sacrifices.

This great number of officials with their families constituted a court nobility entirely new in Israel. The old rulers of the people, the "elders of the city" and "elders of the tribe," still retained certain local authority (1 Kings 8. 1; 20. 7; 21. 8; 2 Kings 6. 32; 23. 1; Isa 3. 2, 14). But they were entirely overshadowed by the new aristocracy, and this aristocracy was separated from the people. It was an officialdom dependent upon the king; and its interests centered at the capital. The speech of Samuel (1 Sam 8. 14f) states the bitter facts when it represents the king taking the best of the fields, the vineyards, the oliveyards, and a tenth of the produce and giving it to his nobles. It was against this avaricious and oppressive aristocracy that the prophets of Israel and of Judah uttered their stern denunciations (Isa 5. 8-12; Jer 5. 26-29; Amos 6. 1-6; Mic 3. 1-3).

The nobles copied the example of the king in the establishment of harems, and the ladies were even more self-indulgent and overbearing than their lords. The prophets particularly denounced those women whose luxury was purchased at the expense of the misery of the poor (Isa 3. 16 to 4. 1; Amos 4. 1-3). It is a significant indication of our dependence on conventions that women, whom we naturally think of as peculiarly sympathetic to misery, have not seldom been even more unconcerned than their husbands about the condition of the poor in those societies where the extremes of wealth and poverty have existed. The Roman empire and the French monarchy are notable instances of this fact.

DIRECTIONS FOR STUDY

1. Read 1 Sam 13, 14, 18, 20, 22, 24, and 1 Kings 3 to 7; 9. 10 to 11. 40, and contrast the kingship of Saul as a social institution with that of Solomon.
2. Look through the kingly histories and note the references to

war. Consider the influence on the kingship, on the nobles and on the people, of war between the two kingdoms, civil war, successful foreign war, and unsuccessful foreign war.

3. What modern kingship seems to approximate most nearly that of the Hebrews? What parallels could be drawn?
4. What were the good and evil elements in the Hebrew kingship? Was the evil inevitable in the institution? Why did certain of the prophets look for an ideal state under an ideal king?
5. How would you estimate the economic results of the system of taxation employed by the kings?
6. What were the elements of social value in the old Hebrew eldership? How far were these conserved under the monarchy? Could they have been more fully conserved and at the same time maintain a strong central government?
7. Compare the development of the Hebrew aristocracy with that of France?
8. Both the Northern and Southern Kingdoms fell before great eastern empires; what elements in the royal and aristocratic organization contributed to the fall?
9. What kind of aristocracy may develop in a republic? Compare it with a court aristocracy. What would be the social influence of each?
10. What is the religious conception of political duty as expressed by the prophets in the book of Kings? How far would this idea modify modern political conditions?

CHAPTER XII

THE PRIESTLY ARISTOCRACY

§ 1. The Development of the Priesthood

During the monarchy the priests both in Jerusalem and in the Northern Kingdom were of two kinds, those who served at the royal sanctuaries and were practically part of the court, and those who served at the high places or local shrines and subsisted on the offerings brought by the people. The Deuteronomic reform, which centered all worship at Jerusalem, disposed of the priests of the high places, and gave an additional dignity to the Jerusalem priesthood.

The deportation to Babylon included the king, the princes, and most of the priests, together with the elders who had been the local dignitaries of the cities and of the tribes. The kingship ceased with the fall of Jerusalem. The nobles suffered a loss of prestige with the disappearance of the court. It was the opportunity for the priests to come forward. They had a great representative in the priest-prophet Ezekiel, who devoted himself to the preparation of a constitution for the reorganization of the state when the people should be able to return to Jerusalem. In his system, the temple became the center of the people's life, and the priests were, of course, the dignitaries of the temple.

During the Babylonian period also was developed the Priest Code now found in Exodus, Leviticus, and Numbers, in which the functions and privileges of the priests were elaborated with great care.

This extended influence of the ecclesiastical leaders did not become operative at once. It is evident that during the captivity the elders, whose dignity had been so much overshadowed by the court nobility, became again significant

(Ezra 5. 5, 9; 6. 7, 14; 10. 8; Ezek 8. 1, 11; 14. 1; 20. 1); and in the development of the Jerusalem community the prince of the Davidic line, Zerubbabel, was for some time the center of the national hopes (Ezra 5. 2; Hag 2. 20-23; Zech 4). Yet already beside him, and practically equal in dignity, was Jeshua the high priest (Ezra 3. 2; 5. 2; Hag 2. 2; Zech 3 and 4). When Nehemiah became governor of Jerusalem it was a fundamental principle of his plan of reconstruction of the Jewish state that the religious constitution provided in the developed Pentateuch should be accepted by the people. Thus in the great covenant which the people made under his leadership the most significant requirements were for the upkeep of the temple service and for the support of the priests (Neh 10. 32-39).

This elaborated law greatly enhanced the significance of the temple and of the sacrificial system. Costly offerings were to be made daily, and at all the great festivals. The worship was to be accompanied with sacred song by great Levitical choirs, for which large numbers of the Levites were to be set apart. The various inclosures of the temple were to be carefully guarded from any profane approach, and for this large numbers of Levitical doorkeepers were required. Moreover, practically everything within the sacred precincts was in charge of ecclesiastical functionaries, the laymen, who had formerly been allowed much freer access, being further and further removed, and the slaves of the temple being replaced by Levites. The insistence upon the priestly mediation between God and man was carried so far that the holy place of the temple and the court of sacrifice were not to be entered by the people at all (Num 18. 1-7).

This ritualistic emphasis required a very considerable number of persons for the discharge of the sacerdotal functions. The list preserved in Neh 7. 39-42 gives a total of four thousand two hundred and eighty-nine priests who returned from Babylon out of a total of forty-two thousand three hundred and sixty people (v. 66), in addition to the

Levites. And it is probable that both the higher and lower orders of ecclesiastical functionaries became more numerous as time went on.

The entire priesthood was divided into twenty-four courses, each of which was to give service for one week (Josephus, Vita, 1), the change being made on the Sabbath. At the three great festivals when the Judaistic religion was to be expressed in its greatest magnificence the whole body of the priests was to be present. At the head of each course was a chief (1 Chron 24. 6; Ezra 8. 24, 29; 10. 5; Neh 12. 7).

§ 2. The Emoluments of the Priesthood

This great hierarchy necessitated considerable provision for its support from the Jewish community. As we have seen, the priest from the earliest times received as his due certain portions of the animals that were sacrificed. The Deuteronomic law increased the emoluments of the priesthood, and the Levitical law added many further provisions in view of the enlargement of the sacerdotal order. In later times, when these two laws stood side by side in the Pentateuch, the problem of harmonizing them arose. This was done for the most part by the simple process of addition, so that all that was given to the priests in each of the codes became the law of Israel.

Schürer[1] summarizes the revenues of the priests as follows: As regards the animals that were offered, they would receive (1) the sin offerings and trespass offerings entire (Num 18. 9f.). (2) The greater part of the meal offerings (Lev 2. 3, 10; 6. 16-18; 7. 9, 10, 14). As these offerings were very frequent, they constituted a large meat and meal provision. (3) The twelve cakes of shew bread which were renewed weekly (Lev 24. 5-9). (4) Of the peace offerings, the festal meals, the priests were to receive the breast and the right shoulder (Lev 7. 30-34; 10. 14f.). (5) The burnt offerings were, of course, consumed entire, yet even of these

[1] History of the Jewish People in the Time of Christ, ii, 1, pp. 231ff.

the priests were entitled to the hides, which, as a great many animals were offered, would yield a considerable revenue.

A much larger element of priestly income was derived from the taxes levied upon the agricultural products. These consisted of (1) the first fruits. Of the seven principal products wheat, barley, grapes, figs, pomegranates, olives, honey (Deut 8. 8), a portion was to be brought to the priests with a confession and thanksgiving (Deut 26. 5-10). (2) A further portion of the choicest of all the fruits, especially of the wheat, wine and oil (Num 18. 12), was to be paid. The required fraction to fulfill this obligation was not determined, but later usage fixed it at about one fiftieth. (3) The tithe. A tenth of everything that grew on the earth was to be paid to the Levites, who were in turn to give a tithe of the tithe to the priests (Num 18. 20-22). This was practically a transfer of the tithe which had been paid to the king (1 Sam 8. 15). (4) The second tithe. The old tithe of the Deuteronomic time was not intended for the priest but was to be used for a family festival for the owner. This still continued as an added religious requirement, though it does not properly belong in an enumeration of the priestly emoluments (Deut 14. 22-26). (5) The third tithe. Once in three years, according to Deuteronomy (14. 28f.; 26. 12), the tithe was to be given to the poor. This was probably originally the only tithe of that year, but later practice made it a third impost on the faithful Jew. This, again, was not for the benefit of the priests, although the Levites shared in it. (6) The dough. The priests were entitled to an offering from the kneaded dough (Num 15. 17-22). In practice this was one twenty-fourth from private persons, and one forty-eighth from bakers.

While the tithe was restricted to agriculture, the increase from flocks and herds of the Hebrews was also subject to taxation. Originally, the first-born male was to be sacrificed to Jehovah. This later became the perquisite of the priests. The first-born of oxen, sheep, and goats were actually brought to the temple when distance permitted. They were otherwise redeemed, while the first-born of unclean animals were always ransomed at the rate of one and a half shekels for each beast (Num 18. 15f.). The first-born child, which in the forgotten primitive past had also been sacrificed, was ransomed for five shekels. There was also a tax on the fleece at the sheep-shearing (Deut 18. 4).

Another source of priestly revenue was the vows. People often consecrated or devoted something to Jehovah as a pious act. These were to be paid to the priests, sometimes for themselves, sometimes for the expenses of the sanctuary (Lev 27. 28; Num 18. 14). Misappropriations of property which could not be restored to the rightful owner also went to the priests, together with the accompanying fine (Num 5. 5-8).

When all these sources of income are taken into account it is evident that they constituted a heavy tax for the not overwealthy population of Palestine, and they gave to the priesthood a provision for comfortable and dignified living far above that enjoyed by the ordinary Hebrew.

§ 3. The High Priest

At the head of the priesthood was the high priest. There had been some such presidency of the sacerdotal officials in the time of the monarchy (2 Kings 11. 9; 16. 10; 22. 10; 25. 18), and the office was probably hereditary in the family of Zadok, who had been appointed by Solomon (1 Kings 2. 35). The high-priesthood received greatly enhanced significance and dignity in the Priest Code. It was traced back to Aaron, the brother of Moses, and was held to be hereditary in his family (Num 35. 25-28).

The high priest held an important place in the earliest days of the postexilic community when the deposition of Zerubbabel removed the only Davidic prince about whom any hope of a renewed monarchy might center. The way was open for the advance of the high priest to the supreme authority. And after the governorship of Nehemiah there was no other Hebrew layman who could divide with the high priest the leadership of the nation.

It naturally came to pass that the Persian governors, and afterward the Greek governors who held suzerainty over Judæa, recognized the authority of the high priest as the representative of the Jewish community. He thus became the head of the state (note Josephus, Antiquities, XI, viii, 4, 5).

The historical records of the high-priesthood are very meager. It is probable that there was just as much intrigue for the possession of that office as there is always for the first position of any government. We know that the Greek kings of Syria assumed the right to depose and appoint high priests at their pleasure (2 Macc 4. 24; Josephus, Antiquities, XII, v, 1). The office, therefore, did not remain strictly hereditary, but there were a few of the greater priestly families from which alone the head of the order could be selected (Josephus, B. J., IV, iii, 6). The members of those families, and particularly ex-high priests, when there were such, constituted a higher caste above the ordinary priesthood, and are properly referred to as the priestly aristocracy.

The high priest was assisted in his government by the Senate, or *Gerousia* (2 Macc 11. 27; Josephus, Antiquities, XII, iii, 3), better known to us by its later title, Sanhedrin (XIV, ix, 3-5). The composition of this body is not definitely known. It consisted principally of members of that priestly nobility to which reference has just been made, but there were also representatives of the secular nobility and of the scribes. As this body while exercising conciliar functions was more important as the supreme court of the Jews, we shall consider its character more particularly in the next chapter.

In general, the administration of the affairs of Judæa tended to come more and more into the hands of the priests. In his eulogy of the Jewish system Josephus, evidently speaking of the practice of his own day, states that the priests were, in general, the administrators of the principal affairs under the presidency of the high priests (Contra Apion, II, xxii).

The secular duties of the high priests naturally carried them into the political intrigues of the courts of Alexandria and Antioch during the long period of warfare between Egypt and Syria, which so greatly affected the fortunes of Judæa. Like the popes of the Middle Ages, they were often more attached to their political than to their ecclesiastical functions, and that not always to the advantage of the people or to the dignity of the sacerdotal office.

The Hellenizing influences were potent from the time of Alexander on, and favor was to be secured from the suzerain by accepting Greek customs, which seemed to the kings so infinitely nobler than the provincial practices of Judaism. In their effort to curry favor certain high priests turned Jerusalem almost into a pagan city. In the rivalries and plots which this attitude fostered the foreign king found opportunity more than once to interfere and to replace the high priest by one more to his own liking.

The opposition between the Hellenists and those Jews who were loyal to the ancient faith and practice reached its climax in the Maccabean revolt. The noble brothers expelled the tyrannical Syrians, and secured freedom for the Jews. As a consequence they exercised the supreme authority which always belongs to military leadership. They were of the priestly order, although not of one of the high-priestly families. So, although it was quite contrary to the Pentateuchal law, Jonathan deemed it fitting to assume the office of high priest (1 Macc 10. 15ff., 59ff.). Simon was so splendidly successful in dispelling the enemy and building up the Jewish state that the people gladly accepted him as "high priest, captain, and governor forever" (1 Macc 14. 27-47). For nearly a century the Asmoneans were the civil and ecclesiastical rulers, and from the time of Aristobulus held the title of king of the Jews.

When the Asmoneans gave place to the Herods the high-priesthood lost its independence. Herod took care that a creature of his own should occupy that influential position, and the Roman procurators assumed a like prerogative. Thus it came about that there were a number of ex-high priests as well as the incumbents of the office (Josephus, Antiquities, XX, x, 1; John 18. 13). The families of these were among the chief of the priestly aristocracy.

§ 4. The Sadducees

The Maccabean revolt had united all the forces of pious Judaism, but when the Maccabees illegitimately took the dignity of the high-priesthood in contravention of the law, the strict constructionists were greatly scandalized. To be sure, they were anxious that the nation should be independent, but they were far more anxious that the law should be scrupulously enforced. On the other hand, the extreme Hellenists had been overcome, and there was a considerable party in the state, including the leaders of the great priestly families, who were in favor of organizing Jewish life in a more practical way than the law seemed to permit. It was impossible to live in that busy Greek world and at the same time preserve the strict exclusiveness of a law that had been devised by ecclesiastical scholars in the remote times and conditions of the Babylonian exile. The rulers of the Jews must make treaties with foreign nations, admit foreign ambassadors to their court, and permit commerce with foreign peoples.

Thus arose the two parties in the state—the Pharisees and the Sadducees, the former standing absolutely for the law, the latter supporting the policy of the new rulers. The name "Sadducees" is probably derived from the Zadokite priests, that is, the priesthood that was descended from the Zadok of Solomon's temple. It is thought that the name, like so many party titles, may have been given to these secularists by their enemies as a term of contempt, indicating that all who supported the Maccabees were mere followers of the priestly aristocracy, which had generally manifested more concern for its own privileges and emoluments than for the interests of pure religion.

It is not germane to our study to follow the history of the Sadducees or of their controversies with the Pharisees. It is sufficient to note that they represented the true character of the priestly aristocracy during the whole period of postexilic Judaism. The wealth of the state was largely in their hands. They were interested in the preservation of the *status quo*. They desired peace and prosperity in order that they might enjoy their privileges. Their ecclesiastical functions were subordinated to their aristocratic enjoyments. They were much like the Roman Catholic hierarchy before the Reformation.

We must consider the teaching of the Pharisees in connection with the teaching of Jesus. Let it be said at this point that while we know the Pharisees in the New Testament as they had hardened into legalists in the later times, yet they sprang from a longing for purity of religion and of life, and to them in those happier days of religious protest we may well believe that a great number of the godly priests of humbler rank always belonged.

The conflict of the Sadducees with Jesus was that of a political aristocracy facing a dangerous social upheaval. Spite of the oppressions of Herod and the iron hand of Rome, the priestly nobles still held much of the wealth of Palestine in their hands. They carried on the temple service and found it vastly profitable. Above all things, they desired to live at peace with Rome. They cared nothing for Jesus's great teaching of love as the fulfilling of the law which came into conflict with Pharisaic legalism.

But as soon as the Galilæan movement seemed likely to take on a Messianic character, and to attract the attention of the Roman authorities, the Sadducees saw its danger and caused the arrest and crucifixion of the disturber of the peace. So always is the attitude of the privileged classes and the defenders of the vested interests, when a revolutionary social gospel is proclaimed.

DIRECTIONS FOR STUDY

1. Read Neh 8 to 10, and with free use of the historical imagination consider what it meant to the Jewish community in Jerusalem to make such a covenant. What place would it give the priests in the national life?
2. Read Lev 21f., and note the careful regulations designed to secure a holy priesthood. How far were these moral and how far ritual?
3. Read Exod 28f., and note the sacred robes and the ceremonies of consecration for the priests.
4. Read Num 3f. for the duties of the Levites.
5. The above selections are from the later priestly law, although the historical setting is in the circumstances of the wilderness journey. In a similar way the book of Chronicles, with its religious idealization of the past, pictures all the arrangements of the second temple as operative in David's time. Read 1 Chron 23 to 25, and note the elaborate arrangements ascribed to David. Picture the temple service of the third century B. C. as there described.
6. Read Num 18, and note the provision for the support of the priesthood.
7. Read Sirach 50 for the impression which a good high priest made upon the religious men of his time.
8. Compare the government of Judæa under the priesthood with the government of the papal states. What are the advantages and disadvantages of such an identity of church and state?
9. Read the Gospels, and note the relations of the priests and Sadducees with Jesus. Why was the social point of view of Jesus objectionable to the priestly aristocracy?
10. Compare the history of the Jewish priestly aristocracy with that of the Roman Catholic and Greek Catholic hierarchies. What is the most satisfactory relation of church and state?

CHAPTER XIII

THE ADMINISTRATION OF JUSTICE

§ 1. Primitive Justice

In our discussion of law we noted how developing custom controls in primitive societies, and how conspicuous advances in legislation are effected. No one is particularly charged with the duty of making laws. They are not supposed to be "made," but, rather, to exist. In the same way no authority is distinctly charged with the administration of justice; and particularly there is no clear distinction between the executive and judicial functions. The judge is the person in authority. First of all, the father, the head of the patriarchal family, is judge even to the exercise of the power of life and death. As the clan develops, the elders jointly settle disputes between the members of the clan; and as the clan enlarges to the tribe, the elders of the tribe are the arbiters.

In Israel, as we have seen, this patriarchal justice prevailed to the time of the entrance into Canaan; and after the settlement in the land the same system continued, except that the elders of the city took the place of the elders of the clan or tribe. A typical case which indicates the mode of procedure is that of Naboth (1 Kings 21).

In order to understand the administration of justice in Israel one should call up in imagination the open place near the gate of a walled city. Here all men come and go, and here are always to be found certain of the older and more weighty men of the community, to whom appeal can be made in difficult matters. A real estate transaction is to be effected; the elders must witness the transfer. A robbery has been committed, and the indignant kinsfolk of the injured man drag the culprit to the gate; there the elders silence their vociferous speech and command the witnesses to relate the facts. An angry dispute arises over a commercial transaction, and it is for the elders to hear both sides and bring about an arbitration of the differences. In all these matters certain precedents would guide the elders in their decisions.

But there was another place of judicial decision besides the city gate, and that was the sacred shrine. There was another judicial authority besides the elders, namely, the priests. The priest's part in the administration of justice was of two kinds, corresponding to his twofold character. He was a teacher and a mediator. As a teacher the priest was able to instruct the people in what was ceremonially right and wrong. He knew when ritual offenses had been committed for which atonement must be made. He was able to decide difficult questions as to what was clean and what was unclean. And probably, besides these external teachings, there were moral decisions which the priests could make out of their experience and knowledge of the law.

But the more potent influence of the priest in judicial matters during the early period grew out of somewhat crude notions of religion. It is always felt by primitive people that a divine decision can be secured when a human decision is impossible. That "man's extremity is God's opportunity" is believed in a very naïve way. The sacred lot, therefore, is the means of deciding the disputed point. As it is understood that this is an appeal to God, the matter is in charge of the priests.

In Israel this was probably effected by two stones, which were called Urim and Thummim, and which were contained in the pouch of the priest's robe (Exod 28. 30). When a question was to be decided a solemn formula was used: "O Jehovah, if such and such be the case, give Urim, but if such other be the case, give Thummim" (1 Sam 14. 41f.;

23. 9-12). The stones would then be cast, and the matter would be definitely decided by the one which came forth (Num 27. 21). The Book of the Covenant probably refers to this method of decision (Exod 22. 7-9).

A somewhat similar function of the priests was in the ordeal of jealousy (Num 5. 17, 27, 28). It was expected that if the woman was guilty, God would intervene and cause a dropsy from the otherwise harmless water that was given her to drink. It is noteworthy that this Hebrew ordeal was not of that harsh character in which a deadly draught is administered and the victim must survive in order to establish innocence.

With the development of a nobler religion under the leadership of the prophets, this resort to the magical duties of the priests became less significant. It is an interesting fact that the meaning of Urim and Thummim was forgotten, so that the people had an idea that it was some mysterious power that would some day return (Neh 7. 65). But in truth, the influence of the priesthood, both in teaching and in judicial decisions, was no longer based on magical powers, but on their study of the law and of its applications to life. The great interest of the priests in the law is evident from the fact that the Book of the Law was placed in the temple and was held to be in their keeping (2 Kings 22. 8).

From the above outline it appears that if dispute arose between two Hebrews, they might carry the matter to the elders and secure an arbitration of their differences; or if a crime had been committed, the offender might be brought before the elders for punishment. If the case were obscure, resort might be had to the priests, who would cast the sacred lot.

But there was still another means of securing judgment, namely, by an appeal to some commanding personality who held authority beyond the local rulers. There was no organized system of appellate jurisdiction. As judgment was supposed to be a matter of wisdom, appeal was naturally made to the greatest man of the nation for his decision. Thus Moses was called upon to decide disputes (Exod 18. 13ff.). It was, therefore, simply in their capacity as leaders of the people that the national heroes in the times before the monarchy were appealed to for judicial decisions, thus receiving the title of judges.

§ 2. Justice Under the Monarchy

The judicial authority of the king was exactly of the kind just considered. Justice is always fundamental in social life. As soon as some members of the group become stronger than others they have the ability to exercise oppression. There must be some umpire to whom to appeal. There is always danger that little men who have judicial authority will pervert it to their own ends. Some great central justice is therefore essential to the stability of the state.

In the narrative of Israel's demand for a king one of the reasons is stated to be the perversion of justice by Samuel's sons, and the consequent desire of the people for a real judge (1 Sam 8. 1-5). A king would be above the petty strifes of the people and would be stronger than the chiefs who were practicing oppression; and his position would enable him to enforce his decrees. Thus the ideal king was always thought of as a just judge (1 Kings 3. 9; Psa 72. 1f.; Isa 11. 3-5; 16. 5; Ezek 45. 9-12).

To say that the king of Israel was the supreme court of the nation in the sense in which that could be said of the Roman emperor, or in the sense in which the English Crown is the fountain of justice, would be incorrect. There was no regular appeal from the local courts to the throne, but the king was accessible to his subjects—theoretically accessible to the least of them. A case of injustice or a matter involving peculiar difficulty might be brought before him. Thus Nathan appealed to David to punish the supposititious rich man who had wronged the poor man, and the king announced his intention to decide the case (2 Sam 12. 1-6). There are many instances of such appeals (2 Kings 6. 24-30; 8. 1-6). The case of the two women claiming the child was brought to Solomon, for none other was wise enough to find the truth (1 Kings 3. 16-28).

The great position and power of the king so overshadowed that of the elders as to reduce them to quite subordinate condition. The development of the new nobility, who had the rule of the land, operated in the same direction. While, therefore, the right to make judicial decisions remained in the body of the elders (Deut 19. 12; 21. 2; 22. 15; 25. 7; 1 Kings 21. 8), there was a smaller group of men in each of the cities who were the rulers and judges (Deut 16. 18; 21. 2; 1 Kings 21. 8; Isa 3. 2; Mic 3. 1, 9, 10). We do not know by whom these judges were appointed, but probably, inasmuch as they were rulers, they were part of the royal system of government (Isa 1. 23). A development took place in the priestly function in legal decisions, for instead of the priests casting the sacred lot they were associated with the lay judges in the determination of causes (Deut 19. 17).

While it is assumed that it was the business of the king to give judgment, and he actually continued to do so (2 Kings 15. 5), it was impossible that he should hear all cases personally. In the early times he appointed a deputy (2 Sam 15. 2-4). Later there was established a superior court at the capital composed of judges and priests, to whom difficult cases could be referred (Deut 17. 8ff.; compare Num 11. 16ff.).

The official judges were peculiarly liable to venality. The development of the landed nobility, the sharpening of the contrast between the rich and the poor, the entrance into the social stage of commercialism—all these things gave opportunities to the judge to render valuable services to litigants who were in a position to give him a bribe.

The vehement denunciations of the prophets indicate that this fundamental social corruption was dangerously prevalent in the later days of the monarchies (Exod 23. 8; Deut 16. 19; Isa 1. 23; 33. 15; Ezek 22. 12; Amos 5. 12; Mic 3. 10).

It was probably to facilitate justice that the Book of the Covenant (Exod 20-23) was composed early in the kingly period. It was the simple statement of the old customs of right which had prevailed in Israel, and were to prevail. The code is throughout deeply religious, for it was God's justice which was to be executed, and the obligation was strongly emphasized.

The great lawbook of the kingly period was Deuteronomy (see pages 31f.). One of the provisions of this law book was the appointment of judges in every city who were to be pure in the discharge of their high duties (16. 18f.). Finding this reference to themselves in the sacred code which they were expected to take as their guide, the judges would naturally be led to realize the obligation of fidelity. The book as a whole was the codification of the developed social practices as the people had become more highly organized, and was intended to summon rulers, judges, and people by its earnest religious appeal to realize the obligation of justice and generosity in the upbuilding of social life.

§ 3. Justice in Post-Exilic Judaism

In the Jewish community, composed of Jerusalem and the small surrounding territory, there continued to be the same need of ordinary justice as between man and man which had previously existed. This need was met, as it had been before the exile, by the existence of a local court in each city composed of several lay judges, perhaps with Levitical assistants. The book of Chronicles is good evidence for conditions in the day in which it was written, and so the arrangements attributed to Jehoshaphat were probably those which existed in the third century B. C. (2 Chron

19. 4-7; compare 1 Chron 23. 4; 26. 29). There was also the need which had previously existed of a superior court composed of more experienced and wiser men who could hear the more difficult cases. This court as it had existed at Jerusalem was perhaps more definitely organized after the exile with a bench of lay and clerical judges (2 Chron 19. 8-10). Ezekiel had already indicated that the priests were to be charged with judicial duties (44. 23f.).

From these courts developed very naturally the local sanhedrins and the great Sanhedrin as we find them in New Testament times. Josephus states that there were seven judges "most zealous in the exercise of virtue and righteousness in every city," with two Levitical clerks appointed to assist them. If any case were too difficult for them to decide, they were to send it undetermined to the Holy City for the decision of the high priest and the Sanhedrin (Antiquities, IV, viii, 14). In larger cities twenty-three instead of seven men formed the governing council. The later Jewish tradition informs us that there were two lesser courts at Jerusalem in addition to the great Sanhedrin, and that most of the ordinary cases came before these, only those of highest importance coming to the supreme court.

The great Sanhedrin consisted of seventy-one members, including the high priest, who was president. It was supposed to derive its origin from the seventy elders appointed by Moses (Num 11. 16). As we have seen, it was the Senate, which administered the affairs of the nation, both administrative and judicial, under the high priest. The leading members of this great court were the chief priests, representatives of the priestly aristocracy which had grown up as a result of the sacerdotal organization of the state. Another element in the court was the elders (Acts 23. 14). These are not exactly to be identified with the elders of the old régime. After the exile the difference between the court nobility and the city or tribal elders naturally disappeared. The term "elder" came to mean one of the leading citizens of the nation. These lay nobles were represented in the high court. A third element had its place in the Sanhedrin neither by hereditary dignity nor by wealth, but by reason of being learned in the law. The highly complex Levitical law, which after its final adoption in the fifth century could never be amended, required great skill in order to understand it and to apply it to the changing conditions of social life. It was the business of the scribes to give this study and interpretation to the law; and while most of them were teachers in the synagogue and in the temple, a limited number of the greatest of them were members of the Sanhedrin.

The high tribunal lost much of its independence and dignity in the reign of Herod, who put to death many of the Sadducean nobles who were opposed to him. Under the Roman procurators, however, it recovered its prestige and was allowed to exercise authority in matters strictly Jewish, although it could not pronounce a capital sentence (John 18. 31). The court could take original jurisdiction in grave cases, and it was before the great Sanhedrin that Jesus was arraigned (Matt 26. 57 to 27. 10; Mark 14. 53 to 15. 1; Luke 22. 54-71; John 18. 12-27). Before this same court, the "rulers and elders and scribes," the apostles Peter and John were brought (Acts 4. 5), and later also Stephen (Acts 6. 12). And it was to the Sanhedrin that Paul was delivered for trial by Claudius Lysias (Acts 22. 30). The apostle had probably himself been a member of the court (Acts 26. 10), and so, knowing that it was composed of the Sadducean nobles and the Pharisaic scribes, he skillfully made use of this knowledge to set the one party in the court against the other (Acts 23. 6-10).

The jurisdiction of the great Sanhedrin was properly limited to Palestine, but so highly was the court esteemed that its decisions had force wherever the Jews were to be found throughout the world (Acts 9. 1f.).

It is customary in our study of the Hebrew law to distinguish between the ceremonial and the moral requirements. It should be carefully borne in mind, however, that the Hebrews did not make any such distinction. All law was God's law, and the breaking of any law was at once a religious and a civil offense. The worship of strange gods was a capital crime equally with murder (Deut 17. 2-5). Jesus was arraigned upon the charge of blasphemy in that he said he was the Son of God, a charge which no modern secular court would consider. It is necessary to take the Hebrew point of view, and to realize that the state was a religious organism in order to sympathize with the complete organization of social life upon religious lines.

The Hebrew law was framed with every endeavor to secure justice. We have noted how bribery of the judges was condemned; and the law was very severe against false testimony. Two witnesses were required to establish a matter (Num 35. 30; Deut 17. 6; 19. 15; 1 Kings 21. 10; Matt 26. 60). False witness was condemned as early as the Decalogue (Exod 20. 16), and in the Deuteronomic Code it was provided that if perjury were proved, the offender should suffer the penalty which he had sought to bring upon the innocent man, a most just instance of the *lex talionis* (Deut 19. 16-21).

DIRECTIONS FOR STUDY

1. Read Ruth 4. What elements does this narrative contribute to our knowledge of Hebrew methods of legal procedure?
2. Compare the use of Urim and Thummim with similar judicial practices among the Greeks and Romans. Why do we find this method early rather than late in Israel's life?
3. Trace the development of the judicial authority of the priests in Israel.
4. Read the speech of Samuel (1 Sam 12. 1-5), and picture the good judge of the ancient times.
5. How far were the legislative, judicial, and executive functions distinguished in Israel? Compare the Hebrew system with

that of England, and with our own. Note the interesting theocratic statement in Isa 33. 22.

6. Read carefully in each of the Gospels the account of the trial of Jesus, and note what is there indicated regarding the procedure of the Sanhedrin.
7. Read the book of Acts, and note what information it affords regarding the Sanhedrin.
8. Read Neh 8. What provisions are therein made for the people to know the law? Note that the Hebrews made as much provision for teaching the people the law, in order that it might be obeyed, as for securing the punishment of those who disobeyed. Is that true of our own practice?
9. What provision was made for the purity and independence of the Hebrew courts? Compare it with our own system.
10. Note the entire absence of a jury system. How far would the elders take the place of a jury? How far did the Hebrew system secure those advantages which the jury system was designed to secure for us?
11. Why did not the Hebrews distinguish between moral and ceremonial law? Compare this with the system of Calvin in Geneva and with the Puritan laws of New England.

RELIGIOUS INSTITUTIONS

CHAPTER XIV

TABOO AND HOLINESS

§ 1. The Common Origin of Holiness and Uncleanness

The religion of Israel, like the law, was a development from primitive custom which had its roots in the prehistoric past. Like the law, again, the religion of Israel had much in common with that of other primitive peoples. The higher elements of that religion came through the experience and insight of great personalities. Such men, pushing through the ritual to the real, either modified old customs, sometimes even abrogating them altogether, or gave them a nobler significance.

A practically universal element in primitive religion is taboo. There are certain things which possess supernatural qualities, rendering them highly dangerous. They must not be touched. Sometimes they must not be seen. They are charged with magical influences, of which it behooves one to beware. Among most peoples a dead body was taboo, probably for the reason that the spirit might do harm to the survivors; and so all contact with the body was to be avoided as far as possible, and various purifications were necessary to remove the consequences of such contact. We need only realize the utterly irrational fear that many people among ourselves entertain toward a corpse or toward a graveyard at night to be able to sympathize to some degree with this feeling of primitive man.

In the same way anything connected with the Deity was taboo, for religion has fear as one of its main roots. A most interesting illustration of this attitude in Israel is seen with reference to the sacred ark, in which it was thought that in some special fashion Jehovah dwelt. The awful danger connected with the ark appears in the narratives of its capture by the Philistines and return to Israel (1 Sam 6f.), and in the fate of Uzzah, who merely touched the sacred box to keep it from falling from the cart (2 Sam 6. 6f.). Again, in the story of the people at Mount Sinai it is required that no one shall come beyond a certain boundary, for God is in the mount (Exod 19. 11f.).

This idea of taboo is the root of two diametrically opposite conceptions—holiness and uncleanness. The original idea of holiness had nothing to do with moral purity. It simply meant the uncommon, the removed, the unapproachable, that is, the taboo. How physical was the conception may be seen in the passage just quoted. If a person trespassed the boundary that was set, he was to be put to death, but no hand was to touch him (v. 13); the mysterious quality was infectious, and the executioner would have been involved in the danger. How from this simple notion of Jehovah as the one removed, whom it was dangerous to approach, there may develop the prophetic conception of ethical holiness—the one who is too good for the evil to come near him (Isa 6. 5)—is typical of the whole process by which the noblest religion of Israel and of Christianity has evolved.

Because that which is taboo imparts its dangerous character to the person who comes in contact with it the idea of uncleanness is developed. He has become contaminated with the forbidden thing, hence cannot mingle with the common people, still less come into the presence of Deity, until by some proper means he has removed the contamination and thus made himself "clean." As holiness originally had nothing of ethical quality to be loved and revered, but came to have that quality as religious experience deepened, so neither had uncleanness originally anything of abhorrence or shame connected with it. It was simply a quality which had become attached to a person, and which was removable by proper means of purification.

§ 2. FOOD TABOOS

The most outstanding type of uncleanness is that of food. Among the Hebrews there were a great number of creatures which could not be eaten (Lev 11; Deut 14. 4-20). The attempt has often been made to show that these prohibitions were of a hygienic character, and, therefore, highly favorable to the development of the Hebrew people. The modern study of similar customs among peoples all over the world requires that this view shall be given up. But the exact reason for the food taboos is not very easy to find. It has been supposed by some that they originated in totemism. Totemism is the belief of a primitive people that they have a blood kinship with some particular animal, which, of course, thus becomes to them taboo. It may perhaps be sacrificed in a sacramental feast, but it cannot be eaten with ordinary food. Inasmuch as the Hebrews were a complex of many clans, each of which may have had its own totem, some scholars are of the opinion that the tabooed food of one became tabooed of all, and so the long list accumulated. We have already noted the possibility that the Calebites were originally the dog tribe. However, this is by no means certain, and it is not proved that the Hebrews ever passed through the totem stage.

Whether or not totemism is the basis of some of the food taboos, it is unlikely that any single explanation can be given for all of them. The same reason that forbade the eating of animals which had not been bled, or which had died a natural death, would forbid eating the beasts and birds of prey who lived upon such food (Lev 11. 13-19; Deut 14. 12-19). The serpent was almost universally regarded with fear, and so the scaleless fish that resembled it would share its taboo (Lev 11. 10; Deut 14. 10). When certain creatures had come to be regarded as unclean a principle of selection could be derived from them to apply to others. This is a basis for the requirement that only those beasts were clean that were cloven footed and that chewed the cud (Lev 11. 3-8; Deut 14. 3-8), and only those fish with fins and scales (Lev 11. 9f.; Deut 14. 9f.).

It was not only the eating of the tabooed animals that caused uncleanness—indeed, it was not expected that anyone would do so abominable a thing—but the mere touching of the carcass of an unclean animal, or any contact with the unclean "creeping things" produced defilement (Lev 11. 24-38).

A fundamental taboo was against eating the blood (Gen 9. 4; Lev 3. 17; 17. 10-14; Deut 12. 23-25; 1 Sam 14. 33). It was regarded as the life. In the most ancient sacramental meals among many peoples the blood of the sacrifice was drunk by the worshipers, and so the most intimate communion with one another and with the god was secured. This practice does not appear in historical times among the Hebrews; the blood was offered to Jehovah or poured out upon the altar. The fat was also considered to be the seat of life, and so was also forbidden for food and was consumed in sacrifice.

It is quite possible that some of the food prohibitions arose from the fact that particular animals were used in heathen sacrifices, and hence were regarded as involving Israel in idolatrous practices. This was certainly the reason for the difficulty that greatly perplexed the early Christians who were so constantly brought in contact with food that had been offered to idols (1 Cor 8).

The prohibition of eating blood made it necessary that animals for food should be killed only in such a way that the blood could flow out. The slaughter was in a sense a sacrifice, the blood being offered to the Deity (1 Sam 14. 32-35). Hence the prohibition of eating anything that died of itself (Deut 14. 21), or that was strangled (Acts 15. 29). The permission that these might be sold to foreigners (Deut

14. 21) simply meant that it was understood that the foreigner was not subject to the same ritual requirements.

§ 3. VARIOUS TABOOS

As already indicated the Hebrew law of uncleanness in connection with the body of the dead was very primitive. The mysterious, cold physical form with the likeness of life but without movement caused man in his early days to regard the dead with fear. The Levitical requirements are very specific in the matter (Num 19). Whoever touched a body was unclean for seven days. Moreover, the condition was so contagious that every one whom he touched was in turn unclean, but the virulence of the condition was diminished so that he was unclean only until sundown (v. 22; Hag 2. 11-13).

It was felt, moreover, that the spirit of the dead was about the dwelling so that every one who even entered the tent was unclean seven days (Num 14). Immediately after the death, therefore, pains were taken to cover every vessel in the house, for the spirit of the dead might enter it and impart to it a dangerous quality (v. 15). Even the touching of a bone or a grave involved the same uncleanness (v. 16). The priests, who were under special necessity to guard their ritual purity, were not allowed to "defile themselves," that is, to come in contact with any dead body, save that of the nearest relatives (Ezek 44. 25f.).

The plague of leprosy was so abhorrent that it was regarded with superstitious fear by many peoples. In Israel the leper was unclean. The most elaborate precautions were taken to decide whether a person was afflicted with the disease, anyone having the slightest trace of it being placed in quarantine for an inspection by the priests (Lev 13). When he was pronounced to have the plague he was required to dwell outside the city, to go with rent garments, and with a covering on his upper lip, and to cry when any approached him, "Unclean, unclean" (vv. 45f.; compare

Luke 17. 12). Inasmuch as the stricken man was thus separated from the people by official action, he could be restored to his place in society in the event of his cure only by specific ceremonial purifications (Lev 14; compare Matt 8. 4; Luke 17. 14).

When the lepers were healed by Christ the word that is used to express it is not healing but cleansing (Matt 8. 3; 10. 8; 11. 5; Mark 1. 42; Luke 7. 22; 17. 14, 17), indicating that the idea of their defilement still existed in New Testament times. Indeed, the idea continued in the Christian Church, and through the Middle Ages lepers were generally looked upon and treated much as in the biblical narratives.

The function of reproduction, which we are only now beginning to regard in normal fashion, and to dignify by realizing its inherent purity, was for primitive people a subject of superstitious regard. Rigid taboos were connected with various aspects of the function. The birth of a child is so mysterious a fact that it is natural that the idea of aloofness, which is the essence of the taboo, should attach to it. Thus among the Hebrews the mother was required to undergo certain ritual purification (Lev 12). The mother of Jesus went to the temple for this ceremonial (Luke 2. 22-24). The older Christian churches still maintain such a prescription.

There was one aspect of this religious relation to the function of reproduction which had a curious development in Israel. Among primitive peoples the attainment of puberty is attended with important religious ceremonies, especially for the boys. One of the most common of these is the rite of circumcision, which is probably intended as an initiation into manhood. But this practice did not prevail among the Hebrews in historic times, the rite being performed in infancy. The later religious explanation of this was that the child thus entered into the covenant with the God of Israel (Gen 17).

The Jews of still later times recognized the religious

significance of puberty in making the boy a "son of the law" at twelve or thirteen years of age (Luke 2. 41ff.). The ceremonies of confirmation or joining the church continue among Christians this appropriate recognition of the transition period in youth.

When a person had become ceremonially defiled he could not resume his normal place in the community until he had been cleansed. This was in many cases accomplished simply by a bath after the appropriate lapse of time. In other cases more elaborate washings were necessary and sometimes sacrifices of a greater or lesser quality were required.

The matter of uncleanness played a great part in Hebrew life. Probably a considerable part of the population at any given time was unclean, that is to say, ceremonially unfit, from some slight cause or other, to participate in the community life (1 Sam 20. 26). Such an attitude would evidently have a tendency to externalize religion. One cannot read the minute and elaborate requirements for the purification of those who were unclean without feeling that the priests who were engaged in such ritualistic practices, and the people who were subject to them, would come to think of religion as a set of arbitrary rules which must be literally obeyed, and that the divine favor was secured by such perfunctory observances. And this is what actually happened in Israel. Spite of all the endeavors of prophets, and psalmists, and of the more ethically minded priests and scribes, ceremonialism conquered; and it has determined the character of the Jewish religion to this day.

The taboo belongs to the lower strata of the Hebrew religion. It was carried over from primitive life, and in the nature of the case could only slightly be ethicized. It gave opportunity to the later scribes, who were concerned with literal obedience to the minutiæ of the law, to exercise their ingenuity in the most subtle refinements. The purifications that were required for all kinds of slight ritual defilements occupied the scrupulous Pharisee to such an extent that he spent much of his time in useless exercises. Those "traditions of the elders," which so greatly extended the already too ceremonial requirements of the law, met with the strong disapproval of Jesus. He insisted that purity is not ritualistic but moral, that not that which enters the man as food, but that which comes out of his heart as sin, was the real defilement (Mark 7. 1-23; Luke 11. 37-41).

§ 4. Holiness

The original meaning of holiness was purely physical. The fact that the word has to-day no physical connotation whatever, but is wholly ethical, is evidence of the development that has taken place in religion. Various stages of this development may be seen in the Bible itself.

When the men of Bethshemesh, who had been smitten because they looked into the ark, said, *"Who is able to stand before Jehovah, this holy God?"* (1 Sam 6. 20), they meant simply to speak of the physical danger of the presence of the Deity. Just as the idea obtained that uncleanness was contagious, so it was thought that holiness could be imparted by contact. The priests were not allowed to go among the people in their holy garments, lest they should make holy the people who might touch them (Ezek 44. 19). The sacrifices would have a similar effect (Lev 6. 28; Ezek 46. 20). The altar and the sacred vessels also imparted the quality of holiness (Exod 29. 37; 30. 29). It is to be remembered that this was a dangerous quality, which it was disadvantageous to the people to possess. Thus the later Levitical legislation provided that the people should be removed from the holy places, and the holy things, these being approached only by the priests, who were carefully to keep themselves ceremonially clean, that is to say, fitted to minister without danger before Jehovah. It is manifest that at this point we are in the realm where there is little difference between the holy and the unclean. Both are simply taboo.

An advance in religious appreciation is made when we find the unclean regarded as an abomination to Jehovah, while the holy is that which peculiarly belongs to him. In the various laws relating to the unclean food and to similar defilements it is indicated that Jehovah hates such things. They are not seemly for his people to eat or to touch. But in the earliest Hebrew legislation that has come down to us the idea has already been reached that Jehovah is concerned with justice and truth. His holiness is, therefore, to some extent ethically conceived. So when the sanctuary with all its furniture is set apart for his worship, and the sacrifices are offered to him, and the priests are dedicated to minister, and the special times, the Sabbath and the festivals, are set apart in his name, all these are holy and have the ethical qualities which Jehovah was conceived to possess.

The prophets advanced to a realization of Jehovah as the God of righteousness, and in so doing took up an entirely new attitude toward the institutions of religion. The sacramental idea, that religious acts are efficacious in themselves, was utterly denounced. Amos declared that Jehovah despises the very ceremonials which were regarded by the people as holy (5. 21). He did not use the word "holy," probably for the reason that it would not have been understood. Hosea in the same way insisted that Jehovah desires "kindness and not sacrifice" (6. 6). But it was Isaiah who especially presented the thought of the holiness of God which he conceived in ethical terms. In the wonderful narrative of the vision of Jehovah (6) may be clearly seen the evolution of the conception of holiness. Isaiah was in the sacred building. He saw Jehovah in his majesty. The seraphs veiled their faces as unworthy to look upon him, and cried, "Holy, holy, holy." The prophet felt the danger of the august presence: *"Woe is me! for I am undone; because I am a man of unclean lips, and I dwell in the midst of a people of unclean lips; for mine eyes have seen the king, Jehovah of hosts"* (v. 5). Here are the very words that come over from the old taboo—the divine king must not be seen; but the whole conception is ethicized, for Isaiah felt only his unworthiness. The uncleanness was not ceremonial but moral.

Isaiah delights in the phrase "the Holy One of Israel," and he means the righteous one: *"Jehovah of Hosts is exalted in justice, and God the Holy One is sanctified in righteousness"* (5. 16). He tells the people that they cannot enter the sanctuary because of their uncleanness, but the purification is to be moral: *"Wash you, make you clean; put away the evil of your doings from before mine eyes; . . . seek justice, relieve the oppressed"* (1. 16f.).

The Levitical law came later than the prophets, and organized elaborate institutions of sanctity. Into the Holy of holies no one could enter but the high priests once in the year. Into the Holy Place none but the priests could come, and so on through the various courts, until in the outermost the Gentiles were permitted. The sacrifices were given added significance, the Sabbath was to be kept with the most scrupulous care, the tithes were to be paid with exactness. The fundamental idea in these holy institutions was that all the world belonged to Jehovah, who gave it to his people on consideration that certain places should be peculiarly set apart for him, certain persons should minister to him, certain gifts and seasons should be reserved for him.

The religious ideal here was that which is always implicit in the sacramentalism of deeply religious men. They believe that by making a few things especially remindful of God, all things would become sacred. How thoroughly this was realized by the nobler spirits of later Judaism may be seen in the psalms. Psalms 15 and 24 make the conditions of acceptable worship wholly ethical. But the danger of sacramentalism is that most people will be satisfied with the externals; because a few things are very sacred, sanctity will be applied only to them, and common things will be altogether profane.

DIRECTIONS FOR STUDY

1. Read Daniel 1, Acts 10, and note how significant the food taboo was for the Jew even in later times.
2. Read Exod 19, and consider how far the idea of holiness there expressed is ethical.
3. Read Lev 10 and 22, and consider how far the ideas of holiness there expressed are ethical.
4. What food taboos are still in force among the Jews? What is the religious significance of such regulations?
5. Compare the food and disease taboos with our modern hygienic regulations. Have they anything in common?
6. Read Josh 6f., the story of the "ban" upon Jericho. The city was banned as an offering to Jehovah. It, therefore, with all that it contained became his. Hence all plunder was taboo. What, then, was the fundamental cause of the execution of Achan? How would you estimate the religious quality of the attitude manifested in the incident?
7. What superstitions are current in modern life that have the quality of the primitive taboo? What is the ethical and religious attitude involved in such superstitions?
8. Read Psa 51, and note the difference between the emotions of the penitent sinner and those of the primitive worshiper who was afraid of the holiness of his god.
9. Read Psa 96, and consider the idea of the holiness of Jehovah that is expressed in this joyous experience of worship.
10. Read Psa 99, and note how utterly ethical the idea of holiness has become. In our modern religious experience, what do we mean by the holiness of God? How far do awe and reverence belong to the religious attitude?

CHAPTER XV

SACRIFICE AND OFFERINGS

§ 1. The Original Sacrifices

The most conspicuous element of ancient Semitic religion was sacrifice. This was of two kinds—the gift to the Deity and the sacrificial meal. It is difficult to say which of these was the more ancient, and we find both of them side by side in the earliest Hebrew records.

The idea of the gift was that the Deity was able to receive and to enjoy the good things which were pleasing to him. Food and drink, especially the flesh of animals, were the chief goods that men enjoy. These, therefore, they gave to their god. The blood as the mysterious seat of the life was poured out as an offering. Perhaps there was some thought that the earth drank it up. Flesh was consumed by fire, the ascending smoke seeming to carry the food upward to God (Gen 8. 21). One of the earliest records of Hebrew sacrifice is that of Gideon, who prepared a complete meal for Jehovah (Judg 6. 19-21). The flesh of the kid with unleavened cakes was laid upon the rock, upon it was poured the broth, and then the whole was consumed. In obedience to the divine command Gideon proceeded to offer a second sacrifice of a bullock burned whole upon the altar (vv. 25f.). This form of gift-sacrifice was called "the burnt offering." It was an expression of thanksgiving, as in the case of Noah (Gen 8. 20), or it might be offered in intercession in connection with the desire for divine aid, as in Samuel's sacrifice of the young lamb (1 Sam 7. 9), Saul's offerings before the battle (1 Sam 13. 9), David's offering at Araunah's threshing floor (2 Sam

24. 22ff.), and Solomon's magnificent sacrifice at the inauguration of his reign (1 Kings 3. 4).

A special form of the gift sacrifice, and one which was conceived to have high efficacy, was that of a human being. The practice was common among the Semitic peoples (Deut 18. 10), but the Hebrews had already grown beyond it in historic times, except on rare occasions when they were highly desirous of securing the favor of God. Jephthah's vow doubtless contemplated human sacrifice, and resulted in the offering of his daughter (Judg 11. 30-40). Ahaz in the time of his dire trouble, when the land was invaded by enemies, sacrificed his son (2 Kings 16. 3), as the king of Moab had done in a similar strait to terrify his enemies (2 Kings 3. 27). The practice became more common in Israel as the national difficulties increased, giving rise to the great prophetic protest of Micah 6. 7f. These incidents, with the possible exception of that of Jephthah, are narrated by the biblical writers with grave disapproval, and the story of Abraham's attempt to offer Isaac with the divine command to substitute the ram for the son was doubtless intended as a protest against the awful practice (Gen 22).

The other original sacrifice was the sacrificial meal. It was a joyous feast attended by the friends and neighbors of the worshiper, and including the Deity as the honored guest. He received his share of the food in the form of the blood poured upon the ground and the fats burned in the fire ascending as smoke. Fellowship between the god and his people, which was all important for the prosperity of the tribe, was thus cemented, and religion had accomplished its purpose of keeping the Deity well pleased with men. This sacramental meal was known as the peace offering.

An early instance of such a festal sacrifice in Israel was that in which Saul and Samuel had their first meeting (1 Sam 9. 11ff.). The people were to have a sacrifice in the high place. Some thirty friends had been invited (vv. 13 and 22) and were waiting until Samuel should come to bless the sacrifice. After this solemn invocation the feast proceeded. There is no specific mention of the portions of the animal which were offered to Jehovah, for this was too well known to need record.

Such sacrifices were also offered as family festivities, as in the case of Elkanah (1 Sam 1. 4). But it was usual to hold them at a sacred place so that Elkanah went up to Shiloh for his annual observance (v. 3). The worshiper himself offered the sacrifice, but there were certain perquisites which belonged to the priest in connection with it. One objection to the sons of Eli was that they did not observe the proper custom in taking their portions, and particularly that they did not burn Jehovah's portion—the fat—before dividing the meat (1 Sam 2. 13-16).

During the kingly period sacrifice was offered throughout the land at the ancient sacred places where the Canaanites had worshiped the Baals, the agricultural gods. The altars were generally erected upon the elevated spots, and hence the shrines were called "the high places." There was grave danger in this practice that in the minds of the people Jehovah would be simply identified with the Baal to whom the shrine had anciently been dedicated, and thus an idolatrous worship should come in. Moreover, the Canaanitish rites were shamefully impure, and the festal meals in which wine was part of the indulgence, would easily degenerate into riotous orgies ending in the most flagrant immorality (Exod 32. 6). The prophets denounced the popular worship because it had these characteristics (Hos 4. 11-14). The Deuteronomic Code attempted to work a reform by abolishing absolutely all places of worship except the temple at Jerusalem (Deut 12. 5-14). Here the great festal occasions were to be kept, but, inasmuch as it was impossible to make the journey to the temple whenever men wished to have a feast, it was provided that animals might be killed anywhere, the requirements of Jehovah being met by the pouring out of the blood upon the ground. In this attenuated form there was preserved the ancient idea that the killing of an animal was a sacred act. The blood continued to be taboo.

After the destruction of the temple, and during the exile in Babylon, there was opportunity for the earnest spirits among the Hebrews to reflect seriously upon their past history. Why had such awful disaster fallen upon them? Why had Jehovah so failed to protect them that even his temple was destroyed and his people prevented from offering him worship? The sense of sin was greatly deepened, and as the priests undertook to put into written form the practices of the interrupted ritual in order that those who followed them might be able to carry it forward correctly, they felt the necessity of elaborating those features which might secure the favor of God. The writers of the Priest Code, therefore, minimized the importance of the peace offering. The sacrificial meal, which was little more than a happy feast, celebrating the goodness of Jehovah, did not seem to them important. In practice it was much like our Thanksgiving dinner, whose religious character is at least somewhat subordinate. It belonged to the older religion of the family and the clan. It admitted the layman to a large share in the ritual, and it was essentially joyous. The new plan was altogether priestly and more serious. However, the ritual for the peace offering was carefully elaborated, and included the sprinkling of blood around the altar, and the burning of the fat (Lev 3).

The burnt offering was continued as expressing the adoration of Israel for Jehovah's goodness and mercy. It was ordained that a public burnt offering should be sacrificed every morning and evening in the temple (Exod 29. 38-42; Num 28. 3). At the beginning and end of every day there was to be burned upon the altar a yearling lamb, with cakes of flour mingled with beaten oil, and with a portion of wine as a drink offering, thus forming a complete meal. Thus Israel through her priests would declare her sense of obligation to a sustaining God. On the Sabbaths and the new moons the burnt offerings were to be more elaborate. In addition to these public offerings, any Hebrew who desired to express his thanksgiving and adoration might offer an appropriate animal or bird, or a meal offering of fine flour with oil and frankincense, for all of which the ritual was prescribed (Lev 1f.).

§ 2. The Propitiatory Sacrifices

While these older sacrifices thus continued, new offerings of a more solemn character were instituted that were particularly concerned to secure the pardon of sin. There had always been the idea that the burnt offering had a propitiatory quality. The bringing of the gift to Jehovah was intended as a symbolic petition for the removal of any estrangement between the worshiper and God.

However, sacrifice was not intimately connected with sin in preexilic Israel. When David committed his great wrong he repented at the word of the prophet, but there is no mention of any propitiatory sacrifices (2 Sam 12. 13ff.). When Ahab was guilty of the judicial murder of Naboth, and repented under the stern rebuke of Elijah, he was forgiven, but no sacrifice was considered necessary (1 Kings 21. 27-29). When Josiah realized that the people had been guilty of what almost amounted to apostasy, he inaugurated a thorough reformation with the destruction of all the instruments of impure worship, but there is no suggestion in the account that it was an appropriate occasion for piacular sacrifices (2 Kings 23). And the prophets were so anxious to make clear that Jehovah was concerned with ethical attitudes, right conduct, and loving loyalty to his righteous will that they spoke in such scathing terms about the useless sacrifices as to raise a serious question among modern students of their writings whether they were not in favor of the entire abolition of the sacrificial system (Isa 1. 10-17; Hos 6. 6; Amos 5. 21-24; Mic 6. 6-8; 1 Sam 15. 22).

The priests in the dark period of the exile were profoundly convinced of the sinfulness of the previous life of the people. They were doubtless influenced by the prophetic teaching to recognize that the injustice, the sordidness, the immorality, as well as the idolatry of the past had been the cause of the national disasters. In looking forward to the reconstructed Jewish state and the rebuilt temple they believed that the danger of sin and the need of repentance ought to be kept strongly and continually before the popular mind. Hence they developed the two great forms of sacrifice, the sin offering and the trespass offering.

It was recognized that much of the sin of the past had occurred through ignorance. Men and nations fall into the sins that do so easily beset them. It is only on reflection that they realize what they have done. At that moment of realization proper means should be taken to make atonement for the sin. The English word "atonement," which means reconciliation of those who have not been *at one,* is used to translate the Hebrew word which means literally "to cover." The idea was that the sin should be covered, not, of course, concealed, but put out of sight by forgiveness (Psa 32. 1). How was this to be done? The prophets had taught that repentance and confession secured forgiveness, but the priests had always been concerned with a ritual that expressed the dependent relation of the worshiper upon the Deity; and, as we have seen, the burnt offering had always been specially designed to secure his favor. What more natural than that they should feel that a more solemn offering would be the ritualistic condition of reconciliation after the commission of sin?

There was a special sin offering for the high priest, for if he offended, he involved the community in his guilt (Lev 4. 1-12). There was another sin offering when it had become clear that national sin had been committed (vv. 13-21). There was still another for the ruler because of his representative capacity (vv. 22-26); and another for the individual who desired forgiveness (vv. 27-35). There were specific offerings which individuals had to offer for certain kinds of sins which were called trespass offerings (Lev 5 to 6. 7).

The ritual of these sacrifices was distinguished by a specially solemn treatment of the blood, which was not merely poured out, but was put on the horns of the altar, and in some cases sprinkled before the veil of the Holy of holies. The fat was burned, as in the older sacrifices, and the flesh was eaten only by the priests.

While these sin offerings were the medium of forgiveness for the wrongdoing that transpired from time to time, there was one great annual sacrifice designed to remove every trace of national sin. The ceremonial of this greatest fast day in the Jewish system is given in Leviticus, ch. 16, and should be carefully examined. It includes the entrance of the high priest into the Holy of holies, the only occasion when this most sacred place was ever seen by mortal eyes. It includes also the strange ceremony of the scapegoat, in which the priest with hands upon the head of a goat confessed the national sins, and then sent the animal away into the desert symbolically to carry the sins out of sight. The solemnity of this Day of Atonement has continued to the present time so far as the changed circumstances of Judaism will permit; and the day is still designated by the Jews as *Yoma,* "The Day."

It is difficult to determine what the writers of the Priest Code intended to imply as to the efficacy of the piacular sacrifices. It is not likely that they thought that the animal died as a substitute for the sinner. Certainly, such noble spirits as Ezra and many godly priests who were concerned in the preparation and elucidation of the law, did not imagine that the sacrifice itself secured divine forgiveness. They would probably have gladly echoed the prophetic protest against any crass sacramentalism. But they believed that the sacrifices had been ordained, and therefore were necessary. It was not for man to discuss those divine requirements. Jehovah had prescribed the method of securing his forgiveness, and it was for man with humble and contrite heart to obey. Thus often a later sophisticated age accepts primitive customs as if they had permanent significance. The postexilic psalms abundantly indicate how compatible true repentance and ethical motive may be with sacrificial observance.

Yet the influence of the sacrifices was no more wholesome in the postexilic period than in the earlier times. The butchery of so many animals in the temple could minister to spiritual religion only for those fine minds that could see through the symbol to the reality. When we realize that, according to Numbers, chs. 28f., there were offered annually one hundred and fifteen young bullocks, eleven hundred lambs, thirty-eight rams, thirty-two he-goats, together with the concomitant offerings which each of these required, and that these were only the officially prescribed offerings to which must be added all the sacrifices inspired by private religious interests, it is evident that the grosser elements in Judaism were made exceedingly prominent.

When sacrifice was a family or clan matter, performed in the high place near the village, to which every one could easily resort, it entered into the people's life, although it was not much conducive to ethical development. But when it became centralized at Jerusalem, and given over entirely to the priestly class, it was formalized, removed from popular interest and played a decreasingly significant part in popular religion. The Jews were very insistent that the official sacrifices should be carried on, but their own religion centered not in the temple but in the synagogue, where the law as it affected their own conduct was carefully elucidated by the scribes.

The scribes themselves had become quite definitely separated from the priests and regarded their own work as very much more significant than that which was accomplished at the temple. The conduct of the priests had not tended to give them a high place in popular estimation, still less in that of the scribes. The latter were obliged, of course, by their theory of the law to accept the whole ritual as a necessary part of their religion. But the practical emphasis was upon those aspects of religion which could be observed by the people in the common practice of life. These were minute and legalistic enough, relating to the punctilious keeping of the Sabbath, the regular hours of prayer, and the many ritual obligations which the law laid upon the individual. But the sacrificial ritual just because it belonged to the priests, to Jerusalem, and to the temple, was less strictly emphasized, and came to be more and more external to the life of the nation.

§ 3. Firstfruits, Tithes, and Gifts

As the slaughter of the animal for the festal meal and the burning of the victim in the dedicated holocaust were the appropriate offerings of a pastoral people, so the presentation of the first fruits of the ground were those of an agricultural people. The Hebrews added these latter to their earlier offerings. We have noted that in the development of the sacerdotal system these agricultural offerings became a special tax on the land and were given to the priests for their support. The tithes, which were probably in addition to the first fruits, were also levied on all the agricultural products for the benefit of the priests. The various other gifts which were of a religious character, and were allotted to the sacerdotal order, have been discussed in connection with the priestly revenues (see pages 127f.).

There were other offerings, however, which Jewish piety prompted and which were reserved for the expenses of the sanctuary. Every male of twenty years old and upward, whether rich or poor, was expected to pay annually one half shekel for the temple service (Exod 30. 11-16). We have interesting evidence that this usage existed in the time of

Christ (Matt 17. 24; compare Josephus, Antiquities, XVIII, ix, 1). This money, collected from the Jews all over the world, was employed for the daily burnt offerings and the other public sacrifices, which, of course, entailed heavy expenditure.

In addition to this tax there were the freewill offerings. Thirteen trumpet-shaped boxes were placed in the temple court, into which the faithful might put what their hearts prompted them for the service of the temple. Jesus was looking at this public offering when he saw the poor widow drop in her two mites and spoke his encomium of her great devotion (Mark 12. 41-44; Luke 21. 1-4).

DIRECTIONS FOR STUDY

1. Read Judg 13. What kind of offering is there described and for what purpose was it offered?
2. Read 1 Sam 16. 1-5. What kind of offering is there described and for what purpose was it to be offered?
3. Read Lev 1. Consider how each element of this ritual arose.
4. Read Lev 3. What was the significance of each element in this ritual of the peace offering?
5. Read Lev 4. 1-12. Consider why the sin offering was developed?
6. Read Lev 5. What was the meaning of each item in the ceremonial of the trespass offering?
7. What was the origin of human sacrifice? Why was it discontinued among the Hebrews? How do you explain Exod 22. 29?
8. Compare the Hebrew sacrifices with those of Greece and Rome.
9. Read Pss 40 and 51. What attitude toward sacrifice do they express?
10. What religious values did such great souls as Ezekiel, Ezra, Nehemiah, Judas Maccabeus derive from the sacrifices? Why did the prophets speak so often against sacrifice? What does sacramentalism mean in modern religion?

CHAPTER XVI

THE SABBATH AND THE FESTIVALS

§ 1. The Sabbath Rest

One of the most distinctive social institutions of the Hebrews is the Sabbath. Even to-day, living in the midst of Christian or of Moslem peoples, who observe other sacred days, they continue to be loyally attached to its observance in spite of much difficulty, financial loss, and occasional persecution.

The Sabbath was not in its origin a Hebrew institution. The seventh day was observed among the Babylonians; the Hebrew people probably brought it with them in their western migration. It is probable that at the first it was a lunar festival occurring on the seventh, the fourteenth, the twenty-first, and twenty-eighth days of the lunar month, while the new moon, which was later separated from the Sabbath, originally occurred on a Sabbath day. The first observance of the day is lost in antiquity, and it can only be conjectured that the mysterious phases of the moon in some way gave to it a mysterious holiness, using the term in the physical sense. Certain common acts could not be performed upon that day. It thus corresponded to the *dies nefasti* of the Romans.

The first Hebrew legislation knows the Sabbath as a day of humaneness: *"Six days thou shalt do thy work, and on the seventh day thou shalt rest, that thine ox and thine ass may have rest, and the son of thy handmaid, and the sojourner, may be refreshed"* (Exod 23. 12). There is nothing said in the early law about religious observance. The Sabbath was to be a cessation from the constant toil which made the unrequited labor of the slave and the ceaseless work of the beasts so heavy. This gracious purpose is a part of that consideration for the weak and unfriended which is so conspicuous in the work of the great religious leaders of Israel.

In the preexilic history the Sabbath was observed as a day sacred to Jehovah, when ordinary work was to be given up. Traders ceased their business, even though some of them would have been glad to continue it (Amos 8. 5). It was considered a convenient time for visiting (2 Kings 4. 22f.). It was counted among the festivals as a day of joy (Hos 2. 11). It was also observed with some religious solemnities (Isa 1. 13).

The Deuteronomic law reaffirmed the Decalogue, and with it the Sabbath commandment, stating definitely the regulation of rest, with the insistence, *"that thy man-servant and thy maid-servant may rest as well as thou"* (5. 14), the reason for the observance being given in the deliverance of Israel from the Egyptian bondage (v. 15). The emphasis is thus upon the philanthropic motive, according to the spirit which runs all through the Deuteronomic Code. The necessity of this reiteration of the old law is evident from the contemporary word of Jeremiah, who rebuked the people because the Sabbath had not been observed. He made it a condition of the future prosperity of the house of David that they release the burden-bearers on the seventh day (17. 19-27). There was doubtless a constant temptation to keep the slaves at their toil without the kindly intermission of the Sabbath rest.

This institution, like all others in Israel, bears the distinctive marks of the exile experience. When the temple was destroyed and the sacrifices ended, the Sabbath remained as the great rallying point for the exiles. They still had the day which had always been regarded as sacred to Jehovah. They could keep it more strictly and give it larger significance than ever before. The exilic prophecies, therefore, bring the Sabbath into greater prominence, making it a day set apart for peculiar religious observance, and as a sign of loyalty to Jehovah (Isa 56. 3-6; 58. 13f.; 66. 23).

§ 2. The Sabbath Sanctity

In the priestly legislation the observance of the Sabbath was not put in the form of exhortation to kindly treatment of the toiler, but made a day of complete cessation from work for the honor of Jehovah, with the penalty of death attached to its profanation (Exod 31. 12-17). The great creation story of the Priestly Document had been put into the form of a panorama of a week of divine activity with the rest of God for his refreshment at the end. Thus a cosmic significance was attached to the keeping of the seventh day (v. 17; Gen 2. 2f.).

Many special observances and sacrifices were ordained for the Sabbath (Lev 23. 3; 24. 8; Num 28. 8f.), and striking incidents were related showing the danger of breaking its solemn requirements of cessation from labor (Exod 15. 5, 22-30; Num 16. 32-36).

Nehemiah's earnest attempts to reorganize Judæa on the basis of the priestly law included efforts for the observance of the sacred seventh day. Those who had remained in Palestine after the deportation of the best people of the land had become lax in many ways and in their poverty had used the Sabbath for profitable work. Moreover, trade, as we have noted, was largely in the hands of foreigners who had no interest in the Jewish Sabbath and would bring their wares as usual on that day. Nehemiah proceeded with his usual vigor (10. 31; 13. 15-22), and seems to have been highly successful in putting a stop to the violations of the sabbatic sanctity.

By the time of the Maccabees the Sabbath had become so significant to loyal Jews that they would allow themselves to be killed without resistance rather than bear arms on that day (1 Macc 2. 31, 38). When, however, it became evident that the great revolt would be crushed by this literal observance of the law they decided that they would defend themselves on the Sabbath (vv. 39-41). Josephus records many instances in which the question of meeting the enemy in battle on the Sabbath was a great element in determining Jewish history (Antiquities, XIII, xii, 4; XIV, iv, 2; XVIII, ix, 2; Contra Apion I, 22). He also notes that the Romans released the Jews from military service on the ground of their religious objection "to bear arms or to travel on the Sabbath days" (Antiquities, XIV, x, 11-19).

The Sabbath of later Judaism was a curious complex of joyous social relaxation and irksome religious obligation. It was a feast day in which the people entertained their friends with good cheer (Luke 14. 1). They managed to do so without actual labor, even serving hot viands by a clever contrivance not unlike our modern fireless cooker. It was a release from toil. From the time that the trumpet blew in the temple at sunset on Friday until it blew again at sunset on Saturday announcing the close of the Sabbath (Josephus, B. J., IV, ix, 12) no labor was permitted of any kind (cf. Mark 1. 32). The service in the synagogue (Mark 1. 21; Luke 4. 16) brought the people the opportunity of spiritual inspiration. It ought to have been a social institution of unmixed value.

But the Sabbath was spoiled by legalism. It is always difficult to keep the golden mean in religious observance. Obligation is either held so lightly as to be ignored or so rigidly as to be burdensome. Manifestly, it was not possible for the Sabbath to pass without any activity of any kind, especially as it was to be a festal day. What, then, were the permitted limits of activity? Might one take a walk, and, if so, how far? Might one feed his cattle, tend the sick, pluck a fruit? To these questions the scribes devoted their best learning and finest ingenuity. Learned doctors devoted their attention to the determination of what kinds of knots could be tied on the Sabbath day. Their refinements and subtle interpretations meet us constantly in the Gospels. The plucking of a handful of grain and rubbing it between the hands was unlawful (Matt 12. 1f.; Mark 2. 23f.; Luke 6. 1f.), for it was held to be essentially reaping and threshing. The healing of the sick was not allowed unless the life were in danger; thus Jesus's beneficent ministry aroused antagonism (Matt 12. 9-13; Luke 13. 10-17; 14. 1-6; John 5. 2-16; 7. 23; 9. 13-16).

These rigid requirements inevitably led to casuistry and legal fictions which destroyed the sincerity of the Sabbath observance. Pious Jews were forever asking whether this or that were permitted on the sacred day, so that, combined with a determination to keep the law to the letter, there was a constant desire to strain its permissions to the limit. Jesus gladly took advantage of the blessing of the day of rest and worship, used it with the freedom which ever belongs to the man of the spirit, and uttered the final word which is applicable to all ritualism, *"The sabbath was made for man, and not man for the sabbath"* (Mark 2. 27).

§ 3. The New Moon

In ancient times the new moon was even more important as a holy day in Israel than the Sabbath. Its original connection with the Sabbath had disappeared before historic Hebrew time, and it remained as an extra monthly day of rest, feasting, and religious observance (Isa 1. 13; Amos 8. 5; Hos 2. 11). Saul had his royal feast of the new moon (1 Sam 20. 5, 24). The annual feast of the Jesse clan was celebrated at the new moon (1 Sam 20. 6). Visits could be made on that day, as the animals were free from toil (2 Kings 4. 23). It was selected by Ezra as the appropriate day for the great assembly when the law was to be read (Neh 8. 2).

In the legislation of Ezekiel and of the Levitical Code the new moon had a high ritual significance (Ezek 46. 1), the sacrifices being even more in number than on the Sabbath (v. 6; Num 28. 11-15), including a he-goat for a sin offering (v. 15). The lunar festival continued to have its place in Jewish social life and religious observance after the fall of Jerusalem, and it is still maintained with distinctive services in the synagogues of the orthodox Jews.

§ 4. The Great Festivals

There were three annual festivals of great significance, the Passover, with which was combined the Feast of Unleavened Bread, Pentecost, and Tabernacles. In the earliest legislation these were prescribed as times of pilgrimage: "*Three times in the year all thy males shall appear before the Lord Jehovah*" (Exod 23. 17; 34. 23); and the same was required by Deuteronomy (16. 16).

The Passover was originally the spring festival of the nomads when the firstlings of the flock and herd were offered as a thanksgiving to Jehovah (Exod 13. 12). The people presenting their gifts, of which the sacred portion, the blood and fat, was reserved for the Deity, would eat the young lambs and calves with joyous festivity. A similar agricultural festival, when the first fruits of the field were offered, was observed by the Canaanites. This was naturally adopted by the Hebrews when they entered the agricultural stage, and the Feast of Unleavened Bread, continuing for seven days, was added to the Passover. In the Deuteronomic regulations these appear as one festival, and, in accordance with the law of the central sanctuary, the Passover was to be observed in Jerusalem (16. 1-8).

Although it originated in a sacrificial feast, the Passover had always a family character, and therefore it could be observed during the exile. It had long been connected with the deliverance from Egypt, standing as a great annual memorial of the covenant relation between Jehovah and his people. The priests felt the great religious and national significance of this aspect of the feast and developed the ritual with reference to such observance. It was a picturesque ceremonial in its public features, including the waving of the first sheaves of the harvest before Jehovah, and the solemn sacrifices (Lev 23. 4-14); and it was a deeply impressive religious spectacle in its family observance. The manner in which this family festival was carried out in later Judaism, which in turn has persisted until the present day, was very nearly in accordance with the description of the idealized observance of the first Passover in the land of Egypt (Exod 12; compare Matt 26. 17-30; Mark 14. 12-26; Luke 22. 7-30; John 13. 1-30).

As the beginning of the ripening grain was marked by the Feast of Unleavened Bread, so the end of the harvest period was celebrated by the Feast of Harvest, "*The first fruits of thy labors, which thou sowest in the field*" (Exod 23. 16). Barley ripened first, and later the wheat and the lesser grains (Ruth 1. 22; 2. 23). Of course the time of the close of the harvest would vary in different years and in different parts of the land, but as the agricultural festivals became nationalized they were arranged at definite periods according to a system of sevens. Thus seven times seven days was set for the harvest period. For this reason it was called the Feast of Weeks (Exod 34. 22; Deut 16. 9f.). From the fact that offerings were made of the new flour, it was called "The Day of the First Fruits" (Num 28. 26). From the fact that it was observed on the fiftieth day after the offering of the wave sheaf (Lev 23. 15f.), the Greek Jews called the festival Pentecost (meaning "fiftieth"), which is the term by which we generally know it (Acts 2. 1; 20. 16; 1 Cor 16. 8).

As one of the great nature festivals Pentecost was observed with freewill offerings in recognition of the goodness of God in the gifts of the earth. It was a time of joyful feasting, and the Deuteronomic Code provided that the entire household, including the slaves, should enjoy the festivities, and that the poor and needy should be invited to partake of the good cheer (16. 9-12). The Priest Code gave to the festival a liturgical character. It was to be observed with cessation from all common work, special sacrifices were to be offered, and in particular two loaves made of the flour of the new wheat baked with leaven were to be waved before Jehovah (Lev 23. 15-21). These ceremonies were very carefully observed in later Judaism, and the Jews flocked to Jerusalem for this feast from all parts of the world (Josephus, Antiquities, XVII, x, 2; B. J., II, iii, 1; Acts 2. 5, 9-11; 20. 16).

The greatest festival of the Hebrew year was the autumn Harvest Home, corresponding to our Thanksgiving Day, when not only the grain was harvested but the threshing was completed and all the fruits, especially the grapes and olives, were gathered in. Such a festival is practically universal among agricultural peoples. Thus the Canaanites before the coming of the Hebrews observed the vintage season with eating and drinking and religious ceremonies (Judg 9. 27). The Hebrews adopted the feast, as we know incidentally from the interesting reference to its observance at Shiloh, where the dancing of the maidens in the vineyards is specially mentioned (Judg 21. 19ff.).

At the ingathering of the fruits it was customary for the people to come from the towns and villages to the fruit gardens where they lived in hastily erected booths (Isa 1. 8), and carried on joyfully the work of securing the autumn bounty. From the practice of living in booths, the feast took its name, Feast of Booths. The translation "Tabernacles" is somewhat unfortunate as obscuring the simplicity of the institution. The Deuteronomic Code, in accordance with its purpose of transferring all ceremonial to the temple, provided that a pilgrimage should be made to Jerusalem and the high festival there kept with great rejoicing. With the customary kindness of that code the provision is made that the family rejoicing should include the slaves, and *"the Levite, and the sojourner, and the fatherless, and the widow, that are within thy gates"* (Deut 16. 13-15).

The Levitical Code, in accordance with its principle of interpreting social institutions, gave to this festival a historic significance, and commanded all the people to make booths and to dwell in them as a solemn reminder of the journeys through the wilderness where they lived in such dwellings (Lev 23. 39-43). Specific offerings were to be made in the temple (Num 29. 12-34), and an eighth day was added to the festival week, "the last day, that great day of the feast" (John 7. 37). This was to mark the conclusion of the annual round of celebrations, and was to be a day of "holy convocation," distinguished by additional sacrifices (Lev 23. 36; Num 29. 35-38). A lively description of the first historical observance of this elaborated festival is given in Neh 8. 14-18.

Further ceremonies were added in later years, two of which, the solemn pouring of water at the altar, and the illumination of the Court of the Women, gave opportunity for significant sayings of Jesus, as recorded in the Gospel of John (7. 37f.; 8. 12).

§ 5. The Lesser Festivals

In ancient Israel an important festival must have been held at sheep shearing. We have only two incidental references to the custom (1 Sam 25. 2; 2 Sam 13. 23ff.), but it is natural that it should have had a place among the pastoral people somewhat similar to that of the threshing feast among the tillers of the soil (Ruth 3. 2, 7).

An interesting festival because of its marked secular character was Purim. It seems to have been borrowed from the Persians during the exile, and to have been originally simply a holiday for good cheer and charity. It was observed for two days as a time of family jollity, when ordinary conventional restraints were somewhat removed. The fascinating story of Esther gave a historical interpretation to the feast (9. 20-28), and in time it became customary to read this story in the synagogue at the festival with the delightful permission that whenever the name of "Haman" occurred in the reading the children might shout and stamp with all the noise they pleased, and the congregation could curse the enemy of their race. In the harsh days of persecution to which the Jews were subjected under the Greek, the Roman, and later under the Christian and Moslem, "Cursed be Haman" may well have been the thinly veiled imprecation upon king, Cæsar, Tsar, or Sultan. Purim is still observed among the Jews as in ancient days as a convivial holiday and with the same service in the synagogue.

The Feast of the Dedication of the Temple had a definite historical origin. The sacred building had been desecrated by Antiochus Epiphanes, and when Judas Maccabeus conquered the Syrians he purified the temple and rededicated it to the service of Jehovah with great solemnities and with feasting and joy (1 Macc 4. 36-59). The thanksgiving lasted for eight days, and it was ordained that it should be kept perpetually as a celebration of the blessed event for eight days beginning on the twenty-fifth day of the ninth month (John 10. 22f.). It was a most joyous celebration, the people going to the synagogues with palms in their hands, chanting as at the Feast of the Tabernacles the great Hallel (Psa 113-118), illuminating their houses every evening, and reciting the great deeds of the Maccabees to stir the patriotism and religious zeal of the youth. Josephus, describing the institution of the festival, calls it the Feast of Lights (Antiquities, XII, vii, 7).

§ 6. The Influence of the Festivals

To these joyous occasions must be added the great annual fast, the Day of Atonement, on the tenth day of the seventh month, five days before the Feast of Tabernacles. Reference has already been made to this solemn celebration (page 164), and we shall return to it in the discussion of fasting.

The social and religious significance of the great cycle

of festivals as they gradually developed through Hebrew history must have been very marked. They cemented the family life. They were times of charitable remembrance of the poor. They turned the thoughts of the nation upon the heroic days of its history. They called the people to the realization of their dependence upon God. The educational value for the children was recognized by the religious leaders, and care was taken that the significance of the celebrations should be explained to them by their parents.

The Hebrew months do not exactly correspond with ours, but the cycle of festivals ran about as follows: At the beginning of April came the Passover, with the Feast of Unleavened Bread, an eight-day celebration of the deliverance from Egypt, and of thanksgiving for the beginning of harvest, which came thus early in that warmer clime. At the end of May came the day of Pentecost, celebrating the end of the grain harvest. In September-October, the great seventh month brought first the Feast of Trumpets, the call to repentance, then the solemn Day of Atonement with its remembrance of sin and its fasting; then within a week the joyous celebration for eight days of a thanksgiving season, the Feast of Tabernacles. About six weeks later in the middle of December was the eight-day celebration of the Feast of Dedication, with the remembrance of the heroic Maccabees. About the first of March the two days' Feast of Purim gave an opportunity of joy and charity, and a remembrance of the divine deliverance of the persecuted Jews. As there were also other minor feasts, more than thirty days in the year had some ceremonial significance in the later days of Judaism.

DIRECTIONS FOR STUDY

1. Compare the Hebrew sacred times with those of the Greeks and Romans (*a*) in point of similarity or differences, (*b*) as to their social significance.
2. What was the essential difference between Jesus's observance of the Sabbath and that of the scribes?

3. Compare the Jewish Sabbath with that of the Puritan. Which was the more ascetically observed? What was the fundamental object of the Puritans in their Sabbath prescriptions?
4. In view of the attitude of Jesus toward the Sabbath and of Paul toward all ritual seasons (Col 2. 16), what is the social and religious value of the Christian Sunday? How is it desirable that it should be observed? How far may legislation secure such observance?
5. Compare the Jewish festival of the new moon with similar observances of other people. Why did not this festival survive in Christianity?
6. Read the Songs of Ascents (Psa 120-134), which were probably sung by the Jews as they went on pilgrimage *up* to Jerusalem. Consider what these beautiful hymns imply as to the spirit in which the festivals were kept, and as to the social and religious significance of these observances in Hebrew life.
7. Compare our own national festivals with those of the Hebrews (*a*) as to number and character, (*b*) as to social significance.
8. Do the Hebrew celebrations suggest any ways in which our own social life might be enriched by ceremonial observance? Consider the educational significance of ritual especially upon young and simple minds.
9. Note that the words "holiday" and "holy day" were originally one. Which element is increasing in the celebration of our own national and religious festivals? Is this a healthy tendency from the largest social considerations? What tendency is manifest in this matter among the foreign peoples in America? What social advantages would accrue from their retention of their own national festivals?
10 Is there any probable connection between the tenacity of the Hebrew in the observance of his national festivals and the continuance of his race as a social entity?

CHAPTER XVII

PRAYER AND FASTING

Prayer and fasting might seem rather to be exercises of religion than social institutions. But without pressing the point that every act of a communal nature may be regarded as a social institution, these two practices had great social significance in Israel. Prayer had a distinctly social origin, and its development in Judaism at once depended on and influenced social movements. Fasting was often a national act, and it entered into the determination of the quality of Hebrew religion to a considerable degree. An understanding of the development of prayer and fasting is very necessary to the appreciation of the evolution of a people whose history was markedly determined by religious considerations.

§ 1. The Prophet as Intercessor

Prayer in ancient Israel was the office of the prophet. Men had not reached the sense of personal religious experience. Their religion was largely external. They could approach their God with a gift as in sacrifice, though even then the priest was generally the mediator; but when they sought to speak with him, and to beseech his favor, they felt the need of an intermediary who was able to secure audience with the Deity. The simplest expression of this fact is in the statement that Abraham as a prophet would pray for Abimelech (Gen 20. 7). So Moses is represented as praying for Israel (Exod 32. 11-13; Num 11. 11-15). Joshua, who was thought of as holding a like mediatorial office, sought Jehovah on the occasion of the defeat of the people (Josh 7. 6-9). Samuel prayed for Israel in the presence of the enemy (1 Sam 7. 5, 8), in this case the prayer being accompanied by sacrifice (v. 9). When the people sought a king they still asked Samuel to pray for them, and he consented (1 Sam 12. 19, 23). Elijah, occupying a noble mediatorial position on Mount Carmel, prayed for the people in connection with the sacrifice (1 Kings 18. 36f.).

The prophets frequently break into prayer in their writings, as Jeremiah when Judah was afflicted with the drought (14. 13-22). The thought of the efficacy of the prophetic pleading is plainly brought out in this incident, for Jehovah answered that even Moses and Samuel could not avail in prayer, so great had been the sin of the people (15. 1). The book of Deuteronomy is both priestly and prophetic. It represents an endeavor to spiritualize the worship at the temple. No directions are given to the people regarding prayer, but there are included two liturgical prayers that are to be said by the layman in connection with his offerings (26. 5-10, 13-15). And in the prophetic history of the kingdom, written toward the close of the preexilic period, the great kings David, Solomon, and Hezekiah are represented as offering noble prayers (2 Sam 7. 18-29; 1 Kings 8. 22-53; 2 Kings 19. 14-19). That of Solomon is especially significant as it plainly indicates the temple as a place of prayer, and represents the pious Hebrew wherever he may be as praying toward that place. It is the thought so nobly expressed in the postexilic prophecy quoted by Jesus, *"My house shall be called a house of prayer for all peoples"* (Isa 56. 7).

It would not be correct to say that there was no practice of prayer by the people before the exile, for Isaiah declares that their many prayers are useless unless accompanied by righteousness (1. 15). But the fact seems to be that religion rather expressed itself in ceremonial, the practice of prayer belonging largely to those who as prophets were accustomed to hold converse with Jehovah.

§ 2. Development of Prayer in the Exile

Like so many other institutions of Hebrew life which were deepened and enlarged by the experience of the exile, the practice of prayer gained an added significance. The opportunity of offering sacrificial worship had ceased, but it was possible to pray even in Babylon. The idea of a local Deity confined to the petty jurisdiction of Palestine gave place to the great prophetic conception of Jehovah as the God of all creation. The exiles, torn from their sacred city, unable to worship according to the prescriptions of their ancient faith, lifted up their voices in confession and supplication, and found peace and refreshment of soul. The noble idea developed at this time, which Hosea had earlier expressed, that prayer is itself an acceptable offering to Jehovah (14. 2). It is finely presented in many psalms (141. 2). Perhaps Psalm 51, personal as it seems, is a national confession, coming from this intensely religious period. And the prayer for mercy and help in Isa 64, in which the Fatherhood of God is pleaded, is a national prayer, wherein the prophet speaks not as a mediator but as one of the stricken people. Ezra's prayer, significantly offered at the time of the evening sacrifice, is of like tenor (Ezra 9. 5-15). Very much later, for the book belongs to the period of the Maccabean struggle, is Daniel's penitent supplication, accompanied "with fasting, and sackcloth, and ashes" (Dan 9. 3-19). The exquisite tenderness of all these prayers, and their marked ethical tone, is an indication of the developing moral power of the Hebrew religion under the great influences of national calamity and prophetic inspiration.

The book of Nehemiah is a remarkable record of the private prayers of an active man of affairs—the more so as it is not an idealized representation by a later historian, but is largely the personal memoirs of the man himself.

Judas the Maccabee also was a man who prayed and "kept his powder dry," as the heroic story repeatedly narrates (1 Macc 4. 30-33; 5. 33; 11. 71).

§ 3. Prayer in Later Judaism

The book of Psalms is really a book of prayers as well as of praises (72. 20). It was very largely produced after the exile, as its constant references to the law and the sacrifices sufficiently testify. The psalms are the expression of Israel's faith and aspiration, many of them having all the elements of true prayer. They are personal yet representative, for the psalmist is always speaking for his people. They are ascriptions of praise, for that is the spirit in which the devout soul ever communes with God. They are cries for deliverance, for peace, for care, and sometimes for vengeance in the face of tyranny and oppression. They are thanksgivings for all temporal and spiritual mercies. Many of them were doubtless written to be chanted by the temple singers, and so come more properly under the category of hymns; but many were probably the spontaneous expressions of devotion which were found expressive of the nation's spiritual needs, and so were incorporated in the hymn book of the temple, as we have added many prayer-poems to our own hymnody.

There was a development of congregational prayer partly on the basis of the psalms, which took liturgical form in connection with the synagogue. The same or similar prayers were employed at the set hours of private devotion. This public and private practice of the forms of worship, while always the medium of religious expression for the nobler spirits, easily fell into the formalism which was so marked a characteristic of later Judaism.

The regular hours had been set when every Hebrew was expected to repeat his prayers (Dan 6. 10). The Pharisees, in their determination to do exactly what was required of them, observed these set times ostentatiously, being often overtaken, as it were, at prayer time in the most conspicuous places of the town (Matt 6. 5). Sirach had already found it necessary to warn against the use of many words and much babbling in prayer (7. 14). Jesus's teaching on prayer was for the most part a serious protest against the forms which it had assumed.

§ 4. Fasting

Fasting is practiced among many peoples as a religious exercise. The involuntary fasts to which scarcity of food often subjected primitive man gave rise to certain strange psychic experiences which he regarded as preternatural. He therefore repeated the fast voluntarily when he desired to secure a repetition of the experience. Thus fasting was often prescribed as the precursor of significant events in the life of the individual. Fasting often preceded the sacrificial meal with the desire that there might be no mingling of the common and the sacred food within the body. Whether either of these purposes played any part in determining the practice of fasting among the Hebrews is not clear.

As with many peoples, fasting was a sign of mourning in Israel (1 Sam 31. 13), perhaps arising from the perfectly natural feeling that in grief one does not care to enjoy food. So in the sorrow occasioned by the sense of alienation from the Deity fasting came to be practiced as a sign of humiliation and contrition. The people fasted and confessed their sins when Samuel prayed for them (1 Sam 7. 6). David fasted when his child was stricken (2 Sam 12. 16, 21-23), and Ahab when he was informed of Jehovah's sentence upon his crime (1 Kings 21. 27). Jehoiakim proclaimed a fast in time of national calamity (Jer 36. 9).

The exile caused a great development in this custom. Four annual fastdays were observed in sad memorial of different calamities that so tragically closed the history of the southern kingdom. The prophet Zechariah declared that in the brighter days impending these should be turned into feasts (8. 19). Ezra proclaimed a fast "that we might humble ourselves before our God" (8. 21). In connection with the acceptance of the book of the law the people fasted and wore sackcloth and stood and confessed their sins and the iniquities of their fathers (Neh 9. 1f.). The penitent prayers of Nehemiah (1. 4), and of Daniel (9. 3), were accompanied by fasting. When the heroic Judas gathered his little host for battle he sought to prepare them by confession and prayer, and this was accompanied by fasting (1 Macc 3. 47).

The Priest Code inaugurated one great annual national fastday that was to be of peculiar solemnity—the Day of Atonement (Lev 23. 26-32). It was to last twenty-four hours—"from even unto even"—and was to be a Sabbath of solemn rest. This was no sham fast of eating fish or eggs, but an actual abstinence from food for the entire day. It was intended to stir in every Israelite the feeling of penitence for all the sins of the year.

The danger that fasting would become a mere form, or, worse, that it would be regarded as a virtuous act, putting Jehovah under obligation, was recognized by the post-exilic prophet (Isa 58. 3-9). With the social passion that breaks through all hollow ritualism he denounces those that fast and oppress their neighbors (v. 3, marg.). With ringing demand he asks:

Is it to bow his head as a rush,
And to spread sackcloth and ashes under him?
Wilt thou call this a fast,
And an acceptable day to Jehovah?
Is not this the fast that I have chosen:
To loose the bonds of wickedness,

. . . .

To let the oppressed go free?

. . . .

Is it not to deal thy bread to the hungry
And to bring the outcast poor to thy house?

The whole history of later Judaism was the enlargement of the significance of ritual. Ritual may always either inspire faith and righteousness or else become a substitute for them. With the one result or the other, fasting in the later times held a very prominent place. It was practiced as an aid to piety and as an expression of concern for national sin. It was sometimes undertaken individually (Luke 2. 37), sometimes under the direction of religious leaders (5. 33). Public fasts were sometimes proclaimed, the days selected for these being the first and fifth days of the week.

The Pharisees, punctilious and ostentatious in this as in all religious practice, were in the habit of fasting regularly on the two fast days of the week (Luke 18. 12). And, inasmuch as the more rigorous fasts included abstinence from washing and anointing, they were conspicuous for their conventional sadness upon every Monday and Thursday, to the great admiration of the populace, who wondered at such religious devotion (Matt 6. 16).

It is an interesting indication of the intimate connection between prayer and fasting that continued in the church that in the great saying of Jesus about the necessity of prayer (Mark 9. 29) there should have been added by some copyist the words "and fasting."

DIRECTIONS FOR STUDY

1. The intercourse of the patriarchs with God as related in the narratives which come from the prophetic period are really expressive of the idea of prayer that was held by the writers. Read Gen 12. 8; 18. 23-33; 32. 9-12; Exod 32. 31-34; Num 14. 13-24; Judg 6. Consider what these imply (*a*) as to the practice of prayer, (*b*) as to the social results that prayer was to effect.
2. Analyze the passages just noted with reference to ethical and religious elements in the conversations with God. Note particularly any passages of high spiritual power.
3. Read 1 Kings 8. 22-53. Note the various references to the history of Israel subsequent to Solomon. Analyze the prayer

with reference to (*a*) its ethical and religious quality, (*b*) its social character.

4. Read Neh 9. 5-37. Note that this is a liturgical prayer with a historical character, intended to stimulate the feeling of contrition in the people.
5. What is the prayer value of Psa 3 and 4 for morning and evening devotion? What social attitude do they suggest?
6. Read Psa 17, 56, 70, 123. If these lyrics express the feelings of the pious victims of tyranny, what is their social significance?
7. Compare Psa 67 and 103. Note that both are praise psalms, but the one is in the form of prayer, and the other of description.
8. What were the religious and social values in the observance of the Day of Atonement? What has been the effect of days of national fasting and prayer in recent times?
9. Why did Jesus fast? (Matt 4. 2). Note that he was a young man at the outset of his public career. Is it possible that we make our life decisions too lightly?
10. Consider the social significance of Lent as practiced in the Roman Catholic countries, and by certain churches in America. What are the various influences of such a period? Can the emptiness of mere formalism be avoided? Is modern religion in danger of losing the element of solemnity?

CHAPTER XVIII

THE SYNAGOGUE

WHEREVER in all the world there is a group of Hebrews there is a synagogue. It is the place of worship, it is the center of racial interest, it is the school of Judaism, it is the most potent social institution of Hebrew life. It has held this place among the Jews for more than two thousand years.

§ 1. THE ORIGIN OF THE SYNAGOGUE

The origin of this institution is not definitely known. There was no special occasion upon which it was ordained that there should be a synagogue. We must go again to the exile, that fertile seed plot of Jewish institutions, to find the development of this congregational body. There had been in the earlier period the council of elders in every city. The functions of a synagogue as a court thus went back very definitely to the previously existing institution. But the exile created a new demand. The loss of the temple and of the sacrificial cultus made the earnest spirits among the Hebrews more solicitous to preserve their religious heritage. They had their sacred writings, they had the Sabbath day, and if they could not offer sacrifices they could pray. All this naturally called for a gathering of the people. We may suppose, therefore, that little assemblies of Hebrews came together as opportunity offered in Babylonia upon the Sabbath day, read the law which their fathers had too lightly regarded, read the prophets whose keen foresight had pictured the very troubles that had come upon them, and then prayed for pardon and deliverance. It was such gatherings that preserved the faith and hope of the people through experiences such as destroyed the racial unity of other peoples, and inspired the devotion that shone forth in the noble work of Ezra and Nehemiah and those who wrought with them.

So valuable were these gatherings for the preservation of the national faith in Babylon that when the people returned to Palestine they continued to meet for worship and instruction on the Sabbath although the temple was rebuilt and the cultus resumed. The synagogue had acquired a place which could not be given up, and it rapidly developed in importance. It supplied the opportunity for community worship, which before the Deuteronomic Reform had been afforded by the sacrifices at the local shrines. These were abolished and all sacrifice was offered at the temple; moreover, it was altogether in charge of a professional priesthood. The people would have largely lost their part in worship if the synagogues had not come in to provide a congregational religious service.

Moreover, the synagogue developed with the scribe. The elaborated law became fixed and unamendable at the end of the fifth century. Its provisions needed elucidation and adaptation. If the people were to be observers of the law, they must know what it meant and how it was to be obeyed. The scribe was able to instruct them. The Sabbath afforded the needed leisure for the instruction. The synagogue afforded the institutional opportunity. The law had been developed about the central institution of the temple and its cultus. The effect of the teaching and practice of the law was to enhance the place and the significance of the synagogue.

§ 2. The Extension of the Synagogue

As the Jews extended beyond Jerusalem to other towns they carried the synagogue with them. Such a simple assembly could be organized anywhere. A special building was desirable, and after a time was usually erected, but it was not essential: the synagogue was the assembly, not the building. As the great dispersion of the Jews throughout the Mediterranean world by colonization, business, or slavery, scattered the people afar they founded synagogues wherever they went. Their one temple remained at Jerusalem, but they could take their sacred books with them. Their liturgies were imprinted on their hearts. The Sabbath could be observed in any land. The Greek period, therefore, saw a wide extension of the synagogue. Alexandria, where there was a very large Jewish population, had a famous synagogue, together with many of lesser importance. Antioch, the capital of the kingdom of Syria, where also the Jews had gone in large numbers as colonists, had a celebrated synagogue in which were later kept the brazen vessels that had been taken from the temple at Jerusalem by the persecutor Antiochus Epiphanes (Josephus, B. J., VII, iii, 3). There were also a number of synagogues in Rome. The narrative of Paul's travels shows that in every city to which he went where there was any considerable number of Jews there was a synagogue carrying on the prescribed worship on the Sabbath days (Acts 13. 5, 14; 14. 1; 16. 13; 17. 1, 10, 17; 18. 4, 7, 19).

In Palestine itself there were one or more synagogues in every city and town (Matt 4. 23), even in so small a place as Nazareth (13. 54). In Jerusalem there was a large number of specialized synagogues. The Alexandrian Jews coming to Jerusalem to visit or to settle would wish to have their own place of meeting, inasmuch as their practices and the subjects in which they were interested were somewhat different from those of the Jews of other places. There was, therefore, an Alexandrian synagogue. And the same was the case with many other nationalities (Acts 6. 9). The later Jewish tradition declared that there were four hundred and eighty synagogues at the capital, including one in the temple itself. While this number is probably far too large, it is an indication of the universality of this important institution, and James was justified in saying, *"Moses from generations of old hath in every city them that preach him, being read in the synagogues every sabbath"* (Acts 15. 21).

§ 3. The Organization of the Synagogue

There was no prescribed form for the synagogue building. It naturally followed the model of the basilica, and in the larger ones, as the ruins still show, there was a double row of pillars. Certain seats were placed at the end of the building for the elders, who thus sat facing the congregation (Matt 23. 6).

In a separate part of the synagogue shut off by a curtain was a box, the ark, covered with a canopy in which were kept the sacred rolls of the Scriptures. A reading desk stood in a convenient position, upon which the rolls were placed for the various persons who officiated in the service.

The synagogue worship itself was of a simple character, although it was somewhat elaborated in later ages. It is partly described in the account of Jesus's attendance upon the synagogue at Nazareth (Luke 4. 16-27) and in that of Paul at Pisidian Antioch (Acts 13. 14-43). It consisted of four elements: (1) The recitation of the Hebrew creed, "Hear, O Israel: Jehovah our God, Jehovah is one" (Deut 6. 4, marg.). This is called the *Shema,* from the first word in Hebrew. It has been the great monotheistic creed of Israel for twenty-five hundred years. In the synagogue the whole passage (Deut 6. 4-9), and a complementary passage (Num 15. 37-41), were recited together with the various blessings. (2) Then followed the prayers, which were led by a person specially selected for that purpose at each service. The Jews had at their hand in the psalms forms of prayer for a large variety of occasions. In addition to these there had been developed very elaborate forms of prayer for the use of the synagogue. It is not possible to determine how early they were employed. Jesus had occasion to warn against vain repetitions (Matt 6. 7), and gave his disciples a simple form of prayer (vv. 9-13). It is worthy of note that the doxology which has been appended to the Lord's Prayer is probably of Jewish origin, for such ascriptions of praise were customary in their liturgy. The various forms of prayer were doubtless gradually developed as time went on, those that were found valuable naturally being preserved. (3) The reading of portions from the law and the prophets was the most important part of the Sabbath worship. Certain persons who were able to read Hebrew were selected to read these passages. Inasmuch as the classic Hebrew was not generally understood, the Palestinian Jews speaking Aramaic and those in other countries generally speaking Greek, the custom arose of translating the Scriptures as they were read into the common tongue, and this required the services of one or more interpreters. (4) After the readings there was often an exposition. No regular preacher was attached to the synagogue, so any visiting rabbi or any competent layman might be invited to address the congregation (Matt 4. 23; Mark 1. 21; 6. 2; Luke 6. 6; John 18. 20; Acts 13. 15). It was the informality of this simple worship that gave to Jesus and the apostles their great opportunity of preaching the gospel to the Jews.

The government of the synagogue was in the hands of the elders. There was no official corresponding to the minister of the modern church. The ruler of the synagogue, who was generally an elder, had the direction of the service. He selected the persons who were to take the various parts (Acts 13. 15), and was charged with the maintenance of order (Luke 13. 14). The attendant had the care of the building, blew the trumpet from the roof to announce the beginning of the Sabbath and of the various festivals, and was intrusted with the handling of the sacred rolls, bringing them from the ark to the readers and taking them back in due form (Luke 4. 17, 20). When court was held in the synagogue he executed the sentence of the council. In later times, when the elementary school was established in the synagogue, he acted as the teacher. While these two officials were all that were requisite in the ordinary synagogue, there might be a number of others where the business and the distribution of alms required their services.

§ 4. The Social Importance of the Synagogue

The identity of the religious and civil life of the Hebrews and of the sacred and secular law resulted in the same body of men acting as ecclesiastical officials and civil magistrates. The chief men of the city or town, the elders, were those who governed the synagogue and also the municipality (Matt 9. 18; Luke 7. 3; 8. 41). Where the city was large enough to have several synagogues the leading men from the various congregations formed the local Sanhedrin, or governing council. The sessions of this body were held in the synagogue building, which thus served as the town hall and courthouse. When Jesus warned his disciples, "*They will deliver you up to councils, and in their synagogues they will scourge you*" (Matt 10. 17; Mark 13. 9; compare Matt 5. 22; 23. 34), he was referring to the police powers of the local Sanhedrins, and to one of the customary punishments inflicted by them. Paul had a part in thus having the Christians beaten (Acts 22. 19), and he himself on five different occasions suffered the same penalty (2 Cor 11. 24). It is interesting that the attendant of the synagogue added to his many other duties that of inflicting this punishment.

The local court had large powers over the people within its jurisdiction, and it might for serious offenses actually exclude a person from the community (Luke 6. 22; John 9. 22; 12. 42; 16. 2). The phrase "put you out of the synagogue" sounds like a simple expulsion from the building, but it refers to an actual excommunication which was tantamount to making the person an outcast from the community.

The synagogue was the center of the people's life; to be outside of that was to be ostracized.

When the elementary school came to be established in the synagogues, still another bond united the people in this significant institution. It is not difficult to understand, therefore, how great was the social importance that it held in every Jewish community. When the temple was destroyed and the Hebrew nation ceased to be, wherever a little group of Hebrews were to be found they still formed the synagogue. There they worshiped, there the lessons of Judaism were taught to the children, there such direction of affairs as the superior political powers permitted them was exercised, there the traditions and hopes of their race were cherished. And so it has been to this day.

The first Christians were Jews. When they formed their first communities they formed them on the model of the synagogue. The very word is used in the Epistle of James (2. 2), and the corresponding verb in the Epistle to the Hebrews (10. 25). The Christian Church was much what the Jewish assembly had been, and the officers of the church were the elders (Acts 14. 23), still preserving the old title which runs back as far as Hebrew tradition extends. The social significance of the church in the old New England community, where the same men were often the ecclesiastical and civil officials, may help us to appreciate the great place which the synagogue held in later Judaism.

DIRECTIONS FOR STUDY

1. Why did the synagogue become more significant than the temple in Jewish life?
2. Read Neh 8. 1-8. Consider whether there is any basis in the passage for an understanding of the synagogue.
3. Compare the worship in the synagogue with that which had formerly been conducted in the high places. What points of similarity and of difference do you find?
4. Imagine such a Jewish community as that of Nazareth. What

were the various values which the synagogue conserved in that community?

5. Read the two accounts of the synagogue service (Luke 4. 16-27; Acts 13. 14-43). What statements in each indicate the character of the service? What do the sermons indicate as to the scope and opportunity of the public addresses that might be delivered?
6. What has been the influence of the synagogue in the preservation of the Hebrew race in its integrity in the various countries in which the Jews have lived since the Babylonian captivity?
7. Compare the Christian Church and the Hebrew synagogue as to the character of the worship, the officials and their duties, the various activities of the institution, its social influence in the life of the people.
8. What advantages did the informal and congregational character of the synagogue service afford? Is it possible that we have lost anything in the development of our one-man ministry? Could the values of both systems be secured?
9. What were the advantages of the union of church, state, and school in the synagogue? What made this possible? Why have we separated them? Is there any way in which a better correlation could be effected in our modern life?
10. Study a modern Hebrew synagogue, as to its worship, officers, activities, and social influence on the Jewish community.

PART II

THE SOCIAL TEACHINGS OF THE PROPHETS AND OF THE SAGES

CHAPTER XIX

THE DEVELOPMENT OF HEBREW PROPHECY

§ 1. The Origins of Hebrew Prophecy

The same elemental conditions that produced religion itself among all peoples produced also the seer, the intermediary between dull mortals and the higher powers. Hebrew prophecy in its origin had the common characteristics of that religious excitability with accompaniments of clairvoyance which is found in many parts of the world. One who has seen the Moslem dervishes to-day recognizes a kinship to their practices in that of the prophets whose contagious emotions so powerfully affected the messengers of Saul, and finally the king himself (1 Sam 19. 19-24). Even Samuel, although he represented a distinct advance in the prophetic character, was looked upon as possessing the mysterious power of finding what was lost in return for a small fee (9. 6-10). The evident dependence of Elisha upon the minstrel's music in order to produce the trance which would enable him to prophesy (2 Kings 3. 15) connects him with those mantic companies that belong on the lower levels of this significant development.

It is probable that the majority of the Hebrew prophets never advanced very far beyond this primitive stage. We have the records and writings of a very small number out of many hundreds who were regarded by the people as possessing the prophetic power. Thus Micaiah, in the reign of Ahab, seems to have stood over against the great company of "medicine men," as they might be called, who were currying favor with the king (1 Kings 22. 20-28). Isaiah and Jeremiah were constantly thwarted in their efforts by those whom they styled false prophets.

The reason why Hebrew prophecy developed from its primitive beginnings into that ethical power which made Jesus feel his kinship with those men of the spirit was the same reason which elevated the Hebrew religion into its unique position above the paganisms of its time. It was the sense and experience of Jehovah as the God of righteousness. The history of religion unhappily shows even to the present day that there is no necessary connection between religious emotion and ethical conviction. Men may think themselves the friends of God, and yet be little concerned about their duties to their fellow men. They somehow think of God as interested in religiosity—sacrifices, prayers, worship and the like. No prophet in Moab would have thought that Chemosh was disturbed if the king of Moab had taken the wife of one of his subjects. No preacher of Nineveh would have had anything to say if the Assyrian king had done a man to death in order to get his vineyard. The pagan gods were never angry with their favorites for such peccadilloes. But the knowledge of Jehovah came to a few gifted souls in Israel as a conviction of his demand for righteousness. The men who gained that insight stand out from the common run of soothsayers in Israel as the representatives of ethical religion. Moses and Samuel were thus inspired by the sense of justice, and after them came a line of religious leaders, not always, perhaps not often, belonging technically to the prophetic order, who stood forth, first as the champions of popular rights, then as interpreters of the world history, and then as the projectors of a future social state.

§ 2. The Prophets and Social Injustice

This ethical sense as a part of the religious experience manifested itself first in a stern indignation against isolated acts of tyranny. Nathan's courageous denunciation of

David is a typical instance (2 Sam 12. 1ff.). When Solomon developed his luxurious court and levied heavily upon the people in taxes and forced labor for his buildings, the popular discontent found expression in the action of the prophet Ahijah, who stirred Jeroboam to rebel against the king (2 Kings 11. 29ff.).

The conspicuous conduct of Elijah on the occasion of the murder of Naboth (1 Kings 21. 17-24), an act of royal tyranny which to the Phœnician Jezebel seemed a mere incident of kingship (v. 7), is a striking instance of the prophetic realization of Jehovah's anger against social oppression.

One is tempted to think that the attitude of Elijah and Elisha in their stern resistance to Baalism may have been prompted by a horror of the sensuality of the Phœnician cultus, although there is nothing in the record to warrant the view. Certain it is that Elisha took so prominent a part in the political aspect of the affair as to be responsible for the rebellion of Jehu and the change of dynasty (2 Kings 9. 1-13).

The development of the court and military aristocracy which we have noted changed the old simplicity of Hebrew life in which the wealth of the land was fairly well distributed among the free men, and produced the contrasts of the rich and poor. With this came all those evils of luxury, oppression, dishonesty, bribery, cruelty, and heartlessness, which inevitably belonged to such a social state, and yet withal there was great religiousness. Jehovah was patronized, and his altars never lacked abundant offerings, but righteousness between men was forgotten. This situation produced the great prophets.

Amos, Hosea, Isaiah, Micah were not concerned with occasional denunciation of individual acts of tyranny; they were the opponents of the whole social system. They were the champions of the oppressed classes against the privileged. Their religious faith was at the same time a social passion. They spoke for a God who is the defender of the poor, the fatherless, and the widow, and who hates the worship of the tyrant.

It was no accident that produced this outburst of brilliant prophecy in the eighth century. The sudden accentuation of the social contrasts in the period of the prosperity of Jeroboam II in the north, and of Uzziah, Jotham, and Ahaz in the south, called for men of passionate and powerful speech who could command the audience of the people. As generally happens, the need produced the men. A rustic man of power felt the call in Tekoa, a young nobleman was stirred to a great sense of duty in Jerusalem, a broken-hearted husband felt the terrible unfaithfulness of the times in Israel, and a bitter critic of the luxury of the cities came out of one of the villages of Judah. Prophecy rose to the high plane of statesmanlike oratory. There could be no greater combination of impulse to public speech than a profound religious experience of the intimate interest of God in the affairs of men, an ethical conviction that immediate and fundamental reformation of national life was necessary, a sympathy with the great population which was oppressed and unable to secure its rights, and a sense of personal mission to be the spokesman of the God of righteousness.

§ 3. The Prophets and the World Powers

But injustice was not only manifest within the limits of the Hebrew kingdom. Tyranny seemed universally victorious and unrebuked. The great world powers were international freebooters. There was certainly in universal operation

> The good old rule, the simple plan
> That he shall take who has the power
> And he shall keep who can.

Yet Jehovah was supposed to be supreme and to be the God of justice. On the basis of the naïve faith which Israel shared with all the peoples of the time this international situation was not difficult to understand. Each nation was supposed to have its own god, who was responsible for protecting his people. He might, indeed, allow them to be defeated by the enemy for the sake of punishing them for some disloyalty, but his own honor and advantage required that he should save them from destruction. When, therefore, one nation conquered another it meant simply that the god of the one people was for the time at least more powerful than the god of the other. (Compare 1 Kings 20. 23-25.) The king of Assyria considered that his mighty Asshur had conquered the gods of all the little nations that fell before him (Isa 10. 10f.; 36. 18; 37. 12).

But the Hebrew prophet could not so interpret the history that was enacted before his eyes. To him Jehovah was God, and the idols of the nations were vanity. Jehovah punished the tyrannies and cruelties of Syria, Philistia, Phœnicia, Edom, Ammon, Moab (Amos 1 and 2) as certainly as he punished Israel and Judah. Why, then, was the brutal Assyrian allowed to crush the nations, rob their treasures, carry their people into slavery, impose heavy tribute upon the inhabitants that were left? Why had the wicked Tyrians gathered a wealth that was the envy of the world? Why were the barbarous Scythian hordes allowed to make their savage raids? When Assyria was at last overwhelmed, was it only that the tyranny of Nineveh was to be succeeded by the tyranny of Babylon?

These questions pressed the prophets to take a world view and a long view. They felt that Jehovah must be working out some great purpose. First of all, he was using the strong peoples to punish the sins of the weaker peoples. But the strong were in turn to be punished. The purpose of the whole process was purification. It was a simple but a noble political philosophy. So Isaiah told the Assyrian that he was but the instrument of God, who should in turn receive due recompense for his arrogance and profanity

(10. 15; 37. 26-29). Obadiah could declare that Edom should feel the heavy hand of Jehovah for her league with Israel's enemies. Habakkuk could declare that the Chaldeans should find their doom for the same social iniquities that had brought woe upon Jerusalem (ch. 2). Zephaniah could summon all the nations to fear the day of wrath that was coming. Nahum could utter his cry of vengeance upon Nineveh, "the bloody city."

Each of the great prophetic collections includes a series of oracles concerning the nations, in which the idea of a divine justice over against the cruelty and inhumanity of the world powers is strikingly set forth.

In the break-up of nationalities in western Asia in the seventh and sixth centuries B. C., the tribal gods of the older times lost their significance. Even Asshur could not save Assyria, nor Bel and Marduk preserve Babylon. Jehovah emerged clearly in the prophetic consciousness as the God of the whole earth. In the great passage, which represents one of the high-water marks of prophecy, Egypt and Assyria, the great hereditary enemies of Israel, are seen as co-worshipers with Israel herself, and equal objects of Jehovah's blessing (Isa 19. 24f.).

§ 4. The Prophets and the Ideal Social State

The final resolution of the hard problem presented by the failure of Israel and the awful tyranny of the world powers was afforded by the prophetic ideal of a social state in which righteousness should dwell. The answer to every cry of distress was, on the one hand, an explanation that the present evil was the punishment of sin and, on the other, a promise that the good times were coming.

This golden age of the future was always conceived ethically and in social terms. In the great Messianic prophecies of the book of Isaiah there is the expectation of a Ruler who, as supreme Judge, will secure that justice for the poor and the unfriended which was fundamental for a prosperous and peaceful community (11. 1-5); and the consequence of his strong government should be universal peace instead of the brutish warfare that was so destructive of all human achievements (11. 6-9). Again, in the brilliant contrast to the foolish, weak, selfish, and quarreling princes that sat on David's throne, there was the hope of a Ruler wonderful in counsel, divine in strength, paternal in his care, and peaceful in his reign (9. 2-7).

Jeremiah, a profound optimist, in spite of the direful messages which it was his unhappy task to carry to his rebellious people, saw that no mere righteousness of government could secure the ideal state. He resolved the antagonism which is often presented to-day between evangelization and socialization by his healthy realization that the two processes are one. In his view individual and social purification go hand in hand, when the new covenant is written on the hearts of the people (31. 31-34) and the state is reconstituted in righteousness (30. 18-22; 31. 10-14).

Ezekiel has the like idea. He lays emphasis on individual responsibility for sin and righteousness (ch. 18). Then he allows his patriotic and priestly imagination to revel in the hope of a reorganized Judaism in which all the tribes shall have their due inheritance, the temple with its elaborated ritual shall dominate the national life, and Jerusalem shall be a city where Jehovah dwells (48. 35).

In the great exile prophecy (Isa 40 to 55) there comes most clearly into view the conception of the universal purpose of Jehovah. Everything looks forward to the redemption of a purified people who are to be the inhabitants of a good land where they shall be established in righteousness (54. 14); and this is not to be confined to Israel but to extend to all peoples (42. 1-4; 49. 6; 51. 4f.). The profound conception of the Servant of Jehovah (42. 1-9; 49. 1-7; 50. 4-7; 52. 13 to 53. 12) has been so generally considered in its Messianic aspect that its social quality has not been recognized. Strictly speaking, the Servant of Jehovah is not a Messiah. This prophecy does not think of a king who would save his people by justice. Josiah had tried to do that and had failed. It presents the view that the prophets and leaders of righteousness will inevitably be misunderstood, persecuted, sacrificed. The path of social regeneration follows the blood prints of those who are wounded for the transgressions of others. It was true of Jeremiah. It was true of Jesus. And Jesus warned his followers that they too must pay the price of becoming the redeemers of men.

Later prophecies which look forward to the glorious future are expressed in such glowing terms that they are often read as descriptions of the life that is beyond this world. But they describe the social righteousness that is to flourish on the earth when Israel has repented of the social sins and idolatries of the past (ch. 59). They picture a happy people building houses, planting vineyards, dwelling together in peace (65. 17-25).

A wonderful vision of the future, which is now included in the prophecy of Micah (4. 1-4) and of Isaiah (2. 2-4), sees Jerusalem obedient to the laws of righteousness given by Jehovah and becoming the teacher of the nations of the earth, while the weapons of warfare are changed into the tools of peace, and every man sits secure under his vine and under his fig tree. As we to-day recognize the part that Israel has played as the teacher of righteousness, we cannot fail to realize the force of this great expectation,

> Out of Zion shall go forth instruction,
> And the word of Jehovah from Jerusalem.

One of the latest prophetic voices was that of Joel. He spoke at a time of calamity, rebuking the people for their unfaithfulness. But he too felt the sense of the awful inequity of human affairs, and bitterly he denounced the cupidity of the Phœnicians who had made profitable traffic in Hebrew slaves with the Greeks (3. 4-6). Jehovah had punishment in store for these national crimes (vv. 7f.), and in the future there is to be prosperity and the divine presence for Israel (2. 26-32).

DIRECTIONS FOR STUDY

1. Read 1 Kings 17 to 2 Kings 9. Note the different activities of the prophets.
2. On the basis of the narratives just read give your impression of the "sons of the prophets."
3. What different types of prophet do these narratives present?
4. Read Amos 1 and 2. Against what nations does the prophet speak? What national crimes are denounced?
5. Read Nah 2, the prophetic denunciation of Nineveh. For what sins is the city punished?
6. Glance hastily through Isaiah 13 to 24, Jeremiah 47 to 49, Ezekiel 25 to 32. What is the general purport of these prophecies? What do they indicate as to the outlook of the Hebrew prophet? Was he a narrow patriot who exalted his own nation and hated all others?
7. What was the prophetic view of the ultimate meaning of human history? Upon what was this view based?
8. What different forms did the Messianic hope assume? How do you account for the divergencies?
9. What were the fundamental ideals in all phases of the Messianic hope?
10. What modern social ideals have any similarity to the Hebrew Messianic hope?

CHAPTER XX

THE RELATION OF THE PROPHETS TO THE SOCIAL PROCESS

THE outline development of Hebrew prophecy in the previous chapter indicates how the outlook of the prophets broadened with the course of events, and how responsive were their messages to the needs of the times. It is further evident that their hopes were always cast in the form of the social institutions with which they were familiar. Under the rule of the kings the prophet, feeling the inadequacy of the royal justice, and seeing how great a power a righteous king might be, naturally saw a vision of the coming social state when God's man should be king. The priest, realizing how far short his colleagues had come in their spiritual leadership of the people, and yet profoundly convinced of the religious value of the sacrificial ceremonial, looked forward to a social state under a noble ecclesiasticism as containing the promise of human blessedness. In the midst of persecution came an insight into the meaning of suffering, and the possibility of the redemption of a people through the sacrificial death of their noblest souls.

The prophets, therefore, must never be thought of as the proclaimers of absolute truth. They were products of the times in which they lived. They spoke to the people and in the language of their day. They were concerned with the future only for its bearing upon the present. Their truth, like all truth, was relative, and that which was spoken for one generation was often inadequate for the next. As we, therefore, face the problems of our day we must not expect the prophets to give us the solutions that we need. That would be too easy a means of working out our salvation. We shall have to fight our way to the light as they fought theirs. But they may help us if we can place ourselves in imagination in the social situations in which they were and enter into sympathy with their spirit, their motives, their outlook, their passion for righteousness.

A moral teacher never comes down out of the sky with a message which is for all time. He grows up from the earth and is a son of his times. Even Jesus must not be thought of as teaching absolute, unrelated truth, which can be mechanically transferred from his day to our own. He spoke to a certain people at a certain time with a certain background; and all these must be estimated if we would understand his message.

The prophet would not have an intelligible message unless he were actually one with his people, sharing their views, their hopes, perhaps their prejudices. That which makes him a moral leader is that he is able to take a wider view than his contemporaries, to see more than the little interests of the passing day, to rise above petty patriotism and provincial prejudices, and that he is able to offer a constructive program of practical ethics to his people with adequate motives into which they can enter.

The Hebrew prophet, therefore, is to be understood as belonging to the social process, and yet as a critic of the social process, and more than that as a religious genius making his own contribution to the social process.

§ 1. The Prophet as a Product of the Social Situation

The student of social institutions will need to have a very clear notion of what is implied in the phrase "the social process." It is the conception of human society as an organism reacting to its environment. Society is never static. It is in a continuous condition of readaptation to the situations in which its life is cast. The study of history by periods and crises and great personalities tends to obscure this. In the foregoing view of the institutions of Israel we have endeavored to see how each of these was the subject of constant modification according to the changing circumstances of the national progress. The nomad wanted a home, and yet because he was a nomad would not brook the restraints of settled government. The adaptation of the nomad instincts to the life of Canaan was a social process that went on for five hundred years, and resulted in a modification of family life, industry, trade, government, judicial procedure, religious practices and ideals.

The prophet was a part of all this. That is why certain social institutions which seem to us fundamentally wrong never met with any reprobation at his hands. No prophet had anything to say against slavery except when wicked foreigners carried off Hebrews as captives—the very thing which the Hebrew was permitted to do to his own enemies. The simple explanation is in the fact that slavery was accepted as a natural condition of human society. The abolition of slavery would have seemed to destroy the foundations upon which civilization was built. A man's property in his slave was as inevitable as his property in his ox. Of course the prophet felt that the ox should be fairly treated (Deut 25. 4), and so the slave should receive kindness at the hand of his master. Our own posterity will be unable to understand how intelligent, kindly people in the twentieth century had so wicked and stupid a system of industrial organization that every year hundreds of thousands of willing workers were prevented from earning their daily bread. We, however, are in the social process, and until very recently we have all accepted the unfortunate fact of unemployment as inevitable. The prophets of the last generation only exhorted us to be charitable to the unemployed.

Thus the Hebrew religious teachers accepted society as it was. They saw no objection at first to a fellow Hebrew being sold in order to pay off his debts, but they stoutly insisted that he must not be kept in perpetual bondage. When in the social process he was inevitably so kept they advanced to the theory that he ought not to be enslaved at all. They had no ideas of social equality, but freely accepted the fact that some are wealthy and some are poor. They felt most earnestly that the wealthy ought to accept their advantages in the spirit of a generous stewardship. When the wealthy made use of their privileges to encroach upon the meager possessions of the poor the prophets thundered their indignation. Whether we should go further than the Hebrew prophets suggested in the democratization of wealth is a question for us to decide for ourselves. We cannot quote the Bible as if it settled such matters for our day.

So the prophets saw events from the Hebrew standpoint. The Israelitish invasion of Canaan was the great struggle for a national home, but when other Bedouin made incursions into the land they were invaders who ought to be driven out. Doubtless the prophetic antagonism against Nineveh, "the bloody city," which one finds in Nahum, represents the righteous indignation of a man who had seen the brutal cruelties of the conquering Assyrians; yet one cannot fail to realize the spirit of national vengeance in the poem, and one cannot forget that the Hebrews practiced awful cruelties upon their own enemies without any prophetic rebuke. Isaiah speaks as a Hebrew when he flings his challenge to the haughty Assyrian, and declares that the virgin daughter of Zion shall laugh him to scorn (37. 22). Obadiah voices the national antipathy to Edom. Even the Messianic hope, so far as it was a mere expectation that Jehovah would give his people prosperity and peace, was part of the popular religion which the prophets inherited from the past.

Again, the prophet was in the social process because he was often the spokesman of the social need. He was often quite as much the representative as the leader. Samuel was the seer because the people needed such an intermediary; he was the judge because some notable person must decide difficult cases; he was the king-maker because he realized, as the people had come to realize, that there must be a single ruler to save Israel from her enemies. Even when the prophets spoke so nobly against the oppressions of the rich they were the spokesmen of the poor. They voiced the poor man's cry. Elijah was not alone in realizing the iniquity of the murder and robbery of Naboth. The people knew that a high-handed act of injustice had been committed.

§ 2. The Prophet as a Critic of Social Conditions

The prophet was thus a product of the social situation in which he lived, and the greater number of the prophets were nothing more. They simply spoke the things that the people wanted to hear (Isa 30. 10; Jer 6. 14; 23. 17; Ezek 13. 10), encouraged the kings on their campaigns (1 Kings 22. 11f.), and painted for the nation a golden future (Jer 27. 16ff.; 28. 3f.). Their words and writings have perished except as a few fragments have been preserved in the writings of the men who rebuked them. There were a few who rose above this mere contemporariness. They were able to look at events objectively and to see more than appeared on the surface. They were the real prophets.

Every man who feels the pinch of social conditions is able to criticize those conditions at the point where they affect him. The true moral leader is the man whose ideals are derived from large and unselfish views of wide interests—much wider than his own personal concerns—and who is able to measure the life of his contemporaries over against those ideals. That was the difference between the real prophet and the so-called false prophet. The latter was a patriot, but he was only a patriot. God's prophet was a man who realized that Israel's purpose in the world was not merely to be a comfortable Israel, but was to exemplify the social righteousness which is the counterpart among men of the character of God.

Hence the prophet was able to evaluate occurrences in different fashion from his contemporaries. Doubtless there were many in Israel who would feel that David played the tyrant toward Uriah, but, after all, David was a king, and that was the way of kings. But Nathan felt that it was not to be the way of Jehovah's kings, and he stepped forth with his stern protest. The worship of Baal, which was popularized by Jezebel with the approval of Ahab, was not intended to deprive Jehovah of his rights. It was a syncretism that was common enough. But Elijah said that such things might be done in other nations but were not to be tolerated in Israel: it must be Jehovah or Baal; there could be no compromise (1 Kings 18. 21).

When social injustice increased, the poor groaned and grumbled, but the prophets said that conditions ought not to be. They dared to denounce prosperity. Even in modern times this is frowned upon as dangerous; but they said that prosperity, when it is the luxury of the few at the expense of the many, is hollow and worthless; and they had the courage to welcome national adversity. They said that a thorough chastisement would do the people good. They believed that the victory of the foreigner over their own people was a needed discipline. The time came when they could even believe that Jerusalem was to be destroyed, and the people exiled, before a purification could be possible.

The national prophets were zealous for the religious ceremonial. The splendid cultus in which the people joined with enthusiasm, and the hope of "the day of Jehovah" when victory and prosperity should be theirs, seemed to be most valuable evidences of religion. But the great prophets declared that it was all empty and vain, and that Jehovah cared nothing for it. As for the day of Jehovah, it would come indeed, but it would be darkness instead of light. Jehovah was supremely concerned only with righteousness.

The pagan gods might be satisfied with sacrifices, but the God of Israel cared only for justice and generosity and reverent obedience.

§ 3. The Prophet as an Ethical and Religious Genius

What is the explanation of the rise of these few men with a world vision out of the common run of Israelites? Why were they able to see those ethical values which are easily apparent to us from the vantage point of time and distance, but which nobody else in their day could see? Whence came that passion for social righteousness so virile, so brave, so keen that it still animates us in our present day and our more complex situation? The only answer to these questions is the answer that must be given to every appearance of genius alike in the moral as in the literary or the practical sphere. The genius is never without natural heritage. He is always, as we have seen was the case with the prophets, a unit in the social process of his time and people. Yet he transcends his time and people by virtue of some great, inexplicable endowment of personality.

We may approach nearer to the answer in the case of the Hebrew prophet when we realize that the fundamentally significant fact about him was his religious experience. He was a man who had an experience of God. To him the most evidently certain fact of life was God. Explain it as we may, the prophet lived with a most intimate sense of community with God.

To him, therefore, the universe was through and through a moral universe. His theodicy and his theology were determined by the culture of his time. The sun, moon, and stars were the lights in the heavens, and were in some mysterious way "the host of heaven," but the solid earth was central in the cosmos. This view doubtless made it easier to think of the universe in moral terms than it may be for moderns. Be that as it may, the prophet believed that Jehovah was in control of the universe and that his central purpose was the achievement of righteousness.

The prophets regarded the Hebrew people as holding a central place in this plan of God. At first it was probably little more than the idea that Jehovah, desiring one righteous people, chose Israel and provided a land where that end might be attained (Deut 29f.). But the idea developed until it reached the splendid conception that the redemption of Israel was to lead to the redemption of all humanity (Isa 49. 5-7).

Psychologically, the religious experience of the prophet is not difficult to understand. He felt himself *en rapport* with the God who is good and is supremely interested in having people good like himself. This God is no respecter of persons. The rich, the powerful, the priests, who are conspicuous among men, are acceptable to him only as their deeds are righteous. Jehovah wills health and happiness to men, and all the good earth has been given to them for this end, and he hates tyranny and injustice. With this divine purpose the prophet found himself in complete sympathy. The only interest in the world that seemed significant to him was the achievement of goodness. Yet he found all about him human injustice. It pressed upon him in its thousand horrid forms at every point. By contrast this deepened his sense of the divine goodness and created a passionate longing that men's minds might be changed to that of God. Thus the divine goodness and human evil acted and reacted in the spirit of the prophet. Each threw the other into clearer outline. The prophet found himself taking the divine point of view, indignant with wrong, eager to chastise iniquity, yet ever hopeful of reformation, and ready to plead with the misguided people. A constructive program stretched out before his eyes with the ideal social state as its goal. Let the great give the weak a chance, let rich and poor combine in the building of society, let family life be purified, husbands and wives in mutual love, parents leading their children in righteousness, let rulers exercise their high responsibility for the good of all. Then it only needed that the evils of foreign aggression should be overcome, and the prophet believed that God could be trusted to see to that if the national life had been purified. So at last men might learn how to dwell together in mutual amity and help. The sense that this was God's plan for the nation and the world filled the prophet's mind, and he was able to declare his message with the divine commission, "Thus saith Jehovah."

DIRECTIONS FOR STUDY

1. Consider the attitude of the prophets on the subject of wine-drinking. How can we reconcile Amos 4. 1; 6. 3-6 with 9. 13-15? Also Isa 5. 22; 28. 1-8 with Deut 32. 14; Isa 5. 1; 55. 1; Jer 31. 12? Why were not the prophets prohibitionists? What does this indicate as to the propriety of the prohibition of the use of liquor to-day?
2. What does the answer to the preceding question suggest as to the meaning of "the social process"?
3. Read Deut 32. 6-9; 2 Sam 7. 22-24; Isa 43. 1-7. Note the intensely patriotic ring of these passages. Only a Hebrew could have written them.
4. How do the prophets illustrate the conditions of ethical optimism and ethical patriotism? How were they distinguished in these respects from the so-called false prophets?
5. On what grounds could a prophet welcome national adversity? Can you conceive a modern prophet announcing in any time of national calamity that a foreign enemy would be victorious over his own country?
6. What was the essential difference in the mind of the prophets between Jehovah and the pagan gods?
7. How in the midst of a people holding an unethical polytheism did the prophets come to believe in ethical monotheism?
8. In what sense is it proper to call the prophet a religious genius?
9. What were the fundamental religious convictions of the Hebrew prophet? How did these determine his social teaching?
10. What type of person in modern times might be compared with a Hebrew prophet?

THE GREAT SOCIAL PROPHETS

CHAPTER XXI

AMOS

§ 1. The Historical Situation

Society has little patience with a pessimist in a time of apparent prosperity. Any man who undertakes to point out social evils with vigor and to indicate their tendency and danger is likely to be esteemed a pessimist. Mild exhortation to improvement of conduct is acceptable; stern denunciation of evil and portrayal of its inevitable consequences is sure to give offense. Amos appeared in Israel as the first stern challenger of the fundamental policies and practices of the nation. Prophets before him had often challenged the particular acts of kings. He went deeper and brought a message to the people that concerned itself with the fundamental basis of their life. An interesting and peculiar combination of circumstances had brought Israel to a position of great prosperity. Her fortunes were determined for more than a century by the conditions existing in the kingdom of Syria immediately to the north. Syria's power was determined in turn by her relationship to Assyria, the powerful monarchy beyond the Euphrates. When Assyria was strong enough to break the power of Syria the latter was unable to trouble Israel, but when Assyria was kept in her own land by internal difficulties or more pressing wars, Syria was free to harass the kingdom of Israel.

Syria and Israel were at war during the reign of Ahab, and it was the campaigns of Shalmanezer II against Damascus that saved Israel from destruction. Jehu was involved with Syria in the payment of tribute to Shalmanezer, but after the death of that great Assyrian there was a period of over thirty years during which no western expedition was undertaken from Nineveh. Syria regained her strength in those years and repaid herself for her losses by a pitiless exploitation of Israel. At the period of Israel's direst distress Adad-Nirari III took the reins of power with a strong hand in Nineveh and made a vigorous campaign against Damascus. Joash of Israel then took advantage of the weakness of Syria to inflict upon her a severe defeat, and his successor, Jeroboam II, followed up this advantage until the beaten nation was obliged to accept the suzerainty of Israel as in the days of David.

§ 2. The Social Situation

There followed in Israel a period of unexampled prosperity. Tribute came in annually from Syria and from other dependencies, perhaps including Judah. Trade developed, rich caravans passing over the highroads of commerce. Architecture flourished as in the days of Solomon, noble dwellings for the king and his courtiers making the cities magnificent (3. 15; 5. 11). The worship of Jehovah was carried on with extraordinary splendor (3. 14; 4. 4f.; 5. 21, 23).

Yet all this prosperity was superficial. It was the luxury of the few at the expense of the toil and poverty of the many. The poor had felt most severely the harsh conditions of the bad times, and now participated least in the opportunities of the good times. During the wars the men had been summoned from their farms to fight the battles. When Israel was defeated and a heavy tribute (or war indemnity, as we should call it) was levied upon the land, the poor were made to pay the largest part of it. We have already noted that as a result of the wars there had grown up a military aristocracy. The nobles naturally advised the king and arranged for the collection of the tribute. Why should they pay it themselves when they could assess it upon their poorer neighbors? If the small farmer could not pay his tax, he could mortgage his land at usurious interest to the nobles. And if he could not pay his debt, the noble could add so much land to his own increasing estate. If the poor man was still unable to discharge his debts, his sons and his daughters could be sold into slavery, and the nobles again were the gainers.

When Israel was successful in war there was rich spoil. But the king and military chieftains would take the lion's share, and it was little likely that the soldier would get enough to pay him for leaving his home and his crops. If he maintained his independence and kept his ancestral inheritance, in spite of the heavy exactions of taxes and imposts, there was always the possibility that the cupidity of the wealthy noble would seek to dispossess him under the form of law. A pretended claim might easily be set up. The judge who was to decide the matter belonged to the upper class himself, and, moreover, the court decision was often for sale to the highest bidder (2. 7; 5. 7, 12; 6. 12). Even ordinary business was unfair. Cheating in weights and measures was notorious (8. 5) and wretched goods were sold for standard quality (8. 6).

The increasing wealth of the fortunate classes resulted in extravagance and debauchery. Splendid banquets afforded every luxury of furnishing, of food and wine, and of amusement (3. 12; 6. 4-6), and there was utter indifference to the poor and to the condition of the land (6. 6). The voluptuous women, as always is the case in such a social system, were even more extravagant than the men (4. 1).

§ 3. Amos of Tekoa

Among the shepherds who tended their flocks in the spare districts south of Jerusalem was Amos of Tekoa. He eked out a livelihood as a dresser of sycamore trees, a fruit that formed part of the food of the poor. He was evidently a man of keen observation. The sale of his products may have taken him to the various cities of his own and neighboring lands. Distances in any case were short, and the journeys could easily have been made. The caravan route from Jerusalem to Hebron passed near his home, and he knew much of the course of the world's life. Familiarity with the traditions of his race, and with the stories which had attained their classic literary form, was his schooling as a speaker and writer in the Hebrew tongue.

Amos looked upon the social evils of his day and grew heavy of heart. He knew what ruthless war had been levied upon the East-Jordanic lands by the savage Syrians (1. 3). He had seen the gangs of hapless slaves driven to market by the avaricious Philistines (1. 6) and Phœnicians (1. 9). He had shuddered at the barbarities practiced by the eastern and southern neighbors of Judah (1. 11-13; 2. 1). But, more than all, his indignation burned against Israel for its rapacity, tyranny, corruption, and empty religiousness.

His robust religious spirit had grown beyond the petty thought that each nation had its own god to whom alone it was responsible. Jehovah was the God of the earth, and the wickedness of every people would be punished by his justice. Amos became convinced that the social corruption of Israel was so great that the doom of the nation was inevitable. He saw it coming and prayed that it might be averted. One peril after another passed, seeming to give opportunity for repentance (7. 1-6), but no repentance came, and the punishment seemed to be at hand.

Amos felt that some one ought to tell Israel the truth. Some voice of protest ought to be raised. But no one dared to speak (2. 12; 7. 10-13). There were prophets enough in Israel, but there was no fearless voice among them. Amos had no connection with the prophetic guilds and naturally hesitated to take upon himself such a mission. But at last the protest of his soul proved too strong. If no one else would go, he must perform the task himself. It became clear that he was the messenger of Jehovah, so he went up to Bethel to speak the word that was given him (7. 14-16; 3. 8).

§ 4. The Message of Amos

The sum of Amos's message was that a society founded upon injustice could not endure. With a fine figure he represented Jehovah as standing beside a wall with a plumbline in his hand (7. 8). The great standard of right is set up in the midst of the nation, and anyone can see the miserable disparity. What can be done with a misbuilt wall but break it down? Again the prophet sees a basket of summer fruit —our own poet's figure of "the goodly apple rotten at the core"; thus he indicates the ripeness of decay. And in Hebrew the figure is more striking, for the word for the fruit has the same sinister sound as the word "end" (8. 2).

Amos does not express the inevitableness of Israel's collapse in the terms of the operation of social forces, as we should explain it to-day. The Hebrew sense of the directness of the action of Jehovah enables him to speak of the coming judgment as a divine infliction. Jehovah looks upon the shameful tyrannies and swears, *"I will never forget any of their works"* (8. 7). It is he who will destroy the wicked nation by sending some other nation to execute punishment (5. 27; 6. 14). The dreadful nature of that punishment is described with terrible impressiveness (8. 3, 8-14; 9. 1-4; 6. 11).

The people, of course, thought that they could purchase the favor of Jehovah by their costly offerings (4. 4f.). Amos had only contempt for such religion. He said for Jehovah,

> *I hate, I despise your feasts,*
> *And I will take no delight in your solemn assemblies.*
> . . . .
> *Take thou away from me the noise of thy songs,*
> *For I will not hear the melody of thy viols* (5. 21-23).

He reaches out to the great truth that Jehovah is only to be served through the social relationships of men. He affirms it in the great word that is the keynote of his prophecy, a permanent summons to every human society, and a rebuke to any religion that would serve God and forget men,

> Let justice roll down as waters,
> And righteousness as an ever-flowing stream (5. 24).

§ 5. The Contribution of Amos

The message of Amos is limited. He declares only the one principle—the doom of the social order that is unjust. The beautiful closing paragraph of the book is perhaps the work of those later editors who sought always to balance the earlier prophecies of judgment with the words of hope. But Amos's rugged word of doom is a good one for our modern day. We too have a prosperity unexampled. We enjoy a peace that has enabled us to grow rich. The wealth and luxury of our cities would put the little splendors of Bethel and Samaria into sorry comparison, and we too "have not grieved for the affliction of Joseph." We have "put far away the evil day" and have allowed among us those "that afflict the just, that take a bribe, and that turn aside the needy from their right." Our religion has too often been carried on with mere magnificence and as if it had nothing to do with social justice. We have not even failed of the parallel that we have commanded the prophets, "Prophesy not," for who is the bold man who dares speak to-day for social justice? We do not expect the collapse of our modern society, but we may well heed the message that reminds us that the foundations of an enduring social order are justice. We may believe that our God, like the God of Amos, will never forget the works of oppression.

DIRECTIONS FOR STUDY

1. Read 2 Kings 13 and 14. Consider what conditions in Israel are there described.

2. Read Amos 7. 10-15. What information is there given about the prophet?
3. What does 3. 1-8 add to our knowledge of Amos and his reasons for preaching?
4. Consider the meaning of the five visions, 7. 1-9, 8. 1-3, 9. 1-4. A lively imagination is needed to see these pictures and their symbolic meaning.
5. One of the greatest of Amos's oracles is 5. 18 to 6. 14, which is a literary unit in three parts. Read the first part, 5. 18-27, and note the prophet's contempt for the religiousness of the people.
6. Note the woe on the nobles (6. 1-7). What social situation is there depicted?
7. What social conditions are described in 4. 1-3? 5. 4-17?
8. What social conditions are indicated in 8. 4-14?
9. Read 9. 7-10. Note that Jehovah is represented as the God of all the nations. What is the nature of the predicted doom?
10. What would we think of such a man as Amos to-day?

CHAPTER XXII

HOSEA

HOSEA is not generally thought of so much as a social prophet because of the intense religiousness of his message. Amos was also religious, but his word from Jehovah had to do almost entirely with the divine demand for just relations between men, while Hosea was intensely concerned with the broken relations between Israel and Jehovah—a broken faith, a broken loyalty. Yet it was still the social evils that gave meaning to Hosea's message. The breach between the people and Jehovah was so evident because of the social anarchy of that terrible time. If Amos had to tell a smug and contented people rejoicing in prosperity that their social fabric was really rotten and was tottering to its fall, Hosea had to call a broken, troubled society back to its religious loyalty as the only hope of political and social salvation. Even the Bull worship which Hosea so strongly denounced was not irreligious alone. Other prophets had tolerated it because it was nominal Jehovah worship, but Hosea saw its utter paganism, its moral worthlessness, and stigmatized it as fundamentally the old Baal worship with all the degrading sensuality of that nature religion.

§ 1. THE POLITICAL SITUATION

Hosea is so far a social prophet that we cannot at all understand him except against the background of the political conditions of the time. Those conditions were terrible. Jehu, a usurper, had come to the throne through rivers of blood. His dynasty went out in assassination. The blood of Jezreel was avenged (1. 4). It was the son of the proud Jeroboam II who reigned only half a year before Shallum slew him (2 Kings 15. 8-12). This conspirator sat on the throne a month when Menahem slew him and established his reign in terrorism (vv. 13-16). He reigned ten years and died a natural death, but his son after only two years was murdered by the commander of the army, Pekah, who in turn was destined himself to die at the hands of the Assyrian overlord from whom he revolted. Well might Hosea say of this wretched travesty upon government, *"I have given thee a king in mine anger, and have taken him away in my wrath"* (13. 11).

The world powers were upon Israel now. No more was there safety during periods of Assyrian weakness. Tiglath-Pileser III, Shalmanezer IV, Sargon, were the mighty tyrants who successively battered the poor little Hebrew kingdom into the dust. And as if they were not enough, there were the Egyptian Pharaohs coming into Palestinian politics, holding out elusive hopes, and flattering Israel into thinking that she could make alliance upon equal terms with the Nile empire against the might of Nineveh.

Hosea looked upon it all with that detachment which moral insight and purity of motive give. He saw the folly of the petty policies and beheld ever nearer the dreadful day of doom.

§ 2. The Social Situation

The prosperity that Amos saw in Bethel and Samaria had, of course, departed, but the end was not yet, and Israel still believed herself secure. Menahem bowed before the Assyrian storm and secured immunity by the payment of a huge tribute, which, in the first instance at all events, he levied upon his nobles (2 Kings 15. 20). Doubtless their luxury was considerably diminished, but there is no reason to suppose that there was any lightening of the burdens upon the people or any attempt to administer the laws with justice. The basket of summer fruit had lost even the appearance of lusciousness and was a pitiful exhibition of decay. But there was enough trade to produce some wealth, and it could still be said of Israel, *"He is a trafficker, the balances of deceit are in his hand: he loveth to defraud"* (12. 7).

The rulers who succeeded one another were too insecure in their tenure of the throne to be able to put down the rude violence that inevitably arises in such troublous times (10. 3). The nobles threw aside all pretense of social order (5. 10). Thieves and robbers ravaged the land (7. 1). The priests were no better than such marauders (6. 9).

Sensuality, ever the sin of the Oriental peoples, and of Israel, became increasingly shameless. The orgies of the popular festivals gave a religious sanction to this debauchery (4. 13). What possibility of a wholesome family life could such a state of things hold out? (4. 14.) It was in this darkest phase of Israel's social evils that Hosea found his inspiration to speak his deathless message to his people.

§ 3. The Tragic Experience of Hosea

The sensuality of the times struck Hosea in his own home. A man of tenderest affection, he had married Gomer in all honor, and hope of the purest family life.[1] She wronged him, left his home with a paramour, shamed him before the people, and wounded him in the deepest interests of his life. He saw the social corruption of Israel epitomized and felt it as no one but a strong, free man could feel it. He might easily have cast off Gomer and been rid of her. He might then have denounced the vices of his nation with the bitterness that would have been so naturally the product of his personal experience. But Hosea found a feeling in his heart other than bitterness—pity for the foolish, misguided woman, the sense of deep responsibility for her who had

[1] The first three chapters of Hosea have always constituted a difficulty to interpreters. The explanation here given is that which has been generally adopted by modern scholars. The literal view, that Hosea married a depraved woman in order to show Israel the awfulness of the relation between herself and Jehovah, is ably set forth by J. M. P. Smith in the Biblical World, August, 1913.

been his wife, a longing for her restoration, not without a hope that she might yet be worthy of his love. So he went after her, found her sold as a slave, bought her and kept her under kindly discipline in his home, hoping that some day he might restore her to the position of a wife.

Could Israel be saved? Was the waywardness of the foolish nation like the waywardness of the foolish woman? Hosea learned from his own broken heart the infinite love of God, just in discipline, endless in hope. It is the profoundest religious truth of the Old Testament. Naturally, Jesus found himself in kinship with this great soul (Matt 12. 7).

§ 4. The Social Message of Hosea

The key word of Amos is *justice*. The keyword of Hosea is *love*. And as Amos treats of divine justice which demands social justice among men, so Hosea believes that the God of love seeks love from men, and love among men. It is not only the love of God for Israel of which Hosea speaks, but love of man to man which he sees as the only bond of the social organism.

Hosea denounces injustice as vehemently as Amos. There is to be vengeance for Jehu's bloody politics (1. 4). Jehovah has a case at law against Israel, *"because there is no truth, nor goodness, nor knowledge of God in the land. There is nought but swearing and breaking of faith, and killing, and stealing, and committing adultery; they break out, and blood touches blood. Therefore shall the land mourn"* (4. 1-3). Priests and people are alike corrupt, and punishment is in store for them (4. 9). Upon the wicked princes shall wrath be poured out like water (5. 10). This prophet has given us a classic expression of social retribution—*"They sow the wind, and they shall reap the whirlwind"* (8. 7).

But Hosea sees some hope. Justice and love may save the state. The awful certainty of reaping what has been sown in evil may be transformed into a reaping of what has been sown in righteousness and love (10. 12f.). The great key word of the prophecy quoted by Jesus finds the heart of religion in human kindness, "I desire love and not sacrifice" (6. 6). The two great words of social salvation are bound together in another exhortation,

> Turn thou to thy God:
> Keep love and justice,
> And wait for thy God continually (12. 6).

Hosea looked for a time of peace when the bow and the sword should be broken and the battles that had harassed Israel so long should be ended (2. 18). As he saw the tangled scheme of things he realized the simplicity of the solution of man's troubles—fairness of man to man and love. Even at the eleventh hour of Israel's history he believed that she could yet be saved. Who shall say if a society so knit together in the bonds of true human fellowship might not endure in spite of Assyrian and Egyptian tyrants? Israel never put the doctrine to the test. Jesus enunciated it again in the great message of the kingdom of God. But no considerable society has ever tried to follow Jesus's teaching either. The world has yet to see whether the social message of Hosea, that a corrupt society may be saved through social justice and love, can be vindicated in human experience.

§ 5. The Religious Message of Hosea

If for convenience we make distinction between the social and religious message of the prophet, we may be well assured that he would not himself have sanctioned the distinction. The great New Testament assertion, "We love because he first loved us," is exactly Hosea's conception of the motive of social harmony. Israel had ever been the object of Jehovah's love. As the bride beloved of her husband (2. 19f.), as the child tenderly nurtured by his father (11. 1), as the burdened animal guided, encouraged, fed (11. 4), so had God loved and cherished and comforted Israel. He sought love and loyalty in return. When he received wickedness instead of love his heart yearned over his foolish people that he might save them (11. 8f.). Israel had supposed with the blindness that had been so common among men that Jehovah was like a jealous monarch asking for praise and tribute and offering, when all his wish was to see them living together in mutual justice and love, acknowledging him with the love that was the answer to his own.

Hosea was right. Increasing experience is bringing thoughtful social workers and reformers more and more to see that we shall never have a socialized humanity except first we have a reverent love for God.

DIRECTIONS FOR STUDY

1. Read 2 Kings 15. Note the historical situation there described.
2. Can you distinguish between the social and the religious experience of Hosea?
3. Read 6. 1-6. Note the hope, the tenderness, the fear, the attitude toward ritual.
4. Read 4. 6-9. What idea of the priesthood does this present?
5. Read 7. 1-7. What political and social conditions are there presented?
6. Read 7. 8-16. To what political policy is reference made?
7. Read 8. 1-6. What conditions does this passage present?
8. Read 10. 4-8. What doom did Hosea anticipate for Israel?
9. Read 11. 8-11. What does this passage reveal of Hosea's character?
10. How would you estimate the social influence of a man like Hosea—then and now?

CHAPTER XXIII

ISAIAH

§ 1. THE POLITICAL SITUATION

THE continuance of the rule of the Davidic dynasty in the south with some kings who were men of ability gave Judah a settled political life which was very different from the turbulent experience of the Northern Kingdom. The geographical position of Judah, moreover, in the rugged hills with her one great city, the easily defended fortress of Jerusalem, gave her immunity from foreign attacks which saved her from many of the harsh experiences of her neighbor. To be sure, she had suffered severely from Syria and had been badly beaten by Israel itself; but comparatively she was less exposed. The extreme weakness of Syria which allowed Israel to regain her strength under Jeroboam II gave also opportunity for Judah under Uzziah and his son Jotham to develop her resources. Ahaz succeeded to a kingdom prosperous and secure.

Two great military powers threatened the independence and prosperity of all the little kingdoms of western Asia. On the south was Egypt, greatly weakened from the days when her conquering Pharaohs marched in triumph to the Palestinian lands, yet still stronger than any other western power, and with the prestige of her ancient glory making her a foe to be dreaded or an ally to be desired.

Far stronger than Egypt, as we now understand, though the fact was not so clear to their contemporaries, were the Assyrians. The period of their greatest military effectiveness covered roughly the century from the accession of Ahaz to the death of his grandson Manasseh. The early policy of the Assyrians was to make robber raids upon their neighbors, looting the cities which they captured, and gathering rich booty of gold, silver, precious stones, and slaves. They would then lay a fixed tribute upon the conquered land, which was to be paid annually as the price of immunity from further molestation. Rebellion against such harsh conditions was, of course, incessant, the tributary states taking advantage of any weakness of the suzerain to seek independence. The later Assyrian kings therefore adopted more drastic measures to insure the stability of their empire. Rebellious peoples were deported from their own lands to some distant district, where, mingled with other races, their national traditions broken, the roots of their national life destroyed, and, according to current religious belief, separated from their national gods, they would be unable to offer serious resistance to the conqueror.

It is this loss of national life that Amos foresaw was coming upon Israel. But the politicians at the court of Samaria believed themselves able to withstand their foe. They, together with their former bitter enemies, the Syrians, realized the danger from Assyria, and formed a defensive alliance. The two urged Ahaz, king of Judah, to unite with them, and upon his refusal undertook war against him. He turned to Assyria for help, which, of course, was readily granted, with the result that Judah became a tributary state. Tiglath-Pileser came west, destroyed Syria, and made Israel tributary. Thereafter the national existence of both Israel and Judah depended upon their willingness to pay the heavy annual tax imposed upon them.

Meantime Egypt was taking active part in the international policies. Her emissaries were intriguing in all the Palestinian courts, endeavoring to combine the various peoples against Assyria. Egypt seemed the one hope of safety to these sorely ravaged kingdoms, though in reality it was a misplaced hope. The Egyptian forces were very slowly mobilized, while the Assyrians moved with lightning speed, conquering their enemies in detail before the Egyptians were able to take the field.

Israel foolishly listened to the seductive assurance of Egypt, and paid the price with her national life. With the fall of Samaria in 722 B. C., the northern Hebrews practically disappear from historical consideration. Had a similar fate befallen Judah, it is difficult to see how the great Hebrew contribution to religious experience could have been preserved for mankind. There is a sense in which it may be said that the religious future of humanity was dependent upon the politics of the court of Jerusalem at the end of the eighth century B. C.

It was in this crisis that Isaiah exercised his wonderful constructive statesmanship. It was a new role for a prophet to play. Hitherto the prophets had been critics of the kings and people, perhaps counselors in special needs. But now their clear insight, which was the result alike of religious conviction and ethical passion, was needed to direct the course of national destiny amid the confusions of selfish and foolish politics.

§ 2. The Social Situation

The course of social progress had naturally been much the same in the south as in the north. Although Judah had not suffered as much from the crushing wars carried on with the terrible cruelty of those times, yet she had by no means been altogether free. Defeats had been inflicted upon her by Egypt, Syria, and Israel, and heavy tributes had been exacted during many years. As in the north, this hardship fell most heavily upon the poor. The military service which took them from their farms, the harsh taxation which was laid on them while the rich went free, the consequent debts, usurious interest, mortgaging and loss of ancestral property, made the lot of the poor extremely bitter in the days of Judah's distress.

But the prosperity which was so marked in the north

had also its parallel in Judah. And again the lion's share of the benefits went into the hands of the military aristocracy, while the poor were little advantaged. Oppression, fraud, and the injustice of the courts gave the wealth of the kingdom to the privileged classes. The writings of Isaiah reveal the sharp and bitter contrast between the rich and poor—luxury, drunkenness, splendid banquets, and the finery of the voluptuous ladies on the one side (3. 16ff.; 5. 8, 11ff.) and the grinding of the poor on the other (1. 17; 10. 2). That worst social iniquity, favoritism in the administration of justice, always the curse of the East, was shamefully common (5. 7, 23). The robbery of the widow and the orphan in the settlement of estates (10. 2) was a flagrant example of this injustice.

The leaders of the people were involved in all these evils (9. 15f.). It was not the ordinary imperfection of social organization; it was high-handed iniquity. Even the prophets, who were supposed to be preachers of righteousness, were mere timeservers (9. 15; 30. 10). When the men set to be moral leaders are more concerned to say the things that are smooth and pleasing than to speak the stern facts of social life the people are far gone in decay.

Religion was splendidly carried on. There was less of the objectionable element in it than was the case at the idolatrous shrines of Bethel and Dan and the other northern sanctuaries. The temple at Jerusalem exerted a steadying influence on the ceremonialism of Judah's religion. No image stood in the temple except in the most degenerate periods. But the worship was formal. It was divorced from human interests. Jehovah was to be satisfied with the multitude of magnificent sacrifices, and with the punctilious performance of ritual duties by the worshipers (1. 10-15). It was a religion without ethical motive.

The conditions in Jerusalem might well have called Amos to speak in the capital of his own country words quite similar to those which he spoke so fearlessly in the north. But he seems to have had little to say about Judah. A generation passed after Amos while the life of Judah gained nothing in moral tone. It was time for some one to speak the summons to social righteousness; and the man for the hour was at hand.

§ 3. Isaiah the Prophet

We know very little of Isaiah's personal life. It has been generally thought that he was high born. There is a Jewish tradition, which, of course, has no value, that he was one of the royal priests. The only ground for believing him to belong to the privileged classes is the fact that he seems to have had easy entrée to the court and to have been thoroughly familiar with the diplomacy of the times, while his early vision would indicate an intimate acquaintance with the temple. It is interesting to think of him as perhaps an aristocrat to whom had come the call of the people's needs.

Certain it is that Isaiah was essentially a man of Jerusalem, of the city. It is with her people, her interests, her dangers, her future, that he is concerned. He knows the life of that city in all its tragic contrasts, and, in spite of the evil which causes him to expect a terrible punishment, he believes that all the future of God's purpose in the world is bound up with the inviolability of Zion. Isaiah's great name gave currency to that splendid, but in less ethical hands most dangerous, doctrine, that Jerusalem could never be destroyed.

Isaiah holds a conspicuous place among the Hebrew prophets as a political guide and a social reformer, but, like all the great prophets, his religious experience was basal in his life. He felt first the presence of God, and the sense of human duty followed upon that experience. This is most clearly shown in the highly picturesque description of the call of the prophet (ch. 6). He is profoundly impressed with the sense of the holiness of Jehovah, and feels himself and his people unworthy to serve the pure God. Perhaps he had grown up in the easy acceptance of the privileges of the upper class, and only gradually a sympathy with the burdens and troubles of the poor had revealed to him the condition of the times. Such social relations were not possible to the people of a holy God. But the ardent young soul longed to be fit for the great task of bringing his people to righteousness, and with the longing came the sense of purification and the sense of being commissioned for the task.[1]

Isaiah's experience soon convinced him that there was little hope of a national repentance and ethical revival. It became evident that no less a sweeping punishment than that which Amos had foreseen for Israel must come also upon Judah. There was, however, this difference—that Isaiah believed that there existed among his people a kernel of the righteous. Whatever might be the devastation, there would be left a remnant which should be the nucleus of the better state[2] (10. 20-22). In the figure which he uses more than once he speaks of Judah as the oak that is to be felled, but out of whose stock a new tree shall arise (6. 13). It is this expectation that gives to Isaiah's words that combination of judgment and mercy that renders them so true and so human in their appeal.

Isaiah was probably the most brilliant orator in the great galaxy of the Hebrew men of eloquence. His poetic feeling, his marvelous command of the Hebrew tongue as it was at its best, his range of poetry, metaphor, simile, parable, his sudden and significant changes of mood—these, with his passion of human sympathy and his sublime conception of the ways of God among men, make him the master orator of Israel and place him among the few really great speakers of the world.

---

[1] It is possible that chapter six was put into its present form some years after the beginning of Isaiah's ministry. It reflects the harsh results that he must have found as soon as he endeavored to lead the people to repentance. (vv. 9-12).

[2] Isaiah, who gave symbolic names to his children, called his oldest son Shear-Jashub, "a remnant shall return" (7. 3, marg.).

§ 4. The Social Message of Isaiah

Isaiah believed that Jehovah was infinitely holy and that he was supremely concerned to have a holy people dwelling peaceably and safely in the land which he had given them. Thus the very depth of his religion gave the social quality to his message. The individualism of religion, with all its wondrous spiritual values, and with its peculiar spiritual dangers, had not yet become a dominant idea. Isaiah felt himself united with his people in a social solidarity (6. 5), and he thought of Jehovah not so much as concerned with individual worshipers as with the people united together in an indissoluble social bond.

To be sure, Isaiah expected the people to be decimated as an inevitable consequence of their sins, and that only a remnant would be left as the nucleus of the new state, but the people were to be destroyed because of their unsocial life, and the remnant were to be saved because they were worthy to live a community life well pleasing to God.

Three main features of Isaiah's teaching as it springs from his fundamental religious conceptions may be noted:

1. The most evident and constant demand upon his lips was for social righteousness. He was concerned with comparatively simple matters. He found no fault with the fundamental constitution of society, although it included masters and slaves, rich and poor. The evil, to Isaiah's mind, was that the strong and privileged, not satisfied with the advantages which they enjoyed by reason of their very condition as such, not only did not realize the fraternal responsibility of generosity to the weak, but actually took every opportunity of exploiting them. He denounced the leaders and princes who should have been the protectors of the people, but who actually filled their houses with the spoil of the poor (3. 14f.). Again and again he spoke with scorn of the bribe-takers who sold justice and honor for money (1. 23; 5. 23). He pronounced woe against the

landowning class who were seeking to get large estates into their hands, crowding out the small farmers, and crowding together the city dwellers (5. 8). Luxury and debauchery upon which the ill-gotten gains were expended met with his stern condemnation (3. 16 to 4. 1; 5. 11, 12, 22, 23). In contrast with this miserable oppression was the prophet's conception of Jehovah. He declared Jehovah to be a God of justice (30. 18). In all the expectation of a better day that was to come for Judah justice and righteousness were made most prominent (28. 17).

2. The second important item in Isaiah's practical teaching was his plea for political wisdom. It was founded in a religious faith that Jehovah was governing the affairs of men, a more naïve view than we should hold with our careful estimate of historical cause and effect. Yet Isaiah's attitude was soundly practical, and was deduced from a careful survey of the political situation in western Asia. He believed that his people had so sinned that they were to be punished, and he saw that Assyria was the power that would accomplish the result. But he also believed that the Hebrews had a part to play in the providence of God which made it certain that Jerusalem should not be utterly destroyed. We are not accustomed to connect the purposes of God with the permanence of any human institution, and we know, in point of fact, that the Hebrew religion not only survived the fall of Jerusalem but was actually purified thereby. Yet it is undoubtedly most fortunate that Jerusalem was captured by the Babylonians, and not by the Assyrians, in the sixth century, and not in the eighth. Isaiah's foresight was justified in his own generation, and as we look back from the long view that the lapse of time affords us we recognize the sober soundness of his political policy.

Isaiah's fundamental political policy might be stated in the words of Washington—"Avoid entangling alliances." The petty courts of Palestine were alive with intrigue. Confederations for mutual defense were formed now against one power, now against another. Egypt stood behind them all, endeavoring to unite all the lesser peoples as a buffer against the Assyrian power which she feared. Isaiah believed that all such combinations were futile, and that if Judah would concern herself with the purification of her own social life she need have little fear of foreign enemies. If the message of Amos was that a society founded on injustice could not endure, that of Isaiah was that a society founded on justice could not be overthrown. Judah gave some little heed to his words, and, as a matter of fact, the little state endured while the mighty Assyrian passed away.

While in general disapproving of alliances, Isaiah was particularly distrustful of Egypt. He constantly warned his people, *"Egypt helpeth in vain, and to no purpose"* (30. 7). He rightly estimated the unreadiness of that ancient and boastful people and knew that reliance upon them would be a costly mistake. Another element in his policy was to keep faith when once it had been pledged.

In pursuance of these views, Isaiah earnestly begged Ahaz to have no fear of Israel and Syria when they tried to coerce him into the league against Assyria, assuring the king that the life of the two northern enemies, "these two tails of smoking firebrands," was nearly burned out (7. 1-9). The prophet was, of course, bitterly opposed to Ahaz's foolish plan of calling upon Assyria for help, and showed the heavy price that Judah would have to pay for such a policy (7. 10-23). The king refused his advice, which he evidently found irksome (7. 10-13). He sent a large present to the king of Assyria and bound himself to be his slave (2 Kings 16. 7-9). So the Assyrian vassalage began, and, having begun, Isaiah insisted that it should be allowed to continue. Egypt was busy promising to free the Hebrews from their degrading servitude, but Isaiah saw that rebellion would mean extermination. He insisted that the payment of the tribute was the punishment for past sin and folly and that the compact with Assyria must be kept. Some of his most brilliant prophecies were concerned with the endeavor to save Jerusalem from futile revolt. On one occasion he went about Jerusalem clothed with the single scant garment of a slave, and when people wondered why Isaiah should be so garbed he told them that all of them would be dressed in that fashion when they labored for the Assyrians as their captives (ch. 20). When at last the accession of Sennacherib seemed to offer opportunity for successful revolt, and the Egyptian party in Jerusalem was in the ascendant, he vehemently denounced them, scornfully describing Egypt as "Rahab that sitteth still" (30. 1-7).

But Isaiah was unsuccessful and King Hezekiah was persuaded to revolt against his suzerain. The prophet saw that it meant defeat and a terrible scourge of Judah, but he still believed in the safety of Jerusalem. In a splendid oration he denounced the cruel enemy (10. 5-33), and definitely declared his confidence that Jerusalem should be preserved (37. 33-35). How remarkably this confidence was vindicated, the Hebrew tradition states in picturesque fashion (v. 36), and the historical records both of Judah and of Assyria sufficiently indicate.

3. The third element in the social message of Isaiah is the vision of the ideal state, or, as it is more generally called, the Messianic reign. It is important that this should be recognized as a social ideal. Isaiah was not thinking of a life after death or of a spiritual kingdom in the midst of the common world of affairs. He believed in the God of justice. He believed that that justice was to be established among men. He believed that the natural agency for that grand reform was a true prince of the house of David, who should be filled with the impartial wisdom of God (11. 1-5). If the king were just, equity would prevail among the people (compare 2 Sam 15. 2-4).

Besides justice the ideal king would bring peace. Isaiah wrote in a time when cruel warfare was the scourge of nations. Following on the description of the righteous king was the exquisite idyllic picture of the age of peace (11. 6-9). The highly poetic character of the language must not be allowed to obscure the very practical meaning that a strong and righteous ruler in God's good time would put an end to wars. More clearly still is this brought out in the great contrast where the king who is to rule in righteousness is actually called "The Prince of Peace" (9. 3-7).

In a passage which Isaiah shares with Micah (2. 2-4; Mic 4. 1-5), the original authorship of which is, therefore, not clear, there is no Messianic reference, but the great social longing for the arts of agriculture to replace those of war is to be fulfilled as a result of the recognition by the nations of the supremacy of Jehovah and of his righteous law.

DIRECTIONS FOR STUDY

1. In what respects was the political and social situation of Judah similar to that in Israel?
2. Trace the varying relations of Judah to Israel, Syria, Assyria, and Egypt, during the ministry of Isaiah, from the death of Uzziah, 740 B. C., to the Sennacherib invasion, 701 B. C.
3. What was the attitude of Isaiah in each political crisis, and upon what political conviction was it based?
4. Should we consider his attitude justified from our own point of view?
5. Give a psychological explanation of the vision of Isaiah (ch. 6). Consider how a modern social reformer might be impelled by a similar religious motive.
6. Read chs. 1 to 5. Consider what social conditions are there revealed.
7. Compare 3. 16 to 4. 1 with Amos 4. 1-3. What special conditions do these passages reveal? Is there anything comparable with these in our modern life?
8. Compare the essential social message of Amos with that of Isaiah.
9. Why did Isaiah believe in the inviolability of Zion? How far was he justified in his faith?
10. Read 2. 2-4; 9. 1-7; 11. 1-9. Consider what social elements are involved in these ideals. How far do such hopes enter into our own social program?

CHAPTER XXIV

MICAH

§ 1. The Times of Micah

Micah was a younger contemporary of Isaiah. His prophetic activity began in those stirring days when the Northern Kingdom was hastening to its fall. Israel had always been stronger than Judah. Its fertile plains and noble pasture lands fostered a far larger population than could be sustained by the rugged hill country of Judah. And Samaria had always been richer than Jerusalem. The south, therefore, must have been powerfully influenced by the north. The certainty that the Northern Kingdom was to come to an end, that the major part of the Hebrew race was to be removed from its ancestral land, must have deeply affected the southern prophets.

With extraordinary fatuity the politicians and people of Israel did not expect disaster. They trusted in the strength of their alliances and in the ability of Samaria to stand the siege. But the prophets believed that great moral forces were operating. Amos had declared that a society established on injustice could not endure. He looked for Israel to disappear. Micah's ministry began with the same conviction. The city of Samaria was to him the center of all the evil in Israel, for he was particularly hostile to the sins of the cities.

What is the transgression of Jacob?
Is it not Samaria?

In the most thoroughgoing declaration he predicted the ruin of Israel's capital: "Jehovah will make Samaria as a heap of the field" (1. 6).

Samaria fell. Amos had seemed the fanatic when he

spoke to the gay crowd at Bethel as the religious festival was being so magnificently celebrated. Even Micah's prediction, in a much darker day, seemed a piece of ungracious pessimism. But Samaria with all its pride and wealth was gone. The leaders of the northern people were gone; princes, priests, judges, merchants, mechanics—all but the poorest had been driven into other conquered lands of the Assyrians and the great social iniquities had ceased by the dreadful process of the removal of the transgressors.

What would happen in the south? Would Judah follow Israel? Would Jerusalem follow Samaria? That was the problem to which Micah especially addressed himself. His messages concerning Israel had been preparatory; his real work was to be done in Judah.

§ 2. Micah and Isaiah

We do not know that these two men had any relation with one another. The prophet is often compared to the modern preacher, but a very important distinction must always be kept in mind. The prophets were not the graduates of schools, prepared for their work according to standard requirements. There were, to be sure, professional prophets, as we have seen, who followed a certain technique of clairvoyance, but the great ethical prophets seem always to have stood aloof from this other type and to have insisted upon their immediate inspiration from Jehovah; that is to say, they were men of individual conviction. They spoke not what was accepted as the great common doctrine, but what was their own inner conviction of truth. Naturally, therefore, the prophets did not always say the same thing. A clear testimony to the independence of these great spirits is afforded by the difference of view expressed by Isaiah and Micah on the same important question. Fundamentally, as regards religious faith and ethical insight, the two men were at one; but with regard to the question whether Jerusalem was to stand or fall they expressed opposite opinions.

Isaiah was a man of the city; Micah was a man of the country. Isaiah loved Jerusalem; Micah hated it. To Isaiah, Zion, though full of iniquity, extortion, and wrong, was to be purified and never to be destroyed (Isa 4. 2-6). To Micah the sin of the nation culminated in its capital, and he saw it doomed, "Zion shall be ploughed as a field, and Jerusalem shall become heaps" (3. 12). How astounding an assertion this was, and how deep an impression it made, are evident from the fact that it was remembered for a hundred years, and quoted in the days of Jeremiah as a precedent for the freedom of speech of the prophet (Jer 26. 18ff.).

§ 3. The Social Situation

The social situation appeared differently to Isaiah and to Micah. The former saw all the evils, but did not regard them as inseparable from city life. He looked for a regenerated city. The younger prophet felt that the rottenness of Hebrew life had come from its urban development and nothing but a return to the simplicity of the earlier days would insure purity.

There was much to justify Micah's view. Solomon had turned the course of Israel's life from the simplicity of agriculture to the more highly organized commercialism of the city, with all the luxury, extravagance, and consequent extortion and heartlessness that characterize it. Jerusalem, like every other city that has ever gained importance, was filled with people desiring to be rich and to partake of the luxuries that were esteemed the highest goods of life. There were more aspirants for wealth than could be satisfied. Those who had much desired more, and all who had anything that could be exchanged for wealth were eager to convert it into money.

When money and all that money can accomplish are the chief ends of life, naturally patriotism, generosity, and justice take the lower place. The exploitation of the poor and the sale of every type of service inevitably result. The merchant robs his customers, the employer drives his servants, the capitalist grinds the last penny from the borrower, the judge sells his decisions, the priest bestows religious consolation on the highest bidder, and the prophet speaks the word that will bring reward. Those who are in power have the opportunity for these extortions and injustice, and pitilessly they make use of their privilege. Wealth flows inevitably from the country to the city, for the man in the country has little chance against the organized greed of the political and the commercial class. Thus the poor of the city are stripped and the country is exploited for the benefit of the luxurious dwellers of the cities. To a greater or less degree all this has been true through history. The prevalence of these conditions in the modern world constitutes altogether the most serious problem of our times. It was the situation in Judah and Jerusalem, and Micah could see no remedy but the destruction of the city altogether.

§ 4. The Message of Micah

They build up Zion with blood,
And Jerusalem with iniquity (3. 10).

Micah's words are against the city aristocracy. He describes them as eating the flesh of the people (3. 3), so terrible was the exploitation of the poor. *"They covet fields, and seize them; and houses, and take them away: and they oppress a man and his house, even a man and his heritage"* (2. 2). Naturally, oppression falls upon the weakest, and the women and children were deprived of their rights (2. 9). So thoroughly does Micah regard all this evil as organized and deliberate that he declares that the sinners plan their iniquity upon their beds, and as soon as morning dawns go out to practice it (2. 1). With fearful terseness he sums up the venal leadership: "The heads judge for reward, and the priests teach for hire, and the prophets divine for money" (3. 11).

Micah could only look for punishment upon all this evil. Poetically he describes Jehovah coming down as a storm to sweep away the iniquity (1. 2-4). When he definitely enumerates the dangerous institutions that are to be removed he includes with the witchcrafts and the idolaters that are to be ended, also the strongholds and the cities of the land (5. 11).

Whether Micah definitely expected that there would be a return to the simple life of the agricultural period of Hebrew history, it is impossible to say. He was not a political economist nor a scientific sociologist. He was hitting hard the evil thing that he saw destroying the national life of his people. That evil thing was the social injustice that had its seat in the city. In our great modern life, in which the city has become so dominating, it would be quite impossible for social regeneration to come through the elimination of the city. But Micah's words may well give us pause, and make us realize that a civilization must purify itself in the city or it will destroy itself through the city.

§ 5. The Great Requirement

Always associated with the name of Micah is the noble statement of the essence of true religion (6. 8), which is the high-water mark of Old Testament religious expression, and remains still a complete and satisfying summary of God's demand upon men. It is unlikely that this passage belongs to Micah of Moresheth, for it presupposes some of the horrible conditions of paganism that did not become common until the reign of Manasseh. In the later editing of the brief prophetic fragments that remained from the sayings and writings of various prophets, certain elements became attached to the writing of Micah, and among them the dramatic dialogue (6. 1-8), which culminates in the great summary.

It would seem that some reformation in Judah was effected by the preaching of Isaiah and Micah under the rule of the good king Hezekiah. But the looked-for prosperity did not result, and under his son Manasseh there was a recrudescence of heathenism (2 Kings 21. 1-7). The most horrible feature in these pagan cults was the offering of human sacrifice (v. 6). It is to this practice that our passage in the book of Micah refers.

The longing to secure the favor of the Deity was often very real and very pathetic in heathenism, as it is still to-day. The good things of life are supposed to come from his hands, and the calamities are the result of his displeasure. Everything, therefore, must be done to secure the divine favor. The most costly sacrifices are the price that is paid for this object, and at last the offering of the first-born son is made as a supreme humiliation before the august divinity. It is this external and most extreme sacramental religion which speaks in the bitter cry of a people, baffled in their endeavor to find God and to secure his favor.

Wherewith shall I come before Jehovah,
And bow myself before the high God?
Shall I come before him with burnt offerings,
With calves a year old?
Will Jehovah be pleased with thousands of rams,
Or with ten thousands of rivers of oil?
Shall I give my first-born for my transgression,
The fruit of my body for the sin of my soul?

The reply to this agonizing question is so simple that like all the greatest words its import may be lost. It puts at once all temple sacrifices, ceremonies, sacramental institutions in their subordinate place as the accessories of religion, and shows a God of righteousness and love asking of man only justice, kindness, and dependence upon him.

He hath showed thee, O man, what is good;
And what doth Jehovah require of thee,
But to do justly,

And to love kindness,
And to walk humbly with thy God?

In these words the prophetic conception of spiritual religion expresses itself at its best, and its profoundly ethical and social character is made clear.

DIRECTIONS FOR STUDY

1. Read ch. 1; 2. 1-11; ch. 3; 4. 9 to 5. 1; 5. 10-15. Note Micah's attitude toward Samaria and Jerusalem.
2. What are the specific charges which Micah makes against the various classes of rulers?
3. Note his denunciation of the prophets (3. 5-8). How can this be justified? What is the basis of Micah's confidence in his own insight? (3. 8.)
4. Compare Micah's attitude with that of Isaiah. In what particulars were the prophets alike and in what did they differ? If they were both genuine prophets, how could they have different views?
5. How far did the social situation in Judah justify the message of Micah?
6. How can Micah's message be applied to modern conditions?
7. What are the reasons for believing that 6. 1-8 is a fragment of later prophecy?
8. Compare this passage with Isa 1 and Psa 51, and consider what Hebrew religion was at its best.
9. What suggestion do these passages make as to the relation of the church to social justice and philanthropy?
10. What is the distinction between justice and kindness? Note that they are not here offered as alternatives.

CHAPTER XXV

JEREMIAH

§ 1. The Silence of the Prophets

We know nothing of the last years of Isaiah nor of the work of the many disciples who had gathered about him, and who had presumably caught his spirit. The splendid hopes of a glorious Israel which was to succeed the Assyrian invasion were not fulfilled. Assyria did not decline after the withdrawal of Sennacherib, but rose to her mightiest strength in the next half century. It seemed as if Isaiah had been wrong in his promises, and that Jehovah was but a weak God in comparison with the mighty Asshur. To be sure, if Isaiah had been living he would not have lost his faith. He would have pointed out that Judah had not learned her lesson, that the corruptions against which he had protested still existed, and that the overthrow of the Assyrian was only delayed. But the people had no mind to hear such explanations, and Isaiah's disciples had neither the boldness nor the ability to offer them.

A period of reaction from the Isaianic point of view resulted. Manasseh, who succeeded his father Hezekiah, reigned for nearly half a century and manifested continuous hostility to the prophets. Many of them were put to death, including Isaiah himself, if the later Jewish tradition is to be accepted, and stern repression put a stop to the freedom that had characterized the great preachers of the eighth century.

In one important respect Manasseh followed the guidance of Isaiah. He came to the throne as a vassal of Assyria and he was wise enough never to attempt a revolt. The great kings Esar-haddon and Ashur-bani-pal made campaigns against Egypt, in which their armies marched through Palestine, but the submissive loyalty of the little kingdom of Judah saved it from devastation. It doubtless paid well for the immunity, both in annual tribute, and in the levies which were made upon it during the campaigns.

To Manasseh and his people it seemed wise to seek aid from gods more powerful than Jehovah. The worship of the heavenly bodies (2 Kings 21. 5), the various forms of magic and necromancy that were so common in the East flourished in Jerusalem, and even the horrid custom of child sacrifice came again into vogue (2 Kings 21. 6). With the development of idolatry came in the unethical conception of deity which was common among the idol worshipers. The lofty idea of a God of righteousness gave place to that of the familiar deity represented by the image, who could be fed with sacrifices, pleased with incense, cajoled by flattery. Instead of the God of ethical demands, Jerusalem had gods who could serve her ends.

The question of idolatry, therefore, was not merely ecclesiastical. It was not a matter of sensuous as opposed to imaginative worship. It went to the heart of the social problem. Gods who could be bought were the allies of the aristocracy, of the privileged classes. All the iniquities against which the prophets had preached could therefore continue without hindrance. One could bribe the gods as he could bribe the judge and live his selfish life in peace. The cry of the innocent blood (Jer 7. 6), the needs of the fatherless, the widow, and the stranger, were not heeded by such deities. It was Jehovah, the God of justice and of love (4. 2), who was concerned with the social morality of his people, and only when a nation realized that the idols were vanities, and that Jehovah was God alone, would the evils of the land be righted. It was from this point of view that we must estimate the assault of the later prophets upon idolatry. All social, ethical, as well as spiritual values were involved in the contest.

The prophets, unable to preach, were earnestly hoping for some opportunity for reformation. The better type of the Jerusalem priests were equally dissatisfied with the course of events. There seems to have been some cooperation between priests and prophets in the great plan to produce another law book which should bring the old law up to date, and should bring the great authority of Moses to bear upon the evil situation of the time. Out of this cooperation was produced the book of Deuteronomy. The death of Manasseh, and the murder of his son Amon after a brief reign of two years, brought Josiah to the throne as a child. The priests and prophets who were seeking the reformation of the national life secured the custody of the young king. In process of time the publication of the new codification of the old law became possible. We have already noted in connection with each of the institutions of Hebrew life the advance in the social ideal which this law sought to bring about.

§ 2. Jeremiah's Warnings

It was when the young king Josiah had been thirteen years on the throne and before the Book of the Law was promulgated, that the impulse to preach came to a young man of the priestly order, whose home was in the village of Anathoth, about four miles northeast of Jerusalem. The explanation of the complex activity of Jeremiah and of those tumultuous utterances which have been so often misunderstood is very simple. It is found in the religious experience of that ardent, sympathetic, and sensitive soul. To him God was the supreme reality. He conceived him very simply as good, just, gracious, ordering the affairs of all mankind with sole regard to righteousness. It was, therefore, the supreme duty of the Hebrews to serve Jehovah with loyalty, utterly disregarding the immoral and senseless gods of the heathen, and to live together in mutual justice and love as became the servants of the righteous God. Instead of such loyalty Jeremiah saw around him a condition diametrically opposed. It seemed to him as he looked at the life of his people that there was not in all Jerusalem a good man, "that doeth justly, that seeketh truth" (5. 1). The nation seemed to be given over to evil. What could God do with such a people but visit them with dire chastisement?

As these ideas formed themselves in the young man's mind an event of fearful portent took place in western Asia. The Scythian hordes broke loose in the north, and swept down upon the civilized peoples in one of those devastating raids which so often disturbed the progress of ancient culture; or perhaps one might also say, which sometimes broke up an effete culture and made way for something better. The occasion was one to kindle the prophetic fervor, and Zephaniah came forward with his message of doom, the *Dies Iræ*. Jeremiah felt the same impulse, and although very reluctant to assume the role, entered upon his long career as a prophet (ch. 1).

The Scythian invasion was to Jeremiah the scourge of God upon his wicked people:

Behold, he shall come up as clouds,
And his chariots shall be as the whirlwind:
His horses are swifter than eagles.
Woe unto us! for we are ruined (4. 13).

But the prophet hoped that the people might take warning:

O Jerusalem, wash thy heart from wickedness, that thou mayest be saved.
How long shall thine evil thoughts lodge within thee? (4. 14.)

Reformation seemed almost impossible, however, as he looked at his wanton people; "they have made their faces harder than the rock." Again and again, therefore, he returned to his threats,

Behold, a people cometh from the north country;
And a great nation shall be stirred up from the uttermost parts of earth.

They lay hold on bow and spear;
They are cruel and have no mercy;
Their voice roareth like the sea, and they ride upon horses,
Every one set in array, as a man to the battle,
Against thee, O daughter of Zion (6. 22f.).

But the immediate events seemed to discredit Jeremiah's message. The terrible Scythians came and went without destroying Judah, yet there had certainly been no reformation of national life. Within five years the great law book was found in the temple, and an impression was made upon the king and people which no words of the prophets had been able to effect. To outward appearance a thoroughgoing reformation took place. The young king, at all events, was heartily in earnest. He removed all the abominations of Manasseh, and directed that every prescription of the law should be rigidly obeyed (2 Kings 22f.; Deut 12).

Deuteronomy is a book of hope. In clear and scathing words it declares inevitable punishment upon iniquity, but with equal insistence promises peace, prosperity, and success as a reward of national righteousness. Josiah was determined to earn the good favor of Jehovah upon the terms of this great covenant. We do not know very well what position Jeremiah took in the matter. It is probable that he saw that the reformation was the work of the king and was utterly external so far as the people were concerned. Yet he loyally preached the doctrines of Deuteronomy and hoped for the best (11. 1-8). We have only a scant reference to his work in those years, and it is likely that others who were more enthusiastic for the new law were more prominent.

Then came that tragic day in Israel's history when the promises of Jehovah seemed to be broken against the rude facts of national experience. Egypt, who had been bitterly humiliated by the Assyrian kings, was eager to take advantage of the rapidly declining power of her old enemy and capture some of the territory of western Asia. The Pharaoh therefore marched along the old route by the shores of the Mediterranean and through the Pass of Megiddo to the plain of Esdraelon on his way to the Euphrates. Josiah decided to dispute his passage. He had great hopes that with the fall of Assyria a real independence should return to Judah. But the Egyptians were victorious, and the best king that had ever sat on David's throne was slain (2 Kings 23. 29f.). Judah became vassal to Egypt (vv. 31-35).

§ 3. The Message of Doom

The religious reaction in Judah was immediate and complete. It seemed to the people that Jehovah had failed against the stronger gods of Egypt. The promises of Deuteronomy seemed to be vain. The people turned back to the old heathenisms, and Jehovah was but one of their many gods. With the revival of idolatry came in again all the selfishness, the sensuality, the injustice of the bad days of Manasseh. Under Jehoiakim Judah was a typical Oriental kingdom with all its worst features well developed.

There was, however, one curious article of faith in Jehovah which was very tenaciously held in Jerusalem. It had never been forgotten that Isaiah had insisted that Jehovah would not abandon his city (Isa 37. 35). The defense of Zion was considered the peculiar province of the national God. The people, as was customary, conceived the whole matter in sacramental and not in ethical terms. Jehovah's favor must be secured by the splendor of the ceremonial; they never understood the prophetic demand for righteousness. Jeremiah made a great attempt to rectify this error. *"Trust ye not in lying words, saying, The temple of Jehovah, the temple of Jehovah, the temple of Jehovah, are these"* (7. 3-11). He not only insisted that there was no certainty of the perpetuity of the temple, but that the house of David which had stood so long would be swept away unless the kings realized their high obligation to see that justice was done (22. 2f).

Jeremiah's plea had no effect. He became convinced that

there was no opportunity of patching up the rags of the national life. He had not been deceived by the hollowness of the Josian reformation, and therefore his faith was not shaken by the fate of that good king. He and the prophets who shared his views gave as an explanation of the seeming failure of the Deuteronomic promise that the evils in Judah had gone too far, and the conditions of the promise had not been met (compare 2 Kings 23. 26f.). Jeremiah came to the conclusion that the only possibility of righteousness was in the complete destruction of the rotten organization of Hebrew society and a fresh start. Then he expected a glorious future. As he looked back upon his call he realized to how radical a mission he had been summoned, "to pluck up and to break down, and to destroy and to overthrow, to build and to plant"—four words destructive, two words constructive, and the work to be done in that order (1. 10).

Thenceforth the message of Jeremiah was one of doom. The temple was to be made like the ruined sanctuary of Shiloh and the city to be a curse to all the nations of the earth (26. 6). The priests and the professional prophets determined that Jeremiah should be indicted for treason. When, however, the matter was brought before the judicial authorities, the precedent of Micah in the time of Hezekiah was cited, and the right of free speech for a prophet was declared (vv. 16-19). It is noteworthy, however, that the king disapproved of the judgment, and soon found opportunity to show another venturesome prophet, who perhaps had not so many influential friends as Jeremiah, that such words were spoken at his peril (vv. 20-23).

Jeremiah spoke his mind freely about Jehoiakim. He denounced the selfish extravagance of the monarch, who was carrying on expensive building operations in spite of the heavy tribute that was laid upon the land. Moreover he was resorting to that most objectionable method of royal extravagance, the employment of forced labor for which no wages were paid. The prophet compared him with his godly father, who did justice and righteousness and "it was well with him" (22. 15-17).

Meantime in 605 B. C., Nebuchadrezzar of Babylon had defeated the Egyptians in the decisive battle of Carchemish. As a consequence Judah became vassal of Babylon. Jeremiah declared that Nebuchadrezzar was the instrument of Jehovah, and that Judah must submit to his power (ch. 25). Jehoiakim foolishly revolted, Jerusalem was besieged, the king died during the siege, his son Jehoiachin succeeded him, within three months the city was captured, and the king, princes, and the best of the people were deported to Babylon (2 Kings 24. 8-16). Zedekiah, another son of Josiah, was made king of the poor remnant (vv. 17f.).

Jeremiah knew that all the hope of a future Israel was with the exiles who had been carried away, but he remained in Jerusalem endeavoring still to serve his people by his counsel. He had the same difficult task that had confronted Isaiah, for Egypt was ever intriguing with the Palestinian peoples and endeavoring to get them to revolt against their eastern masters. Zedekiah and his nobles weakly listened to these seducing counsels, though Jeremiah sternly denounced them. The prophet insisted that for the time Nebuchadrezzar was the chosen ruler of Jehovah and all nations must submit to him (ch. 27).

But tribute was irksome, and Egypt's promises were fair, and probably there were counselors in Jerusalem bought with Egyptian gold. So at last Zedekiah refused to pay the tribute, taking the dangerous position of a rebel against his suzerain. Nebuchadrezzar lost no time in coming with a mighty army, and Jerusalem was again besieged. Jeremiah saw the inevitable end and told Zedekiah plainly that the city would be captured and destroyed (34. 1-5).

Then occurred a remarkable incident that gave Jeremiah an opportunity to show his conception of ethical religion. The rulers were thoroughly frightened at the coming of the Babylonians and were desirous of winning the favor of

Jehovah. They remembered that they had not allowed their slaves to go free at the end of the sixth year, according to the law, so they very piously released them in this emergency. But meantime the Egyptians had at last mobilized their army, and advanced against Nebuchadrezzar, who was obliged to raise the siege of Jerusalem that he might meet the new enemy. The wealthy Israelites immediately took advantage of the occasion to reenslave their manumitted brethren. Jeremiah came forth with a scathing message, "Thus saith Jehovah, You have not proclaimed liberty to your brethren: behold I proclaim unto you a liberty to the sword, to the pestilence, and to the famine, and I will make you to be tossed to and fro among all the kingdoms of the earth" (34. 17). He told them that the Chaldeans would return and would take the city.

Jeremiah was denounced as a traitor. It was said, and with truth, that he weakened the hands of the defenders of the city by his hopeless words. But he was trying to get Zedekiah to surrender, and thus secure some clemency from the conqueror, for he knew that the issue was inevitable. It was a sorry task for a man of tender spirit, and a patriot, but it was duty, and Jeremiah performed it to the end.

§ 4. The Professional Prophets

The task of Jeremiah was rendered the more difficult by the attitude of the professional prophets. It was both to their taste and to their advantage to prophesy smooth things, to tell the kings that they would have success, to tell the people that prosperity would follow adversity. They were the cheerful optimists of their day, using the term in our current connotation of a man who is determined to expect good fortune and to shut his eyes to all contrary facts.

The professional optimist is inevitably a defender of vested interests and of special privilege. He has no brief for the oppressed, for the victim of social iniquity. His emoluments naturally come from the possessors of privilege, and so his interests lead him to be their champion (23. 17). But he is no mere sycophant, for he really believes in things as they are, discounts the evils as incidental, and expects always good fortune to come to his people. With the passionate prophet of justice he has no sympathy. Convention is his master; "justice" is a word for the sentimentalist. He is, of course, a conservative. He believes in the great heroes who are dead, he repeats the great language of forgotten issues (23. 30). He sees old truth but never new truth. That new occasions teach new duties he cannot understand, that time makes ancient good uncouth seems to him not only contradictory but immoral. We have already noted that the professional prophets of the sixth century B. C. were zealous exponents of Isaiah's theory of the indestructibility of Zion. They gloried in that promise, and cited Isaiah's great name in support of their contention. Jeremiah told the people who heard this comfortable doctrine, *"Behold, ye trust in lying words, that cannot profit"* (7. 8).

The professional prophets were patriots of course; that is to say, they were concerned for the independence and prosperity of their country and anxious for the confusion of their country's enemies. But they were provincial patriots. They could not see over the walls of Jerusalem. They never asked themselves whether Judah was worth preserving, whether the world would be advantaged by her success. Their motto was, "Right or wrong, my country." They had nothing but scorn for the pessimist who could contemplate evil consequences for his own people. Jeremiah saw the folly of such vainglorious self-content (14. 13-18).

Not unnaturally they were immoral. The unthinking optimist, the defender of things as they are, accepts the current immoralities of his day, the self indulgences, the corruptions, the "things that everybody does" as permitted. They would say that Jerusalem, as towns go, was a very decent town (6. 14; 23. 14).

These professional politicians were favorites at the court and they had the popular ear. They always had a cheering word to speak of the good things that were shortly coming (14. 13). After the deportation, when Jerusalem was beggared and bereft, Jeremiah felt the obligation to tell the people plainly that the yoke of the Chaldean must be accepted (ch. 27). He put a yoke on his own neck and wore it in the temple courts as a sign of the inevitable submission. When Hananiah broke it he went away, but returned the next day with the grim message that the yoke of the Chaldean was of iron and could not be broken (28. 1-17).

§ 5. The Hope of National Redemption

Yet Jeremiah was the real optimist. He believed in the destiny of Israel more gloriously than any of the timeserving prophets who proclaimed it. He wrote a letter to the exiles telling them of a great restoration that should come in the third generation (29. 10-14). When he was thrown into prison as a traitor during the last siege he spoke exultantly of his great hope for the future day when a king should reign in Jerusalem, who should *"execute justice and righteousness in the land"* (33. 14-16). With a fine patriotism he used the meager funds at his disposal to purchase a piece of land in his native town of Anathoth as a sign of his confidence that houses and fields should yet again be bought in Judah (ch. 32).

But the heart of Jeremiah's faith was that his people should actually come to have a longing for righteousness. He never gave up his confidence that there would be a national penitence, and he knew that that meant salvation: *"I know the thoughts that I think toward you, saith Jehovah, thoughts of peace, and not of evil. . . . And ye shall seek me, and find me, when ye shall search for me with all your heart"* (29. 11-13).

Jeremiah believed in a future social state as a result of a socialized people who should passionately desire it. With a wonderful insight, which we greatly need to-day in our own social endeavors, he saw that this would come about as a result of individual and national regeneration. The inner motive that comes when individual human hearts are stirred in a great enterprise and the social enthusiasm which results from united endeavor were combined in Jeremiah's great expectation of the future. He had seen the failure of the project of imposing the noble Deuteronomic Covenant upon the people. He looked for a deeper reformation, that should come out of the conscience of the individual and of the nation stirred by great religious motives: *"Behold, the days come, saith Jehovah, that I will make a new covenant with the house of Israel, and with the house of Judah: . . . I will put my law in their inward parts, and in their heart will I write it; . . . for they shall all know me, from the least of them unto the greatest of them"* (31. 31-34).

This is one of the noblest words of prophecy. So much of what we call social service and social endeavor is an effort to make other people good. Jeremiah sees men with humble hearts seeking each to do the will of God as he finds it in his own conscience, and thus united together seeking to organize a society in which justice and truth shall prevail. He has been called a pessimist. His is a faith in the reign of God and the possibilities of humanity that is fundamental evidence of ethical optimism.

DIRECTIONS FOR STUDY

1. Read Deut 28, and consider the appropriateness of this appeal to the Hebrews of the seventh century B. C. How far does this accord with our own ideas of social and political philosophy? Is there a truth in this view? If so, what complementary truth is needed to round it out?
2. What estimate of Jeremiah would you make from the account of his call in ch. 1?
3. Read ch. 5, and note the social sins which the prophet denounced. What connection was there between idolatry and these iniquities?
4. Read 18. 1-12. Note the principle that all God's promises and

warnings were conditional upon man's response. What attitude of the people was this intended to meet?

5. Read ch. 36, and consider how different persons in Jerusalem probably regarded Jeremiah.
6. The words "calamity howler" and "muckraker" have come to have an evil significance with us. Could the people of Jerusalem have applied such epithets to Jeremiah? Would they have been justified in doing so?
7. Read 7. 3-11. Was Jeremiah essentially an optimist? What would be the social philosophy of a man of his insight in America to-day?
8. What was the contribution of Jeremiah's individualism (24. 7; 31. 28-30, 31-34) to the development of a right social attitude?
9. What was the relation in Jeremiah's thought of religion and social justice? Is this a necessary relation?
10. Read chs. 37 and 38. Note the reward that a prophet of social righteousness may get in his own day.

CHAPTER XXVI

EZEKIEL

In one of his striking picture sermons Jeremiah described two baskets of figs: *"One basket had very good figs, like the figs that are first ripe; and the other basket had very bad figs, which could not be eaten, they were so bad"* (Jer 24. 2). He explained to the people that the good figs were the Hebrews that had been taken to Babylon and the bad figs were the people that had been left in Jerusalem. His estimate, though not very complimentary to the people whom he addressed, was doubtless correct. Nebuchadrezzar had been careful to take away all the men of ability and initiative in government, in the priesthood, and in industry, for he was determined that Judah should have no leaders who could induce her again to rebel. Jeremiah urged the people not to rebel and turned their attention to the superiority of the Babylonian Jews in order that they might realize that the future of Israel lay in the purification of the exiles rather than in the development of the remnant that had been left behind.

While Jeremiah for the eleven years that elapsed between the deportation of the first exiles and the fall of Jerusalem in 586 was thus endeavoring to keep the city from revolt and to encourage the exiles themselves to expect a long residence in Babylonia, the Jews who had been carried from their own land were by no means willing to accept the situation. It was not that Nebuchadrezzar was a tyrannical master, for with statesmanlike clemency he endeavored to make their condition comfortable and prosperous. But they wanted to go home. However little they might have manifested loyalty to Jehovah, they wanted to worship him in his temple and to seek his favor. And the godly among them bitterly lamented their exile:

> *By the rivers of Babylon,*
> *There we sat down, yea, we wept,*
> *When we remembered Zion* (Psa 137).

There was needed a man with a message to speak to them the deeper meaning of the experiences through which they were passing. This man was found in the young priest Ezekiel. He had probably served in the Jerusalem temple, and had been carried off with the great number of the priests by Nebuchadrezzar.

§ 1. The Social Responsibility of the Prophets

The experience of the prophets is most vividly set forth in the case of Ezekiel, and the psychology of that experience is very evident. The mysterious vision of the first chapter, which often discourages the reader from proceeding any further in the prophecy, is only a symbolic way of describing the prophet's sense of the holy character of Jehovah before which be bows in awe (v. 28). He has a profound religious experience of the reality of the great God of righteousness. Then he realizes the perverseness and rebellion of the people whose history has been one long violation of the good laws that had been given them.

Out of this twofold realization comes the conviction that he must point out to the people their evil ways. But Ezekiel does not express the matter in this prosaic fashion. He must give a picturesque presentation of his experience. A mysterious hand offered him a book closely written with "lamentations, and mourning, and woe" (2. 10). He was commanded to eat the book, and then go forth to speak to the house of Israel; that is to say, he was to make the bitter message of doom his own, and then proclaim it. It was surely a hard obligation. But the prophet was ready to do his duty: *"Then did I eat it; and it was in my mouth as honey for sweetness"* (3. 1-3). The exultant experience of joy in the faithful performance of a difficult undertaking.

But why should a prophet preach? The question is often raised to-day. Men are denounced as busybodies or pessimists when they point out the evils in our social or political life. Ezekiel faced that question and answered it, laying down the great principle of the social obligation of the man of insight. Of course he did it again, as was his wont, in symbolic fashion. He pictured a watchman on the lookout tower. What is his duty when he sees evil coming upon the people? Evidently, he must warn them. If he fails to do so, they will die, but their blood will be upon his hands. If, however, he warns them, and they refuse to believe him, his responsibility is discharged. So Ezekiel declares that the prophet is the watchman. He must warn the wicked of their doom, or he is guilty of what befalls them. Yes, and he must warn the righteous also when they turn aside to evil acts; that is to say, he must speak stern words even to the people whose social life is on the whole decent, but who yet permit bad spots in the social organization, or again he is responsible for the evil consequences that ensue (3. 16-21).

So strongly did Ezekiel feel this obligation to speak forth the truth as he saw it that ten years later, when the imminent fall of Jerusalem was about to vindicate his warnings, he reiterated his defense and repeated his figure of the watchman (33. 1-9). It is a fine picture. The prophet is the man who can see, the man who is raised above the selfishness of personal interest and is able to look out. It is well for any generation when such men of vision are among them and when they dare to speak the things that they see.

§ 2. The Message of Retribution

During the years that Jeremiah was telling the people in Jerusalem that the rottenness of the social order could only end in the complete destruction of the city Ezekiel was speaking the same severe message to his countrymen in Babylon. But Ezekiel was not the only prophet in Babylon. Many of the professional prophets had been among those who were carried into exile, and the people rejoiced in them: *"Jehovah hath raised us up prophets in Babylon"* (Jer 29. 15). These men were expecting some great political cataclysm that should overthrow the Babylonian power and enable the Hebrews to return to their own land. They gave these promises to the people, who eagerly accepted them (vv. 21-32). Ezekiel denounced them as unsparingly as Jeremiah, and warned the people that they could only look for the destruction of Jerusalem (ch. 13).

As one reads the prophecies of Ezekiel it seems as if the greatest emphasis is upon the sin of idolatry and of the worship of other gods. Doubtless the prophet intended such emphasis. But it was no narrow contention about names, such as the English poet cynically suggests in his reference to "Jehovah, Jove, or Lord." One religion is as good as another if it is as good as the other. But Ezekiel knew that the loyal worship of Jehovah, conceived as righteous, loving, infinitely concerned about the good character of his people, produced a certain type of life, while the debased worship of Jehovah under the form of an idol, which could be fed and censed and carried in procession, produced a totally different type of life; and the worship of gods whose rites were cruel and sensual produced a worse life still. Therefore the demands of religion and morality were one.

The social quality of Ezekiel's preaching is clear enough in the great indictment of the sins of Jerusalem (ch. 22). To the Babylonian Jews who were hopeful of the prosperity and independence of Jerusalem he made clear that the wicked city had a long record of iniquity that called for retribution. Ezekiel knew very much more of the details of that history than have been preserved to us; and when he calls Jerusalem "the bloody city" (v. 2) he is referring to gross acts of injustice upon the poor, the defenseless, and the godly patriots. He declares that the nobles have shed blood *"everyone according to his power"* (v. 6). Men have been willing to sell their testimony against the innocent, with judicial murder as the result (vv. 9, 12).

The prophet repeats the age-long charges of wrong committed by the strong against the weak, the rich against the poor (v. 29), of the oppression of the stranger, the cheating of the fatherless and the widow (v. 7), of the greedy, sharp practices of business (vv. 12f.), of the selfish cupidity of nobles that would even murder for money (v. 27), and of prophets so eager for their hire that they cared nothing if their timeserving counsels resulted in widowed homes (vv. 25, 28).

Ezekiel was a plain speaker, and he denounced the horrible immoralities that had disgraced Jerusalem (vv. 9-11). He declared that filial duty, so highly esteemed in the East, had been wanting (v. 7). With these social evils had been combined the religious profanations of idol worship (v. 4), Sabbath-breaking, and ritual defilement (v. 26). He uttered the same extreme statements in the name of Jehovah that had been wrung from Jeremiah's sad experience, *"I sought for a man among them, that should build up the wall, . . . but I found none"* (v. 30).

We have noted in connection with the study of ancient commerce, Ezekiel's brilliant description of the city of Tyre (chs. 26 to 28). As an eloquent portrayal of the princely splendor that had levied upon the earth for the treasures of luxury and beauty it is one of the masterpieces of ancient writings. As a pathetic threnody upon the fall of an imperial city of culture it is worthy of a high place in literature. But the greatest significance of this dirge is the insight of the prophet that a civilization based on envy (26. 2), pride (28. 6), unrighteousness (28. 18), violence (28. 16), with no great moral rightness at its heart—such a civilization, whatever be its wealth or greatness, will inevitably be swept from the earth.

§ 3. The Doctrine of Individual Responsibility

The destruction of the Jewish temple gave the opportunity for a great advance in religion and morality. Hitherto the Deity had been localized and his relationship had been conceived as that of a God with a particular people. But if Jehovah were not in Mount Zion, where was he? And if the Hebrew nation had no longer a corporate entity, where was his Godhood?

Jeremiah had already suggested the individual relationship of the soul with God. It remained for Ezekiel to state the doctrine definitely. Again we must find the explanation in his own experience. He was a priest, but he was forever separated from the temple and its ritual. He was a Hebrew, but he knew that he would never again see his native land. Yet he realized that there was an altar in his own soul, and that the God of his fathers was with him in Babylon.

The book of Deuteronomy had promised blessings for national obedience and punishment for national sins. Ezekiel firmly held this doctrine and preached it. But it seemed to the exiles an unjust doctrine. It seemed to them that they were suffering for the sins of others. The proverb was bitterly repeated, "*The fathers have eaten sour grapes, and the children's teeth are set on edge*" (18. 2). It seemed to them that Jehovah was taking revenge for the past. Ezekiel denied the pertinence of the proverb, and plainly told the exiles that they were suffering for their own sins, and that each man stood alone in his responsibility before God.

It is not to be understood that Ezekiel denied the great fact of social responsibility for the corporate acts of a nation, but he had found in his own experience the divine goodness, and believed that any one of his countrymen who was anxious for a sense of the divine fellowship in his life could enter into that experience. He declared that the wicked should die and the righteous should live, the fate of each being in accordance with his own conduct and not because of any act of his fathers (vv. 5-24). He worked out the doctrine in great detail, showing that the penitent evil worker would be forgiven and the backslider who had been righteous would not be excused.

What did Ezekiel mean by righteousness and sin? The answer to that question indicates at once the practical social problem which the prophets had to face, and the high ethical sense with which they estimated the obligations of social living. The just man is he who has abstained from idolatry, adultery, dishonesty, the oppression of the poor, and robbery, and who has been charitable to the needy, and generous to the debtor, restoring his pledge, and lending without interest—in short, has "executed true justice between man and man" (vv. 5-9).

Perhaps in our day we are so much under the influence of the individualistic point of view in religion that this conception of Ezekiel seems to us commonplace. We need, rather, to appreciate the social emphasis and to feel the consciousness of the sins that are those of the community, of the nation, of the social order as a whole. These are two phases of one truth. Ezekiel preached them both. He knew that he was an exile deprived of his priestly calling because of the failure of his countrymen to preserve their national integrity, which in turn he believed was the consequence of their national sins; but he knew also that he was strengthened, comforted, and blessed as he stood in lonely fellowship with his God.

§ 4. The Ideal Social State

Apparently, Ezekiel secured a hearing among his countrymen, though they did not give serious attention to his message (33. 32). They never believed that Jerusalem would really fall. When that tragic event happened it produced a profound impression on the exiles, and they realized their foolish mistake. Ezekiel immediately changed the tone of his preaching, and began to speak to them words of comfort. He told them that those who had been appointed to care for the flock of Israel had failed of their duty, but Jehovah would be their shepherd (ch. 34). He pictured a glorious future for Israel when God himself should cleanse his people.

> *A new heart also will I give you,*
> *And a new spirit will I put within you;*
> *And I will take away the stony heart out of your flesh,*
> *And I will give you a heart of flesh* (36. 26).

In the wonderful vision of the dry bones that were reanimated and became "an exceeding great army" he pictured the revival of the Hebrew nation. And in the joining of the two sticks, he symbolized the reunion of the two parts of the nation, Israel and Judah, again to be one (ch. 37). He believed that Jehovah overruled the politics of the nations, so he looked for some tremendous executions of wrath upon the savage and brutal people who had beaten the lesser nations into submission. Out of the confusion he saw the emergence of a purified and restored Israel (ch. 39).

But Ezekiel's chief contribution to the conception of an ideal social state is found in the latter part of his book (chs. 40-48), which was probably written some time after the earlier portion. Knowing that he himself and his generation would not return to Jerusalem, he occupied himself in preparing for his countrymen a new constitution for the reorganized nation which should ultimately occupy the holy land. A glance over these nine chapters is rather discouraging to one who expects to find a practical plan of the ideal social state. What is it but a priest's interest in the minute and wearisome details of an ecclesiastical building and an elaborate ritual? It is very much more than that. The priest-prophet hoped for a nation that would accept the law of Jehovah as its guide. He believed that the state could be one great church, a religious community in which everyone should be glad to live with his neighbor as became the members of a common faith. The elaborate ecclesiastical and sacerdotal arrangements were designed to effect the purity of life that was to come from the constant attention to the obligations of holiness. The priests were to teach the people "the difference between the holy and the common, and cause them to discern between the clean and the unclean" (44. 23). The prince was no more to be a tyrant (46. 18), the nobles were to *"remove violence and spoil, and execute justice and righteousness"*; harsh exactions were to be abolished and absolute fairness was to obtain (45. 9-12). The land was to be equitably divided among all the people, and the stranger was to share as the home-born (47. 22f.). There was to be a real theocracy, for the name of the city was to be called *"Jehovah is there"* (48. 35).

Doubtless no such church state could be a practical ideal. Postexilic Judaism organized itself upon the ecclesiastical basis, and made a poor failure of the attempt. The political intrigues and selfish policies of ecclesiastical rulers are, if anything, rather worse than those of laymen. It is to be remembered that Ezekiel believed that the whole nation would go forth purified after their bitter experiences, and that the regeneration of the individuals of the nation would make possible the theocratic ideal. And he was no mere visionary, for he struck the eternal truth when he realized that the ideal social state can never be achieved without individually transformed persons. The idle dream is not that of such a prophet as this old ecclesiastic; the idle dream is that of men who think that human society can be regenerated by a political or an economic program. Only morally regenerated men and women with a realization that this is God's world, and that he is here with his holy and gracious demands, will ever be able to constitute a state in which justice and love will actually prevail. Of course it will not be a theocracy such as Ezekiel saw. That was the matrix in which that son of the temple was obliged to cast his thought, as each of us must think in the concepts of his day. But the kernel of Ezekiel's message lives when the husk of his ecclesiasticism is discarded. It appears again in the message of Jesus. It is the only hope for the human race.

DIRECTIONS FOR STUDY

1. Compare the work of Ezekiel with that of Jeremiah.
2. What is the psychological explanation of Ezekiel's theory of the social responsibility of the prophet? Do you find any parallel in our modern conditions?
3. What opportunities of religious and ethical reformation did the exile experience afford?
4. What was Ezekiel's conception of the relation of morality and pure religion? What do you think of his view?
5. What does Ezekiel's dirge over Tyre (chs. 26 to 28) indicate as to (1) his knowledge of the social conditions of the world in which he lived; (2) his appreciation of the Phœnician civilization; (3) his philosophy of history? What is your own estimate of the causes of the fall of Tyre?
6. Why was Ezekiel's doctrine of individualism an advance in religious ideals? How did he reconcile individual and social responsibility? How far does your own idea accord with his?
7. What was the basis for Ezekiel's hope that Israel would have a glorious future?
8. Compare Ezekiel's theocratic ideal with the development of the priestly aristocracy as discussed in Chapter XII. What was the cause of the disparity?
9. Compare Ezekiel's ideal social state with Plato's Republic, and with Sir Thomas More's Utopia.
10. Does Ezekiel's conception of a theocratic community furnish any inspiration for our own hope of the better social order that is to be?

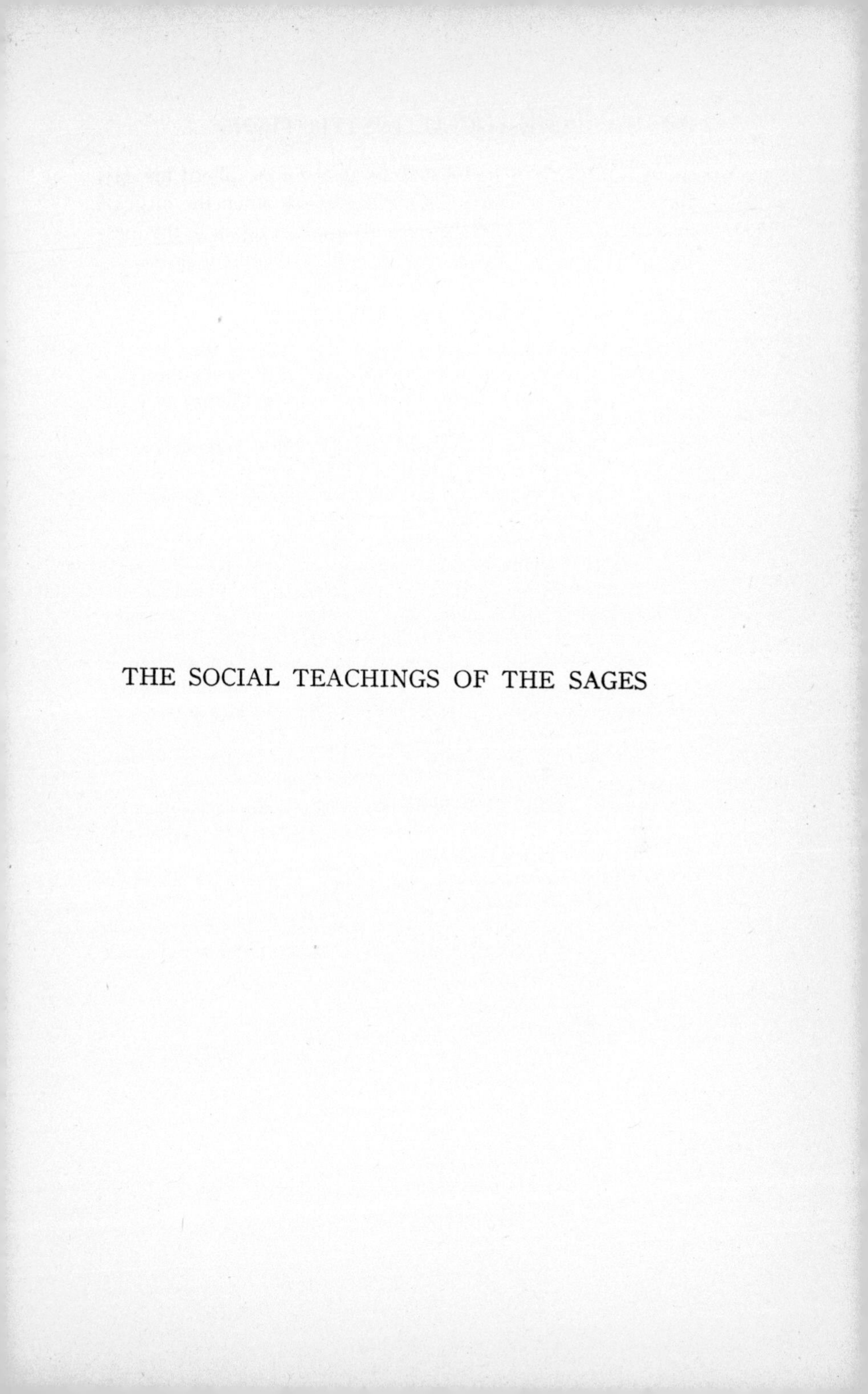

THE SOCIAL TEACHINGS OF THE SAGES

CHAPTER XXVII

THE PLACE OF WISDOM IN HEBREW LIFE

§ 1. The Sage as a Teacher

We have noted the development of three teachers in Israel: (1) the priests, who gave instruction on ceremonial matters, and later had the duty of carrying out the elaborated cultus which was the supreme object lesson in religion and morality; (2) the prophets, who were intermediaries between God and man, and then became exponents and preachers of righteousness; (3) the scribes, who developed from the priesthood, and were concerned with the teaching of the law. The priests appeared early in Hebrew life and continued to the end of the national existence, their greatest influence being in the postexilic times. The prophets flourished especially while the problems of the divine direction of the Hebrew national life were keenly felt; they found little opportunity after the exile. The scribes belong altogether to later Judaism.

There was a fourth class of teachers, the wise men, or sages, who had a different office from any of these three. Hebrew wisdom had a common origin with that sententious, pithy observation of men and things, and shrewd speculation upon practical affairs, which was found everywhere in the East. It was not especially religious in character, and was probably not a little vainglorious and self-sufficient. The prophets do not seem to have highly esteemed the "wisdom" of their day (Isa 5. 21; 29. 14; Jer 4. 22; 8. 8f.; 9. 23). That is partly accounted for by the difference that always exists between the man who reaches truth by the process of thought and the man who comes upon it through vital experience. The prophet is a man with a message; the sage is a man with a counsel.

However, wisdom succeeded prophecy and came into something of its inheritance. The prophet was concerned with the relation of Jehovah to the nation. He was essentially the interpreter of God to the people as a whole. A certain national freedom was essential to his task. There was little place for him in postexilic Judaism, where national life was reduced to the smallest possible dimensions. But Jeremiah and Ezekiel had already seen that there is a relationship between the individual and God, as well as between the nation and God. The sacrificial system carried out both ideas of reconciliation for the people and for the individual. So there was an added significance given to the individual and his duties. The sage, therefore, came forward to point out those duties and to consider the practical problems of life.

Hebrew wisdom really assumes Hebrew prophecy. There was no more question of loyalty to Jehovah. The prophets had fought that battle and won. There was no more question of the fundamentally ethical nature of religion. The prophets had forever settled that antagonism. Legalism might emasculate the significance of morality, but the Hebrew people did not need again to be taught that God could not be bribed by sacrifices. The sages succeeded to the ethical monotheism for which the prophets had contended. It was their task to work out the meaning of the righteousness of Jehovah in practical life.

It is evident that the task of the sage and that of the scribe were near akin. The scribe was concerned with making clear to his disciples the requirements of the law; that is to say, he was dealing with the questions of right and wrong from the standpoint of the divinely given legislation. The sage also assumed the divinity of that legislation, and was concerned with the questions of right and wrong from the standpoint of the experiences of life. Some scholars think that the two teachers were really one, and it seems clear that by the time of the Son of Sirach a complete fusion had been attained.

While Hebrew wisdom had a definite Semitic origin and a long history in its own native strength, it was undoubtedly quickened when the contact between the east and the west came about in the Greek period. With the development of the Jewish community in Alexandria, the process of fusion between Hebrew and Greek thought went forward rapidly, and it is noteworthy that the later books of wisdom emanated for the most part from Alexandria, while Philo, the distinguished Jewish philosopher, belonged to the Alexandrian school.

The wise men were the teachers of Israel during the four centuries before Christ. In that time they produced a considerable literature, the ethical value and literary quality of which should secure for it much more careful study than it generally receives. The influence of the teaching of the sages both in form and in content appears in the Gospels, and particularly in the Epistle of James, which has been well called the wisdom book of the New Testament.

§ 2. The Wisdom Literature and Its Problems

Hebrew wisdom has often been somewhat loosely called philosophy. The Hebrews did not really develop a philosophy, for they were not speculators upon the ultimate meaning of things. They believed in God, the Creator and Governor, who was divinely revealed to them in their law and sacred books. Thus the ultimate questions were settled. The problem before the speculative Hebrew mind was, How shall men live in a world created by the God whom Israel knows?

Thus Hebrew wisdom was fundamentally religious. Its first postulate was always the God of righteousness. This was as clear to the sage as to the prophets. It did not inspire passionate denunciation of unrighteousness and summons to repentance and obedience, but, rather, led to serious reflection upon what is involved in the condition of evil men living in a world created by the righteous God.

The rationality of the universe was also a postulate of Hebrew wisdom. In several beautiful passages wisdom is personified as present with God in the creation. To be sure, it is always insisted that the wisdom of God is more than man can understand, but it is wisdom, and the result is an ordered world. Therefore to obey the order of the world and the revealed will of God, which is conformable with it, constitutes for the wise man rational living.

The general theory of the sages, essentially like that of the naïve prophets, was that goodness produces health, wealth, and length of days (Prov 3. 1f.; 13-18), while evil results in physical and economic calamity (1. 31f; 3. 33f). This is the fundamental appeal of the Book of Deuteronomy as applied to the national life, and appears again and again in the prophets, who believed that Jehovah would take care of the nation if it organized its life in accordance with the demands of justice. The same faith is echoed in the words of the wise,

> *Righteousness exalteth a nation,*
> *But sin is a reproach to any people* (Prov 14. 34).

But they are not so much concerned with the national phase of the doctrine as with its individual application. Their practical wisdom consists in large part in an endeavor to bring home to the individual the wisdom of goodness because of its happy results, and the folly of wrong doing because of its evil consequences.

> *Good understanding getteth favor;*
> *But the way of the transgressor is hard* (Prov 13. 15, compare 10. 3, 16, 27-30; 11. 31; 14. 22; 22. 4f.; 29. 14).

The denial of this great truth was regarded as practical

atheism: *"The fool hath said in his heart, There is no God"* (Psa 14. 1; 53. 1—Wisdom Psalms). It amounted to a practical denial of God's moral government of the world. The Wisdom Psalms are particularly concerned that the reward and retribution shall be constantly evident, in order that the righteous may be saved from *"the reproach of the foolish"* (Psa 39. 8).

Evidently, two objections may at once be brought against this view of life. It may be said that it is not true, and also that it appeals to inferior motives for ethical conduct. But these objections must not be made too easily. There can be no doubt that taking human life all in all, first and last, there is a great truth in this practical wisdom. Sloth, extravagance, sensuality, falsehood, pride are barriers to success and often bring about the complete wrecking of a life; while industry, thrift, sobriety, honesty, cheerfulness, kindness are conducive to prosperity and health. Injustice, tyranny, unneighborliness are responsible for the major part of the world's woe, which generosity and good feeling would remove. Thus the wise man gave to his disciples the advice which every father gives to his sons, and every teacher to his pupils, showing the intimate relationship of worldly success and good character. Doubtless there are direful facts which this optimistic philosophy does not take into account, but as far as it goes it is true, and most significantly true.

Moreover, it is not a fair objection to this philosophy of the wise men to say that it is a merely prudential ethics. "Honesty is the best policy" does not seem to appeal to very lofty motives; and it is always dangerous in view of the examples of success of dishonesty. But to the Hebrew sage this was more than a counsel of prudence—it was a statement of religious faith. Righteousness is urged as the way of success because it belongs to the very constitution of things, since God is God. It is not mere selfishness, it is religion. Consequently, if there seem to be exceptions to the principle, the religious man must regard them as exceptions, and still believe in the great principle. In a world which believed so largely in luck and in the arbitrary favors of the gods, it was a significant advance in ethics that health and wealth should be regarded as the reward of well-doing. The faith was the more significant and religious in that the Israel of the postexilic days was small and poor.

A conspicuous example of this ethical appeal is the book of Proverbs, which consists of a series of collections of "the sayings of the wise," brought into its present form in the Greek period. It is a noble expression of the great half truth that virtue is rewarded and iniquity is punished in the process of human life.

But the wise men realized that this was a half truth. Conspicuous exceptions test the rule and prove it inadequate. Many of the Wisdom Psalms (especially 37, 49, 73) represent the struggle with the great elemental problem that happiness and calamity do not follow upon virtue and vice, as the ethical constitution of the world seems to demand. Various explanations are there put forth in an attempt to resolve the confusion. At last the subject was most vigorously treated in dramatic form in the book of Job, where the older theory is assailed and the impossibility of any complete solution of the problem of suffering is recognized, the whole subject being relegated to the sphere of religious faith in a wisdom that is too high for man.

There is a more serious problem than that of suffering, namely, whether life itself has any significance in view of the unsatisfactoriness of so much of human striving. The book of Ecclesiastes faces this question with no very hopeful attitude. However, Hebrew religion was too well founded to remain long in pessimistic mood, and the teaching of the sages soon regained its happier tone. The Son of Sirach represents a calmer mood, as he finds again that life is good and its goodness is to be found in keeping the law, in obedience to the divine will, and in the values of wisdom. Finally, the noble work called the Book of Wisdom indicates the attitude of the pious Jews who have followed the divine wisdom rather than the maxims of worldly prudence, and finds the resolution of the difficulties that have embarrassed earlier sages in the great reorganization of things in the future life.

§ 3. The Social Quality of Hebrew Wisdom

At first view it might seem that the teachings of the sages are speculative on one side and individualistic on the other. They are concerned with the problems of human life especially in their theological significance, and they are addressed, not to the nation in its solidarity, but to the disciples who gather to listen to the master. Has Hebrew wisdom, then, any social quality at all?

It must be noted that there is a practical interest at the basis of all the speculation. The question with which the sage is really concerned is whether there is any adequate motive for right conduct. He sees first of all a society in which happiness inevitably follows goodness; and if that could be maintained, there would result a very effective social motive. When, however, doubt is cast upon this foundation principle in the social order, the sage is at pains to discover other grounds for ethical motive, but the question remains one of practical moral interest. He is sure that men ought to be good: he is trying to offer them a sufficient reason.

As regards the distinction between individualistic and social teachings, it must be recognized that it is at best a superficial one. We sometimes say to-day that a man is individualistically good but socially bad. Thus he may be an excellent father but an execrable politician. However, this is a question of social degree. Parenthood is a social relation as truly as citizenship. The fact is, rather, that the man has a limited sense of social obligation. He is socialized only within the small group and not within the larger group. Properly speaking, there is no virtue, as there is no vice, that is not social. All conduct that is good and all conduct that is bad is so in its social effects.

It is true that the wise men had little to say of national solidarity. They were not much concerned with national sins and obligations, with the relation of Israel as a whole to God, or with the clash of classes. They saw evil as the acts of individuals, and they saw the opportunities of personal worth and duty. Their teaching was social inasmuch as a man cannot be virtuous or vicious by himself, but only in relation to the members of the society in which he belongs. Industry, truth, honor, fairness, kindness, chastity are social virtues, and their opposites are social evils.

DIRECTIONS FOR STUDY

1. Read Prov 1. 1-6. What does this indicate as the purpose of Hebrew Wisdom?
2. Read Job 28. Note the wonderful comparison between the search for wealth in the mine and the search for Wisdom. Note also the religious basis of Wisdom.
3. Read Prov 8. 1-21. What does this suggest as to the value of Wisdom in the world? How would you modernize the idea?
4. Read Prov 8. 22-31. Note Wisdom as personified and present with God in creation. Compare with this the Alexandrian doctrine of the Logos (John 1. 1-10).
5. Read Eccl 4. 1-3; 8. 9-13; 9. 13-18. What were the social difficulties that disturbed the earlier doctrine of good and evil?
6. Read Job 24. 1-17. Note that this is a declaration of the immunity of the wicked. How would this affect the orthodox theory of the sages?
7. What is the proper place in social ethics for the idea that righteousness brings prosperity?
8. How could the theory of the sages be applied to such problems as those of social diseases?
9. Has the theological consideration of the relation of God to the world anything to do with social ethics?
10. In the practical work of religious and moral education what is the difference between individual and social ethics?

CHAPTER XXVIII

THE ETHICAL TEACHING OF THE BOOK OF PROVERBS

THE necessary limits of our treatment preclude any detailed study of the uncanonical books. We have used these books freely for the light which they throw upon the social condition. Any adequate treatment of the subject of Hebrew wisdom would involve a careful consideration of two of its noblest products—the book of the Son of Sirach, and the book of Wisdom. We must be content with urging the student to make their acquaintance, at least to the extent of reading them.

The books of Job and Ecclesiastes throw much light on social conditions in Judaism, and we have had frequent occasion to refer to them for this contribution. Moreover, they convey incidentally many of the ideas of the wise men upon social matters. Their main purpose, however, is the discussion of the great problems to which reference was made in the last chapter, and therefore a detailed study of them does not fall within our province. For the student who is concerned with the main ethical teachings of the wise men the best course to pursue is to make a study of the book of Proverbs.

§ 1. Wisdom and Folly

The difference between good and evil is presented as fundamentally that between wisdom and folly. Righteous conduct is so eminently sane and reasonable; it conduces to personal and social health; it softens the asperities of life; it promotes all things desirable. Evil conduct to the sage is a stupid thing; its results are all evil; it spoils every condition of human life.

This contrast is carried out very strikingly in the allegory of the Two Banquets (9. 1-6, 13-18). The Lady Wisdom and the Lady Folly each prepare a feast, and offer invitation to "the simple one." This latter is not to be identified in Proverbs with "simpleton." He is, rather, the unsophisticated, the youth who has not yet made the great life choice. He is considered as a candidate for the one way or the other. He may choose which banquet he prefers. Wisdom sends her maidens to summon him with dignity to her goodly feast with the promise that he shall thus come into the way of understanding. But the Lady Folly is clamorous and shameless. She cries out to the passer-by, and her words are seductive,

> "Stolen waters are sweet,
> And bread eaten in secret is pleasant."

The wise man well knows the dangerous fascination of the forbidden. He recognizes also the tragedy of ignorance. The youth may go to Folly's banquet,

> But he knoweth not that the dead are there;
> That her guests are in the depths of Sheol.

In a deadly summary of iniquity the sage describes the "worthless person" (6. 12-15), the familiar "man of Belial," who meets us so often in Hebrew literature. In close juxtaposition he adds his catalogue of the Seven Deadly Sins (vv. 16-19). Here the conduct which is selected as peculiarly abominable is pride, falsehood—including the false witness—cruelty, the sowing of discord, and the general evil attitude of the heart.

It is significant to note how prominent a place was given in Proverbs to the wisdom and folly of speech: *"Death and life are in the power of the tongue"* (18. 21); *"the tongue of the wise is health"* (12. 18). The social effects of angry, unkind, quarrelsome, and even thoughtless speech are so serious that the sage returns to the subject in a hundred forms of warning. The gossip is a social nuisance (11. 13), and *"A whisperer separateth chief friends"* (16. 28). The most dangerous form of evil speech, the false witness which sweareth away reputation, property, and life, may be noted more especially as a political problem.

That sin to which we have come to give dishonorable eminence as the *social evil* is the supreme foolishness. Already the seductions of Lady Folly appear as those of the evil woman who leads the youth astray. The sage again and again warns his disciple against "the strange woman whose house inclineth unto death" (2. 16-19). Most wisely the warning is not put in merely negative form. He is exhorted to devote himself to a study of the words of wisdom, in order that his mind may be full of good thoughts and so he shall be kept from dangerous seductions (6. 20-35; 7. 1-5). The pitiful folly of the youth who goes into the way of sin "as an ox goeth to the slaughter" is drawn out with terrible directness (vv. 6-27).

Various motives of appeal are offered for chastity in addition to the warning of the unutterable folly of unchaste life. There are physical health (5. 11), the waste of substance (29. 3), the high obligation of conjugal fidelity (5. 15-20), and even the risk of jealous anger (6. 27-35).

Gluttony and drunkenness come in for the severe rebuke of the wise man (20. 1; 23. 20f.). A classic passage pictures the seductive attractions of the wine cup, the terrible retribution that follows, the disgusting stupidity of drunkenness, and the folly of the poor victim who goes back to his vice (23. 29-35). The danger of luxurious living, even though it may not reach the point of dissipation, is also recognized (21. 17).

The sage seems to reserve his finest scorn for the sluggard. Delicious bits of humor are found in the excuse that labor is dangerous:

The sluggard saith, There is a lion without;
I shall be slain in the streets (22. 13),

and in the grim hyperbole:

The sluggard burieth his hand in the dish;
It wearieth him to bring it again to his mouth (26. 15).

The description of the woeful state of the field of the sluggard is full of vigor (24. 30-34), and the subject of sloth is considered under many forms (6. 6-11; 10. 4; 21. 25; 26. 13-16). On the other hand, there is earnest exhortation to the virtue of frugality and thrift, for riches are not for ever (10. 4f.; 20. 13; 22. 7, 29; 27. 23-27).

It is probably as an example of thriftlessness that surety is so strongly deprecated in the Proverbs. At first it might seem a niggardly prudence that would refuse to back a friend. It is to be noted that the warnings are generally against going surety for the stranger, although probably the sage regarded the whole matter of guaranteeing the debts of another as unbusinesslike. However, the trait which is denounced is doubtless that easygoing folly of promising anything that one is asked without first carefully considering the character of the obligation. It must have been a very practical problem to call forth so many warnings (6. 1-5; 11. 15; 17. 18; 20. 16; 22. 26f.; 27. 13).

Friendship and enmity are the results of wisdom and folly. The wise man believes in the true friend:

A friend loveth at all times;
And is born as a brother for adversity (17. 17, marg.).

Of course it must be a true friend, for there is danger in promiscuous attachments:

He that maketh many friends doeth it to his own destruction;
But there is a friend that sticketh closer than a brother (18. 24).

Against the fair-weather friends, who go where advantage

is greatest, the sage offers serious warnings (19. 4, 7; 27. 10). Friendliness and peaceableness go hand in hand; it is the fool that is quarrelsome (20. 3; compare 3. 30f.). While, of course, reward of evil for good is an unpardonable iniquity (17. 13), the sage saw the noble blessedness of rewarding good for evil:

If thine enemy be hungry, give him bread to eat;
And if he be thirsty, give him water to drink:
For thou wilt heap coals of fire upon his head,
And Jehovah will reward thee (25. 21f.).

It has been suggested that there is here a cynical suggestion of the delight of humiliating an enemy, but we prefer Paul's interpretation (Rom 12. 20). The wise men distinctly reprobate joy in the downfall of an enemy (24. 17).

§ 2. Family Life

Turning to the specific teachings of the wise men with respect to the social institutions of Israel, it is to be noted that they bring their shrewd counsels of practical wisdom to bear in the direction of elevating ethical standards. In Proverbs family life is held in high esteem. While there is no specific reference to polygamy, the monogamous marriage seems to be taken for granted. The exhortation to the husband to be true to the wife of his youth looks in this direction (5. 18). The good words for the good wife are noteworthy (18. 22; 19. 14), especially the encomium on the worthy woman (31. 10-31). It is quite in keeping with the practical wisdom of the sages that the virtues of frugality and good housekeeping are put in the foreground.

The shrewd observer of life has not failed to notice a common cause of family discomfort, "the contentions of a wife are a continual dropping" (19. 13; also 21. 9; 25. 24; 27. 15f.). The proverb,

Better is a dinner of herbs where love is,
Than a stalled ox and hatred therewith (15. 17),

and its companion (17. 1) may have more than a domestic reference, but they certainly include the happiness of an efficient wife who is also gracious. However, although the Proverbs have the male standpoint, it is not impossible to make an application of this last to the husband also.

The authority of the parents and the obligations of discipline are clearly laid down, as we noted in our discussion of the family. The wise son is obedient (13. 1; 23. 22). The parents are happy who have such, and unhappy indeed if their children are foolish, that is, disobedient (15. 20; 23. 24). Retribution will surely follow filial disloyalty (20. 20; 28. 24). True family life is greatly blessed:

> *Children's children are the crown of old men;*
> *And the glory of children are their fathers* (17. 6).

The family is regarded as a school and its life as a discipline. While reference to the rod of correction undoubtedly includes corporal punishment, the idea that is uppermost is the disciplinary value of a careful training (13. 24; 22. 6, 15; 23. 13f.; 29. 15, 17). It is to be noted that the mother is always recognized as standing with the father in the place of authority and as worthy of respect and obedience.

§ 3. Economic Life

While wealth in general is regarded in the Proverbs as a reward of piety and uprightness, and while poverty is the result of folly, the sage is not oblivious of the fact that wealth may be ill-gotten, and that it has serious dangers. In one noted saying the medium life is commended—"Give me neither poverty nor riches"—on the ground that it is free alike from arrogance and from the temptation to dishonesty (30. 8f.). That the poor are not necessarily wicked is evident from the frequent exhortation to pity them and give them help (3. 28; 11. 24f.; 14. 21, 31; 19. 17; 22. 9; 28. 27).

The dishonesty in business that aroused the indignation

of the prophets still continued in the later times. The sage coupled religion and business in his declaration, "*A false balance is an abomination to Jehovah; but a just weight is his delight*" (11. 1; compare 16. 11; 20. 10). A piece of sharp practice that is very common in our own day is decried in the clever proverb,

> *It is bad, it is bad, saith the buyer:*
> *But when he is gone his way, then he boasteth* (20. 14).

But the most serious economic evil remained still, as in the prophetic times, that the rich and powerful took advantage of their opportunity to oppress the poor and weak. They "*devour the poor from off the earth*" (30. 14), as Micah had already said. There was still the old iniquity of removing the landmark (22. 28; 23. 10). The orphan was especially the subject of such wrong, because there was no adequate means of protecting his estate during his minority. But the sages, no less than the prophets, believed that Jehovah would avenge such iniquity (14. 31; 23. 11). The objection to the taking of interest still continued (28. 8), on the ground that it was taking advantage of the necessity of the needy. The attitude of the Proverbs on the subject of wealth is summed up in a maxim full of social significance for any age:

> *Better is a little, with righteousness,*
> *Than great revenues with injustice* (16. 8).

§ 4. Political Life

While Israel was under the dominance of foreign rulers there was not much opportunity for free discussion of political matters. It is noteworthy that there is not much expectancy in Proverbs of the ideal social state. Rather the wise men seek to point out the duties of rulers and certain of the evils that are manifest in the body politic. The references to kings are very general, and simply declare the blessedness of a good and righteous ruler (16. 12; 20. 8,

26-28; 29. 14). In one strong proverb many of the ills of Israel are spoken:

As a roaring lion, and a ranging bear,
So is a wicked ruler over a poor people (28. 15).

The counsel of the queen mother to King Lemuel (31. 1-9), the origin and date of which are very uncertain, is mainly concerned with caution against unchastity and intemperance, which would prevent the prince from performing the great duties of justice to the poor.

The difficulty of securing justice unless one is able to pay for it, which the prophets felt so keenly, appears again and again in the Proverbs (17. 15; 18. 5; 22. 22f.). The bribe was the source of social corruption (15. 27). It was common then, as it is now in the East, that

A wicked man receiveth a bribe out of the bosom,
To pervert the ways of justice (17. 23).

The evil near akin to this which was noted as early as the Decalogue was false witness, the ready servant of injustice (19. 9; 24. 28; 25. 18).

But the sage was not a revolutionist. His counsel was conservative. He believed that good results would come from the process of education. As a warning to the unquiet spirits who would bring about reforms by violence he says,

My son, fear thou Jehovah and the king;
And company not with them that are given to change (24. 21).

§ 5. Religious Life

As we have already noted, the wise men took the religious institutions of Israel for granted. Stated religious duties are expected of every Israelite. The payment of the tithes and of the first fruits is regarded as giving honor to Jehovah and as a condition of his favor (3. 9f.). But religion is much more than external duties. The ethical significance of religion is declared in Proverbs in words that echo the prophetic fervor:

> *To do righteousness and justice*
> *Is more acceptable to Jehovah than sacrifice* (21. 3),

and the sacrifices of the wicked are regarded as an abomination (21. 27).

If it was within our purpose to consider the religious teaching of the Proverbs, it would be found that the wisdom of the wise included that genuine piety and spiritual understanding, upon which all their doctrines of practical prudence were based.

DIRECTIONS FOR STUDY

1. Why did the wise men discuss good and evil conduct as wisdom and folly?
2. What was the basis of the Proverb writers regarding conduct as good or evil?
3. What influence may Greek life have had in producing social conditions, which caused the wise men to speak so often of immorality and intemperance?
4. What social problems are involved in the matter of suretyship? What principles ought to determine our conduct in the matter?
5. Attempt to construct from Proverbs an idea of Hebrew family life as it then was.
6. Make a similar attempt for Hebrew economic life.
7. What is the attitude of the wise men toward Hebrew religious institutions?
8. Compare the teachings of the sages with those of the prophets.
9. Why is there little social idealism in the book of Proverbs?
10. Would we do well to make larger use of the Proverbs in religious education?

PART III

THE SOCIAL TEACHINGS OF JESUS

CHAPTER XXIX

THE SOCIAL SITUATION IN THE TIME OF JESUS

§ I. Hebrew Institutions as Affected by the Græco-Roman Civilization

Jesus's life at Nazareth was typical of the Galilæan experience of his day. It was of strictly Jewish character, but all surrounded by the influences of the wider civilization that had swept over Palestine without being able to submerge it. The dress and language of Jesus and of his fellow townsmen were Jewish, but the Greek tongue was spoken and understood by all. The copper coins that were used bore the name of the Idumæan ruler at Tiberias, who had built his capital after the models of Greece and Italy, had named it after the Roman emperor, had gathered about him a little court in imitation of that of Rome, and yet professed himself a Jew and scrupulously attended the festivals at Jerusalem.

The synagogue at Nazareth was Jewish after the custom that had existed for centuries, and the Sabbath was kept with rigid exactness; but the land was full of heathen who cared nothing for the Sabbath. It might well be that on that day a caravan of traders would pass across the plain in full view from the hill behind Nazareth, or couriers from Rome would be on their way from the coast, or soldiers would enter the town to carry out the orders of their master. At the great feast-days of the year the Jewish pilgrims would go up to Jerusalem, and the temple with all its magnificence would impress them with the glories of their ancient faith; but the tower of Antonia filled with the barbarian soldiery of Rome reminded them that their city was in the hands of strangers and that they carried on their ritual under sufferance. The presence of the hated publican, the renegade Jew in the pay of Rome, wringing taxes from his own people for the oppressors, was ever a bitter evidence of their servitude. The very priests who represented the sanctity of their religion were living luxuriously in almost pagan fashion. Games and theatrical exhibitions that were little in accord with Hebrew notions of propriety were attended by the aristocratic youth even of the priestly families. It was well known that the high priest himself, the official head of Judaism, was the creature of the Roman procurator, who had appointed him and might depose him at his pleasure.

The old institutions preserved their continuity through all these complex changes, yet there was ever a strong influence, especially upon the young, the ambitious, the pleasure-loving, to yield to the challenge of the freer life of the pagan world. The cleavage had appeared in the third century, when the Hellenizers had looked with contempt upon their sterner brethren. The fierce days of persecution had forced the issue and Judaism had come forth under the Maccabees purified from the conflict. But the old antagonism reappeared. The strict Jews were always against the policy of the court. With the fall of the Asmoneans and the triumph of the Herods the Hellenizers were in complete control. There was nothing for the strict party to do but to fall into opposition and endeavor by the severest literalism, and the strongest emphasis upon the sanctity of the law in its minutest particulars, to stand against the tide of levity and laxity which threatened the foundations of Hebrew life.

It was thus a little world in ferment into which Jesus came. Palestine, notwithstanding its obscurity and political insignificance, was in the current of the great world life. All the social problems were there, though on a small scale. Not the least problem was afforded by the conditions of the national life itself, and the moral uncertainty caused by the contact of two diverse civilizations, and by the consequent presence of different moral standards and customs. Something of the difficulty that confronts us in America in the presence of peoples from all over the earth, who are losing their own racial standards without acquiring ours, and who are consequently weakening the significance of all standards, was present in Palestine, where the Greek, the Syrian, the Roman, and the barbarian from a score of lands mingled with the Jew, who was tenaciously seeking to live his own peculiar life.

§ 2. The Sense of Impending Crisis

As if this mingling of peoples were not enough to confuse social ethics, another element even more disturbing was ever present. There had been developed during the dark days of persecution a passionate hope that God would soon save his chosen people from their miseries. We have noted the long history of the Messianic hope through the prophetic times. The insignificance of the Jewish community during the Persian period, and the extraordinary interest in the development of the law combined to obscure this great expectation. But the awful experiences of the Syrian persecution revived it. Prophecy had already in Zechariah taken on the form of apocalypse. This obscure type of literature seemed well suited to express the mysterious longings of a persecuted race.

The book of Daniel was the first splendid example of this new philosophy of history. It pictured the succeeding empires of the world as ravening beasts, each more terrible than his predecessor; but the last kingdom was to be the everlasting kingdom of righteousness. It was a fine interpretation of the confused political process. It enabled the little community of baffled, harried saints to believe in a moral government of the world. The reign of the tyrants would soon end; the kingdom of God would soon begin. Later apocalypses followed upon the book of Daniel more specifically proclaiming the advent of a King who should be God's servant in the great redemption. Rome and the Herods took possession of the little Hebrew state, but still the Messianic hope survived, and the Messianic apocalypses were written and eagerly read. When, therefore, John the Baptist came in the strange likeness of the old prophets, and proclaimed, "The kingdom of God is at hand," the nation was stirred to its depths, for the end of the old age, with its dire distress, seemed to be approaching.

The coming of the Messiah was associated with the idea of Judgment. The kingdom of God was to be entered only by those who were worthy. John the Baptist himself expected that there would be a fearful dividing of the wicked from the righteous (Matt 3. 10-12). A practical problem, therefore, of the greatest moment was to discover how one could be acquitted in the Judgment and admitted to the glory. The scribes insisted that the minutest obedience to the law was the ground upon which the judgment would be made. Every infraction of the law was a debit on the great book of accounts, and every observance was a credit. The question of the balancing of the account was, then, of the highest importance. Social values are easily minimized when conduct is considered from this transcendental point of view. It is difficult to hold a natural relation toward one's neighbor when one is forever calculating how his acts will be estimated on the heavenly records. Moreover, what did social values particularly matter when the whole world was trembling on the edge of the great gulf that should separate forever the common ways of the past from the utterly new and infinitely significant conditions of the future?

Human history was to be divided by the cataclysm into two great ages—the present age and the coming age. The phrase, "the end of the world" in our English Bible (Matt 24. 3, see marg.) is confusing. The Jews had no such expectation as the traditional Christian idea that this human life in the world would end and a new life of the soul would ensue in heaven. They believed in the resurrection of the body, not in the immortality of the soul. They expected a new and wonderful age in this world. But everything was to be different. Enemies were to be destroyed, oppressions were to be ended, peace and prosperity were to be universal, the law was to be absolutely obeyed, the heathen were to be converted, the righteous dead were to be restored to life to share in the glorious régime. The Son of David was to reign over a regenerate humanity.

There would be an inevitable unnaturalness and disturbance of ordinary standards of value in the feeling that one was living at the near approach of such a complete transformation of mundane conditions. At any moment extraordinary events of the most portentous character might occur, overthrowing every human calculation. How insignificant the efforts of men to better the conditions of social life when shortly God would take the matter in his own hands, and everything would be changed and rectified!

Of course there was a certain saving sanity that prevented most people from living exactly according to these expectations. They carried on their affairs just as if the stability of social conditions was entirely to be relied upon. The premillenarian doctrine in modern times has only in sporadic cases affected the practical life of men. Professing to believe that the Lord may return at any moment, they still carefully make investments that look to the far future, and shrewdly carry on their business on practical principles. Yet there is inevitably a different estimate of social values when people believe that at some near day God will bring about by instantaneous and miraculous intervention the reconstruction that human effort has failed to accomplish by years or centuries of difficult endeavor. It must never be forgotten that Jesus was speaking to people who held these views.

§ 3. Types of Social Attitude

It is necessary to recognize that in the time of Christ

there had developed from various political, economic, and religious causes several distinct types of social attitude among the Jews. It would be scarcely correct to say that there were sects or parties, for they were not organized in opposition to one another.

Perhaps the most outstanding and unique of these types was that of the select righteous few who devoted themselves with steady and punctilious exactness to the observance of all the requirements of the law. As we have noted in our discussion of the oral law (see pages 34f.), the obligations of the Mosaic legislation had become extraordinarily extended by four hundred years of elaboration. In order to keep every minutest detail of these traditional prescriptions one could do little else but give attention to his own personal righteousness. Manifestly, the common people, occupied in earning a living, could not so devote themselves. Thus the full observance of the law was confined to the few. There are two dangers of such legalism and literalism. The first is bigotry, an intense appreciation of one's own particular practice. This is the effect upon the sincere devotee. But the worse danger is that the effort of the punctilious observance of the rule may be combined with a desire for personal ease and self-indulgence. The result then is casuistry, which readily becomes hypocrisy. When the mendicant monastic orders accepted riches, but nominally kept their vows of poverty by holding their wealth in common, thus leaving the individual monk without possessions, there was an exhibition of the same quality that operated so harshly in the case of the Pharisees. The Pharisaic attitude was essentially unsocial, for it cultivated the feeling of class consciousness and of contempt for the masses who could not keep the law.

The second attitude to note is that of the political opportunists. They were the outward conformers to the conditions of the times. In our discussion of the Sadducees (see page 123) we have noted that as the wealthy class they were especially desirous of maintaining their privileges and, therefore, were opposed to anything that might cause political disturbance. This was true, however, not only of the priestly aristocracy, but of many who in one way or another, finding their position comfortable, were unwilling to be led away by Messianic hopes or religious programs into any resistance to the Roman power. Of this type were the so-called Herodians, that is, the creatures and followers of the Herod family. Naturally, a host of people held office or secured immunities or privileges by the grace of one or other of the Herods. It was easy for such to maintain that their masters were Jews by faith, and that it was patriotic as well as wise to uphold them. The opportunist attitude was also unsocial, for it was concerned with personal advantage rather than with the public good.

The mass of the people believed in religion and gave some heed to its requirements. The exigencies of business and the pressure of daily cares prevented the constant washings, prayers, fastings, synagogue attendance, and all that was prescribed for piety, so they contented themselves with admiring the righteousness of the scribes and Pharisees and living a life that was largely secularized. It was not a socially healthy attitude, for they knew themselves to be violators of the law and knew that it was inevitable. It was among the common people that the Messianic expectations in their most glowing colors had the greatest vogue. It was so natural for them to have a kind of easy religious faith that the Lord would miraculously inaugurate conditions of righteousness which would guarantee the observance of the law.

The fourth attitude was that of the irreconcilables—the revolutionists. They were weary of waiting for the kingdom of God to appear. They wanted to overthrow the tyrants who held them in political bondage and to restore the Jewish state to independence. Again and again they broke out in fierce fury only to be harshly put down. It was they at last who forced the rebellion against Rome which brought about the destruction of Jerusalem. Jesus called one of these "Zealots" to membership in the apostolic band (Luke 6. 15).

There remains to note a soundly healthy social attitude that cannot have been uncommon in Jesus's day, and which is somewhat obscured to us because no name was attached to it, and there was no group that professed it. It might have been found in any of the groups into which the nation was divided. It is met in the godly priest Zacharias and in his wife, Elisabeth; in the Nazareth family of the good carpenter Joseph and of his wife, Mary; in old Simeon and Anna, the frequenters of the temple; in the sturdy fishermen Andrew and Peter and the sons of Zebedee; in Nathanael of Cana and his friend Philip; in Lazarus and his sisters; in the good Aquila and Priscilla; in Lois and Eunice, and in Timothy their child. The religion of the prophets, the faith of the psalmists, the longing for the kingdom of God as a reign of righteousness and love had not ceased in Israel. There were many, very many, who shared the experience of the great religious leaders of their race, and endeavored to do justly, to love kindness, and to walk humbly with their God. It is out of the circle of these people that Jesus came.

DIRECTIONS FOR STUDY

1. Endeavor to reconstruct in imagination the life of Jerusalem when Herod was building the superb temple, and was at the same time seeking to make the city an imitation of Rome.
2. What inducements would the Græco-Roman life offer to the Jewish youth?
3. What could the pious Jews do to offset the attractions and seductions of the richer civilization about them?
4. Read Dan 2. 31-45. Note that a series of kings is described. Consider the attitude of people who thought themselves living immediately upon the eve of the events described in v. 44.
5. Read Matt 3. 1-12; Mark 1. 1-8; Luke 3. 1-18. Consider what John thought about the coming of the Kingdom.

6. Read Matt 24, which probably reflects the evangelist's interpretation of Jesus's teaching. Consider the expectation of impending crisis which it presents.
7. Read Matt 23. Make an estimate of the Pharisaic attitude on the basis of this chapter.
8. What is said of the Sadducees and of the Herodians in the Gospels? What do these references imply as to their character?
9. What conditions justified the attitude of the Zealots? To whom do they correspond in various nations of modern times? How do you estimate such attitudes?
10. Read Matt 1. 18 to 2. 23; Luke 1. 5 to 2. 39; John 1. 35-51; 2 Tim 1. 5. Consider what kind of people are here described. How could the prophets affect the Jewish life of Jesus's day?

THE UNDERLYING PRINCIPLES OF JESUS'S TEACHING

CHAPTER XXX

THE TEACHINGS OF JESUS AS A PRODUCT OF HIS EXPERIENCE

ALL ethical teachings that are of any value are the product of experience. It would be no difficult task to draft a code of rules whose ethical demands would be most exacting. But the consciences of men are not stirred by such prescriptions. The great teachers have learned the meaning of life in their own moral struggles, and thus have earned the right to speak the words that men will hear. It was out of the life among his fellow townsmen of Nazareth and in the tetrarchy of Galilee that Jesus brought forth the message that has compelled the attention of the world.

§ 1. His Religious Experience

While distinction may be made for the purpose of analysis between the religious and the social experience of Jesus, it must be remembered that the distinction is not fundamental. In the largest sense social experience includes fellowship with God. In the life of Jesus comradeship with God and with men constituted a fused experience. He went from God to men, and from men to God, without any break in his sense of reality and of duty.

The beautiful story of the boyhood of Jesus preserved by Luke (2. 41-51) indicates a religious experience that had its foundations in the noblest faith of Israel. The son of Mary entered into the heritage of all that prophets and psalmists had bequeathed to their people of the knowledge of God as a reality in human life. The upright and gracious Joseph gave to the young boy such an exhibition of fatherhood that that great relationship expressed to him naturally the attitude of God toward men. Evidently, the surest element in the experience of Jesus was that of sonship toward God, whom he knew and loved and trusted as his Father.

This must not be identified with the theological idea of the Fatherhood of God. It is possible to hold that doctrine as a doctrine without any very definite realization of its value in life. An experience of God as Father is a very different matter. Jesus felt that he was in God's world, where it was safe to live without anxiety (Matt 6. 25-34). He held converse with the Unseen not as "an infant crying in the night, and with no language but a cry," but as a confident son talking with one who heard and whose answer could be understood (Matt 6. 6; 7. 7f.; Mark 1. 35). He had one clear maxim of conduct: to do what would be pleasing to God (John 8. 29). God's concern with the affairs of this world was a very definite and practical concern in the mind of Jesus (Matt 6. 32; Luke 12. 32). He therefore believed that he could actually be a copartner with God in every good work that fell to him to do (John 5. 17).

Jesus found this experience so satisfying, meeting all the needs of his life, that he felt that it was the supreme need of other men. He found his neighbors worried and harassed because they had no strong faith. He found them acting upon impulse, upon petty motives, and evil motives, for self-indulgence, because they had no sense of the divine plan in human life. Jesus saw that there were people all around him to whom God was not a Father, and knew that they suffered loss in that lack. To share his experience with others was therefore an inevitable outcome of the nature of the experience.

There was a sense in which that experience could not be shared. Jesus had no personal sense of a broken relationship with God. The filial attitude had been so continuous, so uninterrupted, so eminently natural that the experience of penitence had not been necessary. In his ministry he called on others to repent and to pray for forgiveness (Matt 6. 12). But with all his clarity of moral insight, he never felt the need of forgiveness for himself. This unique moral experience is the great fact in the personality of Jesus. But it did not separate him from other men. He always summoned others to share with him the sense of God as the common privilege of every human soul. All his teachings grew out of this religious attitude and faith.

§ 2. His Social Experience

Nazareth was a commonplace village (John 1. 46) where humanity ran its little course guided by mingled motives. Men helped one another and cheated one another. Children played and quarreled. Women sacrificed for their children, loved their kindred, performed neighborly acts, and manifested envy, hatred, malice, and all uncharitableness. Perhaps it was one who had lived at Nazareth who spoke of the deadly sins of speech, of the bitterness of jealousy, of the horrid facts of lust and covetousness (James 3. 2 to 4. 2). But Jesus found himself friendly with all his neighbors. He knew that God loved them, and he loved them. When the inevitable aggressions and insults of social and business life met him he was sorry for the offender (Luke 23. 34), and not only refrained from retaliation but gave more than was demanded (Matt 5. 39-42). He found that in many cases people responded to such treatment, and even when they did not he felt that he had done his best. He achieved the extraordinary experience of loving his enemies (v. 44). He hated nobody. The teachings of Jesus must be understood on the basis of this social experience, of regarding all people whom he met as persons and treating them as such. Whatever he felt would be due and proper conduct toward himself, that he accorded to others (7. 12). The inevitable reaction of such conduct was, of course, the still further experience of social values.

So, again, it is not enough to say that Jesus believed in the brotherhood of man; that is all too easily the cant phrase of our modern social gospel. Jesus not only believed in it; he experienced it. He found that men *were* his brothers. He felt and acted toward them as if they were members of the same family. If they were happy, he rejoiced. If they were sad, he was troubled; if they were ignorant, he was sympathetic; if they were wicked, he might be stern, but he was always fraternal. All kinds of men were his brothers; all kinds of women were his sisters; all kinds of children were his friends. Because he had tried brotherhood for thirty years, and found it satisfying from every standpoint and in every test, he was able to preach brotherliness.

§ 3. The Experiential Nature of His Teachings

Evidently, there was no one else in Palestine who was living with God and with men as Jesus was. Evidently, he had found a great secret of life. Happiness was the universal quest, and he had found it. Strangely enough, he had found it in the sense of need, in grief over moral evil, in teachableness, in longings after goodness, in tenderness of human judgment, in utter sincerity, in efforts after peace, in the willingness to suffer for the right (Matt 5. 3-11). But he knew the issue was blessedness, and he saw that men who were proud, self-sufficient, aggressive, covetous, harsh, insincere, quarrelsome, timeserving, while they might gain things, never gained life's supreme values. The world was on the wrong track, but Jesus knew the right way (John 14. 6). What could he do but summon men to follow him?

We cannot think of Jesus as a social reformer in the ordinary sense. The Social Contract Theory aimed to put society on its feet by proclaiming a certain doctrine on the basis of which society was to be organized. The socialist considers our capitalistic system fundamentally wrong and has a different theory of the social order to propound. The philosophical anarchist believes that human ills arise from the fundamental mistake of controlling men by government, and he has a theory of freedom to suggest. Jesus had no social theory. As we endeavor to study his attitude toward the various social institutions we shall find a surprising absence of rule or program. He had some principles of personal living which he had wrought out in his fellowship with God and with men. He was concerned not with schemes of life but with life itself. He believed that the way to get fruits was to give attention to roots (Matt 7. 17f.). Truth, freedom, righteousness, love were the values that he had himself experienced, and these he offered to all men as the highest good.

Therefore the teachings of Jesus are not systematic. We do not find any such thing as the Five Relations carefully worked out in the Confucian system. Jesus was not concerned to give people a body of rules to be applied externally. The old law had done that, and Pharisaism had been the result. He would rather inspire men to take his attitude of filial, obedient trust in God, of fraternal, generous trust in men, knowing that all social problems could be worked out on that basis. Many of his teachings were, of course, specific, but even so, they were not laid down as rules. They are illustrations of right relationships; they are challenging applications of life principles.

§ 4. The Interpretation of the Teachings

Therefore the teachings of Jesus are not to be interpreted as if they were statutes. He did not overthrow one literalism in order to establish another. A character in a popular novel who wishes to be a Christian receives two blows without retaliation, but half kills his opponent when he strikes a third time. The attempt to be obedient to Christ has produced ritualisms and technical observances, with the inevitable casuistic refinements and bitter bigotries, so that a new Pharisaism has often flourished in Christianity.

Jesus did not give to the world a body of religious doctrine and of social teaching that was to be obeyed. He gave to the world a life, whose great qualities are needed in every changing situation in human history. The application of that quality of life to one single human situation, namely, that existing in Palestine in the reign of the Roman emperor Tiberias, is afforded us in the words and acts of Jesus. We must know, then, the social situation of that particular time, the mode of thought and interests of the people. We must see what Jesus had to say to them, and how he lived among men. We may then deduce the principles in accordance with which we must act in our own greatly different modern environment. Jesus may be our Master, our inspiration, our motive power, but not our dictator, our lawgiver, our system-maker. He never offered a ready-made program to save men the trouble of social effort. He offered men a Spirit that should guide them into all the truth, declaring that the truth should make them free.

DIRECTIONS FOR STUDY

1. Read Luke 2. 40-52. Compare the experience of Jesus with that of a modern boy at the time of his entering into full membership in the church. What are the social duties of a boy of that age? How did Jesus meet them?
2. Read Matt 6. 24-34. Think of this as an expression of the religious experience of Jesus. Try to imagine the practical effect upon his own disposition and conduct of such a philosophy of life.
3. Read Matt 5. 3-12. Think of this as a description not of a series of individuals, but of one type of character. If Jesus believed from his own experience that such a quality of life would yield the highest happiness, what does that reveal regarding his own attitude and conduct?
4. Read Matt 6. 2-18. Think of this as a product of Jesus's experience and character in prayer and in religious observance. What type of religious life does it exhibit?
5. Read Matt 5. 22f., 28. Note that these words refer to the motives behind wrongdoing. If they express the experience of Jesus, what do they suggest as to his attitudes toward people?

6. Read Matt 5. 13-15. Consider what this implies as to Jesus's own sense of having a mission to perform in the world.
7. Compare Jesus with the prophets as to the experiential nature of their teachings.
8. Read Matt 7. 28f. Note that Jesus's authority was that of experience. What were the differences between the teaching of Jesus and that of the scribes?
9. What type of men teach with authority to-day? What kind of authority do we recognize? What kind of authoritative teaching is compatible with the freedom of the learner?
10. Why should the student of modern social conditions be at pains to reconstruct in imagination the exact social conditions and modes of thought and conduct of the times of Jesus?

CHAPTER XXXI

THE KINGDOM OF GOD AS A SOCIAL IDEAL

IT is important to remember that Jesus did not originate the term "kingdom of God." It was the current phrase of the Messianic expectation. The kingdoms of the tyrants had succeeded one another on the earth; at last there should come a kingdom of God (Dan 2. 44). It was sometimes called the kingdom of the saints (7. 18). Inasmuch as the divine name was avoided among the Jews from motives of reverence, the word "heaven" being substituted, the phrase "kingdom of heaven" was employed as the equivalent of "kingdom of God." It so appears in the Jewish Gospel of Matthew. It does not refer, therefore, to a condition that should exist in heaven, but always to the great new era that was to be constituted on earth. Jesus, in employing the phrase, was addressing himself to the current belief and endeavoring to give ethical quality to that popular notion. It has been suggested that if he were speaking to our own day he might very well speak of the "republic of God."

§ 1. THE SOCIAL CHARACTER OF THE JEWISH CONCEPTION

As we have seen in the study of the prophets, they looked forward to an ideal social state, a reign of righteousness which was to come in this world by the transformation of human relations on the basis of a great justice and love. They generally thought of it as taking place in Palestine, though some of them had a wider vision and believed that it should include all the peoples of the earth. After prophecy came apocalypse, less ethical, more supernatural, but still the Messianic hope retained its social character. There was to be a mighty cataclysm that should end the present era and usher in the new time with extraordinary celestial phenomena—"*The sun shall be turned into darkness, and the moon into blood*" (Joel 2. 30f.). But the apocalyptic Messianic hope was still for a reconstituted earthly life with the old evils and tyrannies removed (3. 18-21).

The disciples of Jesus always expected that he would reestablish an independent Jewish monarchy (Matt 20. 20f.; Mark 10. 35-37; Acts 1. 6). Even the great Christian apocalypse seems to picture the bright future as a reconstructed earth in which a new Jerusalem would be the capital. It was a walled city with open gates, to which the kings of the earth bring presents, to which the glory of all the nations turns, out of which all violence and falsehood have been cast, and where the ills of humanity are healed at last (Rev 21f.).

The Jews, therefore, had a very definite social program. They looked for a great prince who should expel the Romans, overthrow the Herods, put an end to all tyrannies and oppression, bring freedom, peace and prosperity, permit every man to dwell under his own vine and fig tree with none to make him afraid. In such a transformed social order they believed that men would live in amity and justice, and the righteousness of God would prevail.

§ 2. Jesus's Experience of the Kingdom of God

In such an expectancy Jesus grew up. He shared with his neighbors the golden hope of the golden age. But he more and more realized that it was not necessary to wait for the future in order to have many of the blessings which men so eagerly sought. The righteousness of the kingdom of God anyone could have for himself; and, after all, that was the supreme object for which to strive (Matt 6. 33). He eagerly longed to live the kind of life in Nazareth which men dreamed was to be lived in the coming age; and he attained his object (Matt 5. 6). So far as the reign of God was concerned, the victory of right, truth, and love, the conquest of evil, crookedness, and hate, Jesus found that one could have it in his own life (Luke 17. 21). The satisfaction of doing God's will, and of knowing that he was doing it, was to him like food to a hungry man (John 4. 34).

Jesus realized that his countrymen were making a grand mistake in looking up to the clouds for the kingdom to come down to them, or looking around for some conquering prince to win it for them. Doubtless he believed that only God could give them the perfect social state for which they and he longed. But there was no need to wait for that divine consummation. The life of the Kingdom could be entered upon at once. The supreme good was attainable by anyone that wanted it. Jesus had achieved it for himself. He knew that anyone who would might have it (Luke 17. 20f.). The whole problem was already epitomized in Nazareth, and Jesus saw it more and more as he grew from youth to manhood. The Nazarenes suffered more from one another than from the Romans. It was the hatreds, the vengeance, the lust, the falsehood, the meanness, the dishonesty of the people of Nazareth that spoiled the life of that town. If the Romans and the Herods with all their crew had been expelled, Nazareth would not greatly have been sweetened. A pure, unselfish family life was needed. A fine chastity, honor, and love in the individual soul were needed. Fair and generous business, right neighborliness, charitable judgment, and above all and as a motive for all a genuine confidence in God—these were the needs of Nazareth. And the people could have all these if they would. There was no need to wait for a Messiah. Probably this was the process of thought by which Jesus was led to recognize that all the hopes of the prophets for a Messiah might be better fulfilled through himself.

When the inevitable objection arose in his mind that righteousness and love do not provide food and clothing he looked around him on the world of nature which seemed to speak to him of an infinite care, and he believed that if people would ever put first of all the search for righteousness, God could be trusted that all necessary things should be added unto them (Matt 6. 33).

What, then, of the Messiah? Jesus saw that the people did not need a prince but a teacher. He would be their Messiah and prepare them for the kingdom of God. He read the prophets and saw the deeper meaning of their words. The Servant of Jehovah, misunderstood and rejected, yet saving his people in spite of their blindness, was to him the prototype of the leadership which the times demanded. He entered, therefore, upon a mission which was a summons to his countrymen to make ready for a kingdom of God on earth by living as the citizens of such a kingdom ought to live.

§ 3. The Kingdom of God and Eternal Life

Not only was the phrase "kingdom of God" a common expression which Jesus adopted, but the great phrase "eternal life" was also part of the current Messianic vocabulary (Matt 19. 16; Mark 10. 17; Luke 18. 18). Everybody wanted eternal life. By that they meant that they wanted to live through the present age into that coming age when death and disease should be abolished. Or, if they were to die, they wanted to be sure that they would be raised from the dead to share in the glory of the blessed time (Dan 12. 2; John 11. 24).

Jesus experienced eternal life; that is, he experienced the life that belongs to the kingdom of God. He saw that the common idea of an unending life had no ethical significance. It is not quantity of life but quality that is important. Real life is likeness to God (Matt 5. 48). If one feels toward his fellow men as God feels, and acts toward them as God acts, he has become a sharer of God's life. It was part of Jesus's religious experience to believe that such a life possessed the eternal quality. It was good enough to endure (Matt 19. 29; Mark 10. 30). This is the resolution of his wonderful paradox, "Whosoever would save his life shall lose it: and whosoever shall lose his life for my sake shall find it" (Matt 16. 25).

To put Jesus's paradox in modern speech: The only true life is the socialized life. The law of self-preservation here gives place to the higher law of self-dedication. Jesus believed that one could so preserve himself as to lose everything that was worth preserving, and could so sacrifice himself as to achieve a quality of life that would be indestructible. When we press further in our eagerness to know what this social ideal of living may be Jesus goes to the heart of our problems by laying his emphasis upon motive. All politics, office-seeking, personal ambitions, professional jealousies drop away, and the question remains, What is the yearning desire of a man's inmost heart? If that desire is for the highest welfare of his fellow men, he has attained the social attitude of Jesus, he has entered into eternal living; that is to say, the kind of life that is to be lived in the great coming age may be commenced in the present age.

Jesus did not speak in abstract terms about motives. The type of life to which he summoned men is made clear in repeated specific teachings, all of which lay emphasis upon the motive of high social obligation. Among many may be noted the golden rule of justice (Matt 7. 12), the inner attitudes more important than the outward acts, as the murderous quality of anger, and the duty to love enemies (5. 21f.; 44), the inner chastity (5. 28), the defilements of life (Mark 7. 17-23); the importance of supreme loyalty to the highest good (Matt 6. 33), with its striking demand upon the rich young ruler (19. 16-22); the true neighborliness shown by the good Samaritan (Luke 10. 25-37), and parabolically represented in the last judgment (Matt 25. 31-46); the sacrificial quality of duty shown in the devotion of the Good Shepherd (John 10. 1-21), and of the poor widow (Mark 12. 41-44); the awful negation of these attitudes exhibited by the Pharisees (Matt 23; Luke 11. 29-54); the great summary of duty in the law of love to God and love to man (Matt 22. 34-40).

§ 4. The Relation of the Individual to the Kingdom

The relation of the individual to a social reformation is always an interesting problem. In our modern dreams of a better social order we rather assume that everybody will be included in the new order just because there is nowhere else to be. In a thoroughly established republic a monarchist is a mere malcontent who is out of joint with the system of things. So if there should be a socialistic state, everybody would of necessity be a socialist. So in Jesus's day the kingdom of God was thought of as an inheritance, sometimes conceived as belonging to every Jew (Matt 3. 9), sometimes more ethically as conditioned on a certain quantum of righteousness (19. 16).

Manifestly, if the most significant fact about the kingdom of God is a certain quality of life which is some day to be universal but which may be entered upon now, it cannot be a gift whether to Jews or to all men. Character cannot be bestowed apart from human will and striving. Jesus, therefore, always presented the idea of the necessity of personal choice. Men must be willing to become sons of their Father by living the gracious life of the Father (Matt 5. 43-45). The Kingdom must be set up, and that involved a willingness to act righteously (6. 33). Men were to repent of their sins and believe in the ethical nature of the Kingdom (Mark 1. 14f.). The choice involves a cost which must be measured in advance (Luke 14. 33-35), for the way of right living is not careless and easy, but is ever exacting (Matt 7. 13). So Jesus made the most severe demand upon the young nobleman and then told the disciples that the path of righteousness involved inevitable sacrifice (19. 16-30).

Therefore it might easily be that many would miss the kingdom of God. In the parable of the sower Jesus indicated that if people did not care about the great ideal of social righteousness, they would never know that the Kingdom was open to them; if they wanted it but were afraid to pay the price, they would lose it; if they wanted it but were preoccupied with other interests, they would miss it; only if they were ready for it would they obtain it (13. 1-8, 18-23). He reminded the Jews that their entrance into this great new life was dependent upon their choice, and that others of far less opportunity might become partakers of what they neglected (8. 11; 22. 1-10). Jesus always insisted that anyone, even the most unlikely, might enlist in the great enterprise and enter upon the Godlike life, and that the heavenly Father was infinitely desirous of receiving even the outcasts into the new social order (Mark 2. 13-17; Luke 15).

In the discourses of Jesus recorded by John the kingdom of God, or eternal life, is presented in many striking figures, each illustrating the idea that a person who is willing to follow the summons of Jesus shall have a new dynamic for true living. It is a new life inaugurated by a new birth (John 3. 1-8). It is sustained by the inspiration of the leadership of Jesus as one's body is nourished by food and drink (6. 26-58; 7. 37-39). The great problems of life are illumined (8. 12). Men realize truth and thereby enter into moral freedom (8. 31-36).

§ 5. The Progress of the Kingdom

The Jews thought that the ideal society would be inaugurated in a moment by the power of God. Jesus told them that individuals must make the great choice and become partners with God in reconstructing society. He did not, of course, tell them that it was a social order to be worked out by men. It was to be produced by the power of God, but only as men were workers with him.

In the parables by the sea (Matt 13) the progress of the Kingdom was wonderfully sketched. As seeds are sown on many soils the social ideals are offered to many minds. They fail to make progress because men are careless or timid or preoccupied; they do make progress as men are receptive. Again, as wheat and tares grow together in the field, so good and evil grow together in the world, intermingled and not easily separated. We do not have good nations and bad nations, good cities and bad cities, good industries and bad industries. We have the good and bad together, and we shall have to wait for the separation. But the great social ideals will spread as the fast-growing herb, will permeate the institutions of men as the leaven permeates the flour, for when men see their worth they will give up everything to secure them, as anyone would sell his goods to secure a greater treasure, as a jeweler would sacrifice all lesser gems for the priceless pearl. Moreover, the progress of the great social ideal shall be effected by the destruction of the institutions of unrighteousness, as fishermen throw away the worthless fish that have come into their nets.

DIRECTIONS FOR STUDY

1. Review the prophetic teaching on the ideal social state, and consider why the Jews came to use the phrase "kingdom of God."
2. How far was Jesus's conception of the kingdom of God the same as that of current Judaism? Why did he not avoid the use of the expression in order to avoid misconception?
3. What did the experience of Jesus lead him to feel were the supreme needs of men?
4. What kind of life in the modern world could be characterized as eternal life on the basis of the teachings of Jesus? In what respects would that designation seem to be socially significant?
5. Study the passages referred to as implying Jesus's emphasis upon motive. Consider the significance of these teachings as regards modern social motives.
6. Consider some person whom you regard as sincerely endeavoring to follow Jesus in the betterment of human life. Does his conduct seem to bear out our interpretation of the teaching of Jesus regarding the relation of the individual to the kingdom of God?
7. Can the conduct of men who seem to be standing in the way

of social progress to-day be explained on the basis of Jesus's teaching? What does this suggest as to the possibility of relating such people to the kingdom of God? What does it suggest as to the opportunities of religious education?

8. What does Jesus teach as to the possibility of the social derelict becoming a social force?
9. Read Matt 13. Consider such a social ideal as the abolition of slavery. Note that slavery only gradually disappeared because so many people did not care about the matter (the seed on the pathway); because those who did care were afraid of getting into trouble (the seed in the shallow earth); because others were too busy with their own concerns (the seed was choked); but many were really anxious and willing to pay the price (the good seed). Consider how the other parables would apply to this particular social reform.
10. Apply the parables by the sea to the progress of the temperance reform. Work out the analogies in detail. Apply them also to other social reforms with which you may be familiar.

CHAPTER XXXII

THE WORTH OF THE INDIVIDUAL

§ 1. The Higher Individualism

The old Hebrew religion regarded Jehovah as the God of the nation. It was the nation that was blessed for its loyalty and the nation that was punished for its sin. Individual wicked men might prosper because they were part of a righteous people, and individual good men might suffer because they were compatriots of a disobedient people. The earlier prophets presented very much this view. Amos, Hosea, Micah for the most part spoke their warnings and their promises to the people as a whole. To be sure, acts of tyranny against individuals were rebuked, and the righteous acts of individuals were rewarded, but the idea of national or racial solidarity was very strong. We have seen that Jeremiah, and particularly Ezekiel, saw the further truth that the individual human being had a relationship to Jehovah, and was blessed or punished according to his own deed. We have noted that wonderful social conception of the Servant of Jehovah, wherein the great doctrine of the higher individualism is presented. It is not the doctrine of the sacrifice of the individual for the good of the whole, but of the self-sacrifice of the individual for the good of the whole. And this was the teaching of Jesus.

The speculations of the sages into the meaning of life led them to put emphasis on the significance of the individual. In the Proverbs it is the wise man, the prudent, the thrifty, the honest, the God-fearing who is blessed, and the foolish man, the sluggard, the liar, the cheat, the godless who is troubled. The law combined the two ideas of individuality and solidarity, for the sacrificial system had its national and its individual significance. The apocalyptic literature was like the prophetic in its conception of God's relation to his chosen people whom he was about to redeem, but in its doctrine of condemnation and acquittal at the Great Judgment it looked to the conduct of the individual.

Jesus at the beginning of his ministry quoted the description of the Servant of Jehovah as applicable to himself (Luke 4. 18f.). In a notable utterance he laid down the principle of the higher individualism, "*whosoever would become great among you shall be your minister; and whosoever would be first among you shall be your servant*" (Matt 20. 26f.; 23. 11; Mark 10. 43f.).

Individualism, upon the maxim "Every man for himself," is anti-social. Group solidarity, upon the maxim "The group is everything, the individual is nothing," is unsocial, for it exalts an abstraction and subordinates to it the human personality. We have the former in modern times in the competitive system, which gives the world and its wealth only to the strong. We have the latter in all systems of organization that make the individual a mere unit of a complex whole. Most notably we have it in the industries that regard the workers as hands, to be used and thrown aside like machinery, and in the military systems which regard men as soldiers to be massed, and moved, and sacrificed like the pieces on a chessboard, for the advantage of the state.

Jesus's conception of his own individual worth was supreme. He believed himself to be the Son of God (Matt 10. 32f.). He called himself the Son of man, as if it were infinitely significant to be a human being. One cannot read his wonderful words without feeling an extraordinary egoism, showing that Jesus had a rare sense of individuality. But it is never egotism, for Jesus's conception of the value of supreme human worth was that there was so much more to be dedicated to the service of men.

This higher individualism Jesus expected in a certain

degree of others. He called them the sons of God (Matt 5. 16, 48; 6. 1, 6-15). In the great passage in which he declared his own life ministry he summoned the two ambitious disciples to a like eminence of sacrifice with himself (20. 20-28). When Peter objected to his Master's expectation of death at the hands of the rulers Jesus told him that self-realization was to be obtained only through self-sacrifice, and that the way of selfishness, even if it should result in gaining for a man all that the world holds, could only result in the loss of himself (16. 21-26).

This profound view of life rests in the religious experience of Jesus. He achieved a filial relationship to God which he realized fraternally with men. He did not think of himself and he did not think of those whom he summoned to follow him as atoms to be contributed to the cause of humanity. He considered himself and them as individually precious in the sight of God, and as privileged to yield personal ease, comfort, even life, for the good of the other brothers whom they might thereby bring into fellowship with the Father and with one another. It is the higher individualism of social service.

§ 2. Jesus's Faith in Human Worthfulness

The only ground for the sons of men to give their lives in ransom for the many must lie in the worthfulness of the many. It would be folly to sacrifice the good for the bad. There could be no social justification for that. The great biological law which has been expressed in the phrase "the survival of the fittest" was practically the sacrifice of the bad for the good. The weaklings perish that the strong may endure. Only thus could progress have been made. If Jesus had a sentimental interest in the unfortunate who would go to the wall by the relentless operation of biological law, his teaching might be kindly, but it would not be socially efficacious. However, such an interpretation of Jesus's teaching entirely misses his point of view. He did not believe that publicans, and sinners, and demoniacs, and neurasthenics, and criminals were worthy, but he did believe in their capability of worthiness. He did not excuse them on the ground that they were more sinned against than sinning. He made his appeal to the best that was in them, confident that the best could be evoked. Everybody hated Zacchæus in Jericho. He was a mean, unpatriotic grafter. High-minded people felt toward him as we feel toward the corrupt political boss. Jesus believed that Zacchæus had in him great possibilities of good. He made him a friend by the simple process of asking his hospitality. Zacchæus experienced a complete revolution in his sense of life values, and immediately made restitution to those whom he had wronged and embarked upon a career of philanthropy (Luke 19. 1-10).

The demoniacs, poor creatures, who were popularly supposed to be tormented by evil spirits, and who were consequently experiencing serious mental instability, were cured by Jesus through an appeal to their sense of personality. One demoniac instead of being a social menace became a contributor to the healthy life of his community (Mark 5. 1-20). Mary of Magdala, whom tradition has most unfairly dealt with as a sinner, but who really was afflicted by the delusion of demonism, was completely restored, and transformed into a leader of the new Christian society (Luke 8. 1-3; Matt 28. 1-10; John 20. 1-18). The unfaithful woman, whom the old law would have put to death, was sent forth by the skill of Jesus and by his faith in her reformation with new motives of righteousness (John 8. 2-11). The twelve men whom Jesus associated with himself were developed into extraordinary power by his belief in their possibilities. Several of them were the common fishermen of Galilee; one was an excise collector; none were men of note or learning (Acts 4. 13).

Faith in men is the basis of those teachings of Jesus that have been the most difficult to understand. To submit to be struck, to offer no defense to unjust litigation, to give to anyone that asks seem to be the directions of a teacher who knew nothing about human nature. Jesus believed that ultimately men would not take advantage of love. At Sing Sing Penitentiary there was recently an election for officers of the Mutual Welfare League. The counting of the returns was not completed until one o'clock in the morning. The warden invited those engaged in the count to come over to his house for supper. The convicts walked outside the prison walls without guards, spent an hour with the warden, then went back unguarded to their cells; and some of them were serving life sentences. They were criminals, but they were not mean enough to take advantage of confidence thus reposed in them. Dr. Arnold, of Rugby, governed his difficult school of boys by trusting them. It was commonly said by the boys, "It is a shame to lie to Arnold because he believes you." That is precisely the teaching of Jesus. Of course it does not always work. He failed himself with Judas. But modern scientific pedagogy, penology, and philanthropy are approximating more and more to the principles of Jesus as the methods of social education and redemption. His teaching is that the life of the kingdom of God can be secured only by the great adventure of putting faith in men.

The chief expression of Jesus's faith in human nature was seen in his attitude toward children. When everyone was desiring the kingdom of God he said the children already manifested its characteristics; and he added, "Verily I say unto you, whosoever shall not receive the kingdom of God as a little child, he shall in no wise enter therein" (Mark 10. 13-16). The problem of the regeneration of society is clearly that of the religious and moral education of the next generation.

§ 3. The Treatment of People as Persons

When Jesus's principle of the worth of the individual is

translated into a social program it simply means that each individual is to be treated as a person. It is to be remembered, of course, that in his own case the social experience preceded the formulation of the teaching. It was because he had actually found the significance of treating people as persons that he laid down the doctrine. It needs only to examine the words of Jesus with some care to realize that he said nothing about the masses and nothing about the classes. He did not deal with people in the mass. He thought of each as individually the child of God. He acted toward each person, therefore, with that respect which one accords to a person individually known and esteemed. In the cases of the Samaritan woman, Zacchæus, the rich young ruler, Mary and Martha, the adulteress, there is evident a courtesy and consideration which is entirely compatible with rebuke for wrongdoing.

The Golden Rule, which an American senator curtly dismissed as an iridescent dream, and which is often rather easily postponed to the golden age as an impossible counsel of perfection, was in the mind and practice of Jesus a perfectly simple social attitude. It means, in effect, that we shall have the same sense of the personality of others that we have of our own. In the finer relations of life when they are at their best, notably in that of husband and wife, parent and child, friend and friend, these reciprocal relations of personality are realized. Jesus believed that this attitude could be universalized. The Golden Rule as a social maxim can be stated: "I wish to be treated as a person, my individuality respected, my hopes, aims, efforts appreciated, my failings not excused but forgiven, my rights generously conceded. I never want to be regarded as one of the masses. I shall, therefore, remember that each other person feels as I do, and comport myself toward him, and use all my endeavors that society shall comport itself toward him with respect to his personality."

The most bitter evils of our modern industrial system

arise from the employment of labor in great aggregations so that the personal relation disappears. One of the great difficulties in education is in the fact that children have to be taught in such numbers that the true education, which is the development of persons in all their social relationships, is almost impossible. The failure of the old systems of correction for the vicious and the criminal is in the fact that there is no appeal to the better manhood and womanhood in them. Repression, disgrace, punishment, suspicion never brought about the regeneration of the evil man or woman. Jesus has pointed out the only way of success as the reaffirmation of personality. To work this out is the great problem of modern society. The task of the church is presented in that supreme aspect of Jesus's teaching, that the strongest appeal to personality is in the faith that every person is a child of God, and ought not to be wandering away from his Father (Luke 15).

DIRECTIONS FOR STUDY

1. Review the teaching of Jeremiah and Ezekiel on individualism. What advance did that represent on previous prophetic teaching? How was the thought of Jesus related to that of those prophets?
2. Read Isa 52. 13 to 53. 12. Note that it is a description of the exaltation of the Servant through the willing acceptance of the burdens and woes of others.
3. Compare the philosophy of Victor Hugo's Les Misérables with the teaching of Jesus.
4. Read John 13. 1-17. Note Jesus's teaching of the way of greatness. How does this illustrate the higher individualism?
5. Read Luke 15. Compare the attitude of the scribes and Pharisees and of Jesus regarding the publicans and sinners. What does this indicate as to Jesus's method of social regeneration? Who are our publicans and sinners? What are we to do with them?
6. Read Luke 7. 36-50. Compare the attitude of the Pharisee and of Jesus toward the woman. What was the basis of Jesus's treatment of the woman? Does his method seem practicable?

7. How far does the Golden Rule obtain in a well-constituted family? Could this relation be extended?
8. How far does modern society in its various aspects recognize the worth of the individual, for example, in education, in industry, in penal institutions? What is the trend in this respect?
9. It is sometimes said that Christianity has failed, or that it is impracticable, or that it has never been tried. Which of these statements would be true regarding Jesus's teaching of the worth of the individual?
10. Consider how personal sin is in every case a violation of the personality of somebody.

THE ATTITUDE OF JESUS TOWARD SOCIAL INSTITUTIONS

CHAPTER XXXIII

THE FAMILY

§ 1. The Status of the Jewish Family

No Hebrew institution developed in a more healthy and socially efficient manner than the family. In comparison with other ancient peoples the Jew had a home life that was decidedly significant. Polygamy, which was permitted by the law and had flourished in the earlier periods, had almost disappeared by the time of Christ. The position of the wife had steadily risen in dignity. The children were expected to give honor to both their parents. We have noted that the Jewish system of education centered largely in the home, and that it had some very valuable characteristics. There is every reason to believe that the Jewish home was, in general, a place of large freedom, with a religious atmosphere that had in it much of joy, and that a sincere affection bound together the members of the family (Matt 7. 9-11). Down to the present time the Jew has preserved high ideals of family life, and has fostered them by the precepts and examples of his religion.

The Jewish family in the time of Jesus was not, however, a fully developed institution. While the mother was held in high esteem, yet the inferiority of woman was definitely recognized. The Jew thanked God that he was not born a Gentile, a woman, nor a slave. The children were subject to the father, even though he might be unworthy to exercise authority. Hebrew law had left the provision of divorce somewhat obscure, and there was a marked tendency to interpret the permission with great laxity. The Græco-Roman customs had exerted no little influence in this direction, and had extended the right of divorce to the wife, while the Hebrew law had confined it to the husband. The breaking up of homes by divorce had probably become common enough to constitute a serious menace to the purity of family life. Even the disciples of Jesus thought that marriage without the possibility of escape if necessary would be inexpedient for any man (Matt 19. 10).

§ 2. Jesus's Conception of the Family

The family was to Jesus the significant institution from which he could draw analogies of the kingdom of God. The name for the Infinite Spirit which has become the familiar title on the lips of Christians is the name with which Jesus was first familiar as applied to the humble carpenter in the Nazareth home. The wisdom and love which Joseph exhibited in his family gave to Jesus the sufficient word to express his own experience of God. It was because of what Jesus knew about fathers that he could picture the gracious reception of the foolish prodigal in his father's arms (Luke 15. 11-24), and that he could find parellels between the kindness of human parents and that of God (Matt 7. 9-11).

The family institution was universalized in the social thinking of Jesus, for he spoke of God as the Father not only of himself but of his disciples (Matt 5. 16, 48; 6. 1, 4, 6-15), and he spoke of men as his brethren (Matt 25. 40; 28. 10; compare Heb 2. 11), and as brethren of one another (Matt 5. 22-24; 7. 3; 18. 15, 35). Evidently, he found in the family the nearest approach among men to the social attitudes which he desired to make universal.

Jesus had a large experience of family life, although he did not found a family of his own. If Joseph died before all the children were grown up, Jesus as the oldest of the sons may have had the responsibility of the headship of the home. It would seem that Mary had become accustomed to depend on him in the emergencies that might arise (John 2. 5). He knew, therefore, what it meant to call men brethren.

It is very certain that Jesus did not refrain from marriage on ascetic grounds or because of any light esteem of the institution. In his discussion with the Pharisees (Matt 19. 3-6) he refers to marriage as an original relationship divinely ordained. No word ever fell from his lips of slightest disparagement of family life. For himself with his brief and specific mission, loneliness was part of the supreme sacrifice which he felt called upon to make.

In the teaching of Jesus the normal family relations are rather assumed, but on a few occasions there arose questions of the relations of the members of the family to one another. Once a brother brought before him a matter of a disputed inheritance. He, of course, refused to take the position of judge on a question involving legal rights, but he forcibly laid down the danger of covetousness. Families have become poor indeed through loss of mutual faith and love because they forgot that life consisteth not in the abundance of the things that one possesseth (Luke 12. 13-15). The interesting case of the busy Martha and the meditative Mary exhibits Jesus's tactful defense of one who was misunderstood, but scarcely contributes to our knowledge of his conception of family duties (10. 38-42). More to the point was his condemnation of the casuistry of the scribes who discharged a man of his obligation to provide for his parents if instead he gave the money to the temple (Mark 7. 10-13). Jesus here reaffirmed the law of family duty.

§ 3. Divorce

It is on the difficult question of divorce that the teaching of Jesus on the family is most clearly seen (Matt 19. 3-10; Mark 10. 2-12). He approached the subject from the standpoint of the real meaning of marriage. This he found not, of course, in a consideration of its social origin—Jesus was not a sociologist; nor did he regard it as a contract—he was not a jurist. He saw its fundamental meaning—the union of one man with one woman for life in a bond indissoluble. Whatever permission of divorce the law and society may find it necessary to give, Jesus's conception of marriage is the only tolerable conception if the family, the fundamental unit of society, is to be preserved.

This view of marriage involves the absolute condemnation of polygamy. One person cannot be united in such a bond with more than one person. Divorce practically involves remarriage, for one of the parties if not for both. Jesus assumed that to be the case, and all experience bears out his view. Divorce, therefore, means polygamy, not legal polygamy that a man has an obligation to more than one wife, or a woman to more than one husband, but practical polygamy, for a man has an actual wife and a discarded wife, or a woman has an actual husband and a discarded husband. Such a practice, Jesus said, was virtually a violation of the seventh commandment (John 4. 17f.).

A score of objections immediately suggest themselves to this serious view of marriage. The disciples insisted that in such case it were better for a man not to take the risk of marriage at all (Matt 19. 10). It is to be remembered that Jesus was not concerned with social teaching in the sense that he was offering a program of social organization. We cannot take the teachings of Jesus and make them the laws of the state, or even the *laws* of the church. He was preeminently a religious teacher. He was making appeal to the deepest motives of the human heart. He was telling people the way to live, not the way to make other people live. Indeed, the Pharisees very properly objected to Jesus's teaching that the Mosaic law distinctly permitted divorce (v. 7). Jesus answered them that legal requirements must always be lower than moral obligation. The law can only exact bare justice; it cannot require the generous remission of just dues. The law must permit a debt to be exacted; it cannot require the debtor to forego his rights. But the child of God must forgive.

We see at this point that the social teachings of Jesus really apply only to those who are, first of all, willing to belong to the society of the kingdom of God. It is not society in general that Jesus discusses. He has nothing to say about the kind of rules that it should enact for its government. He says always, first of all, that men and women should be children of God, and then he shows them what is involved in such a relationship as to social attitudes and conduct. The exceedingly significant matter of the relations of the sexes to one another will be based on purity of heart (Matt 5. 8, 27-32). Marriage will be governed by the law of love; not merely love in the sense of passion but patient love, forgiving love, unto seventy times seven, a love that refuses to be vanquished. His teaching was the outgrowth of his experience. He had not the experience of marriage out of which to speak, but it is not difficult to imagine what would have been his attitude if he had been unhappily married. The sublime self-sacrifice of Hosea, whose unconquerable love sought to win back his wayward wife, is an indication of the kind of spirit that Jesus believed must prevail in marriage. It is even possible that he did not sanction divorce in the case of positive unfaithfulness. In the statement as recorded by Mark (10. 11) the exception expressed in Matthew (19. 9 and also 5. 32) does not occur.

It has been the constant error of legislators, both civil and ecclesiastical, to endeavor to embody in law the high family ideal of Jesus. If two people hate each other, they are not likely to be led into a life of love by the legal requirement that they live together. If one breaks the marriage bond, the other on the ground of justice has a right to release. It is for religion to encourage us to forego our rights, not for the law to settle the matter. The state must regulate marriage as best it may in view of the various rights of man, wife, and children that are to be conserved. The teaching of Jesus will ever be the higher demand for the conservation of the great social values of true marriage. The wife of a convicted criminal may be fairly entitled to release from one who has proved unworthy. But noble women who have stood by men who have thus fallen have led them back into righteousness.

With all its shortcomings the family is the strong, sound institution that for the most part it is to-day because of the sacrifice of husband and wife, the mutual patience and forgiveness, the willingness each to see the best in the other, the realization that the great pledge was "for better, for worse." The Christian family is permanently to make its great contribution to human society.

§ 4. The Limits of Family Loyalty

The kingdom of God, that so greatly depends on family love, may also suffer from it. A keen essayist has called attention to the danger of worship in marriage. A true marriage is so infinitely satisfying that it may take the place of infinite interests. Perhaps more often, however, the comfortable seclusion and peace of the home are so attractive that the sheltered members of the family do not care to have a part in the struggle for righteousness. The affection for our own may be essentially selfish if we limit our interests to their welfare and their needs. Jesus saw that sacrificial service to the highest interests of men would often involve a subordination not only of personal interests but of those of the family. It was in connection with the great saying, that one must lose his life in order to find it, that he said that the love of the cause for which he stood must be greater than the love of father, mother, wife or child (Matt 10. 37-39; Luke 14. 26f.).[1]

Jesus went even further than this. He saw that the great

[1] Of course the strong expression that a man is to *hate* his kindred is only a hyperbole to call attention to a comparison of loyalties. It is sufficiently explained by the fact that he is to hate his own life also, which no one would literally do who was using his life in a noble ministry.

ideal of the Kingdom would bring conflict among men. The tyrannies, cruelties, selfishness of human life will not yield without a struggle. He strikingly declared that he had come to set a man at variance against the members of his family (Matt 10. 34-36; Luke 12. 51, 53). He himself experienced want of sympathy among his brothers (Mark 3. 20f.; John 7. 3-5). They did not believe in what he was trying to do. Evidently, there may be higher duty than family loyalty, and when these clash the man who weakly chooses the easier part is unworthy. So men have left fathers who were engaged in unsocial business; they have left home and fortune for some great social crusade; they have taken sides opposed to family interests on questions of social reform. Out of such sacrifice the world has grown better. In the greater movements of social righteousness that are before us in the future it is altogether likely that sacrifice of the same kind will often be required. It was no disparagement of his family when Jesus found his true kindred not in those of his flesh and blood, but in the companions of the spirit (Matt 12. 46-50; Mark 3. 31-35; Luke 8. 19-21).

DIRECTIONS FOR STUDY

1. Review the chapter on "The Family," and consider what kind of institution it had come to be in Jesus's day. What were its points of excellence? In what respects was it unsatisfactory?
2. In what particulars did Jesus use the analogy of the family to illustrate the character of the kingdom of God?
3. Read Rauschenbusch, Christianizing the Social Order, Part III, Chapter II, for a discussion of the way in which the family has reached a marked degree of socialization.
4. To whom did Jesus address his teachings on the subject of marriage? to mankind generally, or to those who were willing to make choice of the kingdom of God? Upon what grounds do you hold your view? What does your view involve as to the significance of Jesus's teaching for modern life?
5. Are those who wish to be followers of Jesus justified in per-

mitting legislation such as that of divorce which they consider contrary to his view of the sanctity of marriage?

6. What would you think of the consistency of a person who, although very unhappily married, should refrain from divorce, and yet should approve of divorce in the case of another person equally unfortunate? Are there any principles which we must apply to ourselves more rigidly than to others?
7. If for reasons which seem socially necessary the state permits divorce, should the church refuse the sanction of its ceremony to divorced persons desiring to remarry? Should the church teach such persons that they are breaking the seventh commandment?
8. Consider the bearing on the subject of divorce of such words of Jesus as Matt 5. 9, 43f.; 6. 14; 7. 1-5, 12; 18. 21-35; Luke 17. 4.
9. Consider the problem of conflicting loyalties to a socially-minded son going into business with a father whose factory employed little children for long hours and in unhealthy conditions.
10. Does the teaching of Jesus upon the family provide us with a social program, or are we still left to study our own problems by the best scientific methods that we can evolve? If the latter is true, what contribution does Jesus make to the modern social problem of the family?

CHAPTER XXXIV

WEALTH AND POVERTY

§ 1. The Absence of an Economic Program

Many schools of economic philosophy have claimed Jesus as their own. Because he told the rich young man to sell everything and give to the poor it has been held that he was a communist. Because he said, "How hardly shall they that have riches enter into the kingdom of God," he has been regarded as an opponent of private ownership of property, and reckoned a socialist. Because, in the parable of the pounds he noted the reward of industry, he has been regarded as a champion of capitalism. Because he said, "The poor ye have always with you," he has been considered an apologist for the inequalities of economic life. But, of course, all these were incidental sayings applicable to the particular circumstances in which they were spoken.

Jesus was not an economic philosopher. He was a religious teacher seeking to show men how to live together, and recognizing the stupendous difficulties in the way of social living which economic conditions create. As in every other case, he went to the heart of the problem and made no effort to settle its special phases.

Jesus accepted the social conditions of his time. He dined with the rich who were highly esteemed (Luke 14. 1), with those also whose wealth was not reckoned respectable (19. 1-10). He was a friend of those of moderate means (Matt 26. 6ff.), even when they were of the despised classes (Luke 5. 29). He accepted financial help from well-to-do women (8. 1-3), and made no suggestion to any of them that they should give up their wealth. There were rich friends to minister to him at the last (Matt 27. 57f.). He himself earned money and knew the responsibilities of economic life. The apostolic band had a common purse in which they kept their funds for their necessary expenses, and out of which there was always something for the poor (John 13. 29).

The relation of wealth to the kingdom of God was, of course, a most important consideration, and Jesus clearly presented the principles which must control those who are seeking this condition of social righteousness.

§ 2. Wealth a Secondary Good

His most fundamental principle was that wealth is not a primary object of desire. He saw in his own day what is so evident in ours, that a large part of the tyranny, cruelty, bitterness, misery, that brutalize society arises from the fact that wealth is regarded as a primary good. Of course when men say they do not want money for its own sake but for what it can procure they are only confusing the issue. Wealth is not gold and silver and bank notes. Wealth *is* what money procures. Men and women greatly desire good things—houses, lands, furniture, jewels, comforts, luxuries. Jesus insisted that life does not consist of things (Luke 12. 15); they are secondary. We want to be served, and money can procure all kinds of service, removing the disagreeables from our path, supplying us with all those conditions that make life easy and pleasant. Jesus found for himself and taught out of his experience that the richest blessing of life consists in rendering service rather than in securing it (Matt 20. 26-28).

It is important to remember that Jesus's teaching about wealth was not directed toward millionaires. There were probably none such in Palestine. He was speaking to prosperous farmers (Luke 12. 13-21), to men who could afford to live well (Luke 16. 19-31), to theologians who were money-lovers (16. 14). He was speaking quite as much to people who greatly desired money as to people who possessed it (Matt 6. 24-34; Luke 12. 22-34). He said that the kingdom of God does not come—that is to say, the right social order does not come—because men are so engrossed with money-getting that they are not willing to give attention to preparing for it. The supreme good is lost because we are so busy about subordinate goods (Matt 13. 22).

Wealth was not the great object of Jesus's own life. He spent himself in the endeavor to bring men into such relations with one another and with God that love should obtain among them, and all the fruits of selfishness should disappear. He urged as the supreme end, "Seek ye first the kingdom of God, and his righteousness" (6. 33).

It is for each generation to decide what is involved in a social order founded on the great principle of love and then to bend every effort to bring it to pass. We cannot go to the teaching of Jesus to find out how industry should be organized, but we can derive from his life and words that the supreme considerations must not be dividends, but must be the manhood of the workers, the sweetness of their homes, the womanliness of their wives, the hopefulness of their children. We can quote no teaching of Jesus on the subject of the tenure of land, but the principles of generous justice and of love make it clear that we must use the land to grow men, while speculative profits to a few people are unimportant.

In general, wherever a human good and an economic good are in opposition, Jesus's own practice was to choose the human good. That is his teaching to the men of to-day. He believed that this would prove a practical doctrine. It is important to remember the second member of the great sentence, "Seek ye first the kingdom of God and his righteousness, and all these things shall be added unto you." He expected that the kingdom of God would have an economic basis. He knew that people required food and clothing. He reminded them that God also knew it. He insisted that a rightly organized society careful of human values would be an economically prosperous society (Matt 6. 24-34).

§ 3. THE MORAL DANGER OF WEALTH

Jesus's advice to the rich young ruler to sell his possessions and give to the poor (Matt 19. 16-22) is doubtless to be explained as a special discipline which that luxury-loving young man needed. But the discourse that followed was very pointed on the moral danger of wealth (vv. 23-30). Great pains have been taken in the endeavor to explain away the serious statement, "It is hard for rich men to enter into the kingdom of heaven." Indeed, the phrase seems already to have been softened in the Gospel of Mark (10. 24). But Jesus was stating a perfectly simple fact. Great social reforms involving economic changes are not easily contemplated by men whose interests are bound up in the constitution of things as they are. It is much easier to believe in the abolition of slavery if one does not happen to own any slaves than if one has a fortune invested in that type of property. It is a simpler matter to work for the prohibition of child labor if one has no stock in a mill that employs children. We can vote any amount of old-age pensions if somebody else is to pay the taxes. We have been recently reminded that Macaulay cleverly said that the law of gravitation would not have been accepted down to the present day if it had interfered with vested interests.

Let it be repeated that Jesus was not speaking of millionaires but of the people who had goods in contrast to the people who had not. The very possession of goods constitutes the moral danger, that we shall care more for them than for great social interests. It is the danger of selfishness.

There is the added danger of obtuseness. The facts of wealth and poverty become so common that men grow used to them. The rich man clothed in purple and fine linen knows nothing of the poor wretch lying at his gate (Luke 16. 19-31). It is no concern of his. He regards his property as his own to be expended as he pleases. If other people are not so fortunate or so clever or so industrious, so much the worse for them. It is a fact that the poor are more likely to aid one another than the well-to-do. The urgency of the kingdom of God is not felt by those whose lives already are guarded and surrounded with comfort. *"The care of this world, and the deceitfulness of riches, choke the word"* (Matt 13. 22).

§ 4. The Responsibility of Wealth

Jesus's admonition to the young ruler was not a universal teaching. He never suggested that all wealth should be abandoned. It cannot be supposed that he would not see the futility of distributing all wealth to the poor. It would mean a collapse of industry with no gain except the temporary easing of some misery. Moreover, it is evident that while he regarded wealth as involving danger, he recognized its power, and consequently the responsibility of its administration. He used the strange parable of the unjust steward (Luke 16. 1-13) to point out that shrewd men employ money to make friends who will stand by them in the future, so good men ought to use money in such a way that the great human friendship may be furthered.

In a complex society this principle must have many and large applications. In the society of Jesus's day, where there were no philanthropic institutions, educational foundations, missionary enterprises, he made the only application that was available—generous and sacrificial giving. His conception of the fraternal character of the society of the children of God led to the conclusion that the wealthy brother must give to the poorer brother. Wherever there is need there must be responsibility (Matt 5. 42; 19. 16-22; Mark 10. 17-22; Luke 6. 30; 12. 33f.; 18. 18-23). When Zacchæus caught the spirit of Jesus he began to be generous with his money (19. 1-10).

Jesus did not deal with the problem of the danger of

pauperizing men by liberal gifts. It was part of his fundamental faith in men that they would respond to love, love begetting love, sacrifice begetting sacrifice. But here, again, we must not think of Jesus as offering us a program. It is as necessary for us to apply our sociology and economic science to the conditions of our life as to make use of antiseptic surgery for the wounded instead of pouring in oil and wine. We follow Jesus when we have the spirit of the good Samaritan.

§ 5. Wealth and Justice

We are more concerned to-day with economic justice than with any kind of charity. Why did not Jesus speak more clearly on this subject? We miss in his teaching the burning words of the prophets against the rich who oppressed the poor, the monopolists who joined field to field until there was no room. He did not even speak against slavery, that great curse of the ancient world, but he went deeper than that. He laid down the Golden Rule of justice (Matt 7. 12). He put persons above property. If he had himself possessed a slave, he might not have freed him, because conditions were not ripe for the general manumission of slaves. It would have upset the whole social order. But Jesus and his slave would have lived together on fraternal terms, and the problem would have worked itself out in mutual service.

He did not denounce the rich, but, rather, laid the responsibility upon the rich to meet the conditions created by the institution of wealth. He also reminded the man suffering from injustice that his clamorous demands for his share had likewise their moral dangers (Luke 12. 13-15). He expected that the kingdom of God would be economically sound, not by an uprising of the poor to confiscate the possessions of the rich, but by the generous realization of the rich that the responsibility of removing all injustice was in their hands. It worked out that way immediately with Zacchæus (Luke 19. 1-10). It is our best hope for a new social order to-day. Unlimited competition, industrial war, class antagonism will not help us. Our only hope is that on both sides of all economic questions we shall have a generous resolve to do justice. Then we shall have to determine scientifically with great pains and experiment what that justice will be. Jesus will not do that work for us. We must not expect to find in his teachings schemes of profit-sharing, plans of industrial democracy, details of minimum wage and maximum labor. These matters change with social conditions, and must be the subject of continual readjustment in accordance with scientific knowledge. But the great human motives of mutual respect and mutual friendship, the emphasis of duties above rights, the supremacy of persons over property—these come to us from Jesus; these are the crying need of the social life of to-day.

DIRECTIONS FOR STUDY

1. Read Luke 1 and 2; Mark 6. 1-3; John 19. 25-27. Note each statement that gives any suggestion as to the financial condition of Jesus's family.
2. Consider modern conditions in which wealth is made the supreme good in family and social life, in industry, in national policies, in international relations. What are the consequences of that attitude?
3. When Jesus said that the cares of this age and the deceitfulness of riches choke the word (Matt 13. 22), could his message have any application to a poor man? Is it possible for the poor to make wealth the supreme good?
4. Consider the moral dangers of wealth in modern society on the basis of Jesus's teaching. How much would one have to own in order to become subject to these dangers?
5. Consider how vested interests in modern life halt the progress of the kingdom of God.
6. Note that the parable of the rich man and Lazarus (Luke 16. 19-31) was spoken in response to the scorn of the Pharisees (vv. 14f.). Using the common imagery of the time regarding the future life, Jesus taught not that all rich men are bad and all poor men are good, but that when true values are really

measured they may be very different from what our superficial property system assumes. What did Jesus really condemn in this particular rich man?

7. Read Luke 16. 1-13. The trickery of the steward was not, of course, commended by Jesus. This is a case where a moral principle is illustrated from an immoral example. Jesus shows that worldly men know the value of money in making friends. What, then, is his teaching about the use that a good man ought to make of his money?
8. Why did not Jesus discuss right and wrong ways of getting wealth? Does his teaching have anything to do with this pressing modern problem? On what grounds would you say that a man who gets money by oppression and gives it away in charity does not follow the teachings of Jesus?
9. Consider the possibility of settling economic differences when both sides are more anxious to give justice than to get it. Is it conceivable that earnest Christians may adopt that attitude in commercial transactions, industrial organizations, and even in international affairs? Is there any great hope for human society except in this attitude? Do we not, then, see why the social teachings of Jesus are religious?
10. Why has slavery disappeared from Christendom? What similar conditions of social injustice are sure to disappear? What is the practical program to secure such results?

CHAPTER XXXV

ORGANIZED SOCIETY

§ 1. THE ABSENCE OF A POLITICAL PROGRAM

JESUS grew up in a political order that was full of social complication. There was the municipal jurisdiction of the Jewish elders who administered the Mosaic law. This was accepted without question as satisfactory. There was the higher jurisdiction of the temple authorities, which Jesus recognized in common with his countrymen by paying his taxes (Matt 17. 24-27), and by commanding obedience to its regulations (Matt 8. 4; Mark 1. 44; Luke 5. 14; 17. 14). There was the territorial sovereignty of Herod Antipas which was essentially alien and pagan and for both reasons highly objectionable to the Jews. There was the overlordship of the Roman empire, which was bitterly resented because it meant the contemptible subjection of the proud Hebrew race. There was in all of this the intense political expectation of national independence through the coming of the kingdom of God.

Jesus accepted the political situation. He did not denounce the Herods or the Romans. He accepted the friendship of the publicans, though their business was to levy taxes upon the people to support a foreign tyranny. When the politicians tried to make him take sides on the question of paying tribute he said to them, "You know what you have to give to Cæsar; do you also know what is due to God?" (Matt 22. 15-22; Mark 12. 13-17; Luke 20. 20-26). Jesus looked for the new kingdom, but its political aspects he did not discuss. Who should rule in an ideal social order? This question he did not answer. He did not offer a political program, because he went deeper, to the discussion of motives.

It is particularly to be noted that Jesus did not consider the possibility of a state becoming nominally Christianized with Christian men in positions of responsibility. He told the Pharisees that political organization had inevitably involved compromise of moral ideals. The Mosaic law was not satisfactory for a society in which men and women should wish to live as the children of God. It could not be, for the reason that real righteousness cannot be exacted by statute (Matt 19. 7f.; Mark 10. 4f.). The practical program for the government of a state whose people are not yet Christian Jesus did not work out. He was content to insist upon the principles that must apply to the healthy organization of society.

§ 2. Love Instead of Force

The world has always believed in force. People must be compelled to obey law. Nations must get what they want by the exercise of superior power. Justice must be secured by compulsion. The ultimate force in human society is physical. The sword is the symbol of sovereignty.

Jesus had seen this method in operation, and doubtless had seen that it produces a fairly workable society. The strong hand of Herod the Great had put down the bandits of Galilee, and had brought order into the affairs of Palestine. The might of the Roman empire had brought peace into the world over a large area, though it was the peace of the suzerain over the dependent. The fact that a man who sought to injure his neighbor was in danger of being injured himself did much toward preventing aggression, though the strongest generally gained the day. In fact, the world of Jesus's day was much like the world of our day. A fair degree of justice was secured by the organization of society on the principle of securing people in their rights by force· yet still, to some extent, inevitably might made right.

Jesus saw the inadequacy of the policy of force. It may prevent a man stealing if he thinks he will be found out, but it does not prevent him from wanting to steal. If he is caught stealing and imprisoned, it makes him sorry that he was caught, but not sorry that he sinned. One may obtain legal redress for an injury, but he has gained the enmity of the beaten party and the issue is hatred and the hope of revenge. Blow for blow may satisfy the feeling of outraged dignity, but the quarrel is increased by the conflict.

Jesus dared to believe in the kingdom of God. He believed that men could live together in mutual respect and love. He believed that a society could be founded on love. His countrymen wanted the kingdom of God when freedom, justice, peace should reign. He told them that they could have the life of the kingdom if they would make the great adventure. He said that it was better to forego rights than to fight for them. He put it very definitely in the prohibition of the resistance of him that is evil (Matt 5. 39). Aggression upon one's rights is best met by yielding more rights; tyranny and oppression are best met by giving to the oppressor more than he demands; importunity is best met by compliance (vv. 40-42). It is not merely non-resistance, not merely a passive acceptance of wrong, it is a positive endeavor to overcome evil with good.

This fundamental teaching was put into its most extreme form in the statement, "The meek shall inherit the earth" (v. 5). In Jesus's day the Romans inherited the earth by the might of their legions. As the apocalypses showed, the world empires had all, like ravening beasts, taken the world by force. The Jewish hope of the kingdom of God was that celestial armies should destroy the terrestrial tyrants, and the saints should inherit the earth under the strong hand of the Almighty (Dan 2. 44; 7. 26f.; 8.25; compare the description of the destruction of Rome (Rev 18). But Jesus proposed the principle of love as the conquering power in human society. He believed that men would yield to love and that by love alone could society be regenerated.

If we really want to understand Jesus, there is nothing

gained by attempting to explain away his words. Apparently, there was no one present to ask the questions that men immediately ask to-day: Shall we allow a woman or a child to be beaten without interfering? Shall we abolish our police, leave our property unprotected, and tell the criminals that we love them? Shall we disband our armies, let our battleships decay, and invite the nations to a love feast? Perhaps these questions were not worth asking, and were not worth answering. When they did ask him a question of that kind Jesus told them that they were living in a society founded on force and they knew perfectly well what it implied (Matt 22. 21). We must note again that the teaching of Jesus was not directed to human society as a whole. It was for those who were willing to become members of the kingdom of God. The principles of that kingdom cannot be made prescriptive for a mixed society. Just as a Christian might take Jesus's attitude toward divorce so far as he was himself concerned, but ought not as a voter, a legislator, a judge to force it upon others, so we have no right forcibly to insist that our fellow men shall follow the law of love.

Jesus was not a teacher of political science any more than of political economy or of sociology. His teachings were not offered as a substitute for careful scientific endeavor to find the best means of organizing human society. He pointed out that selfishness and force are crude and inefficient agents, which will never be competent to bring about a socialized humanity. We must learn how to apply the universal solvent to the problems of the social organism. For himself Jesus dared to begin to live as if the kingdom of God were here, and to treat men as if they were members of the Kingdom. His summons to his followers is a challenge to join him in that great adventure of faith.

§ 3. The Cost of Social Regeneration

Jesus did not choose this apparently impracticable ideal

without careful consideration of all that it involved. The story of the temptation, given to us in picturesque parable, indicates that he saw the possibility of a successful revolutionary movement (Matt 4. 8-10; Luke 4. 5-8). Why should he not have been another Judas Maccabeus, leading his people in a splendid fight for freedom, and then with all the prestige of military success organize a society in which the principles of justice should be supreme? Why should not the kingdom of God be brought about in some such fashion? Why should he not ally himself with the Prince of this world, and "to do a great right, do a little wrong"—wrong, at least, for him? That it was a real temptation to the young patriotic leader of men is evident from his presentation of the experience in parable form to his disciples. But he saw the futility of a policy of force and definitely renounced it.

Yet Jesus did not expect that love would succeed at once. Indeed, he said very clearly that it would not. He promised his followers persecution (Matt 5. 10-12). He soon realized that his own teaching would lead him to the cross. When Peter objected he recognized a renewal of the old temptation to adopt the methods of current politics instead of the methods of spiritual obligation (Matt 16. 21-26; Mark 8. 31-37; Luke 9. 22-25). Jesus never said that it would be an easy matter to overcome human passion and selfishness by love. Indeed, he told his disciples that he sent them forth *"as lambs in the midst of wolves"* (Luke 10. 3).

Did Jesus himself fail or succeed? He was crucified. The preaching of love and righteousness brought him only to the cross. Yet after many years Julian said, "Galilæan, thou hast conquered!" We are afraid that the meek will not inherit the earth, so we do not dare to attempt the experiment. The difficulty is that we want to cash in our meekness too soon. The spirit of Jesus has made some progress in human society. Love has largely superseded force in family organization, in the discipline of schools, in the treatment of the insane. We are just beginning the experiment in the treatment of the delinquent, the vicious, the criminal, and with extraordinarily encouraging results. This might be a pertinent question for scientific inquiry: Where has the method of Jesus ever been seriously and patiently tried without significant success? Of course nations have never tried it. That seems impossible: if any nation would go to war with thee and take away a province, surrender another province also. The long, wicked story of national greed seems to establish the futility of such an attitude. It will be interesting if the experiment of a Christian nation can ever be tried. Of course mere pacificism is not Christianity. A nation that wished to test Jesus's faith in love would have to do more than refuse to fight. It would have to live, first of all, in sacrificial service, and in generous justice toward the peoples of the earth. In fact, the members of that nation would have to choose to be members of the kind of society that Jesus established. We only confuse the significance of the teaching of Jesus when we think that we can make a single element of it effective, especially when the element selected may be one that saves us from trouble and expense.

§4. The Duty of Aggressive Righteousness

Love is least of all negative. It is not a mere endurance of evils without protest. It is concerned with human welfare. It is eagerly solicitous to bring about what is good. Jesus wanted to bring his people to God, that they might live in filial love and obedience with him. But he found them treating God as a Judge from whom they were trying to secure acquittal by fulfilling legal obligations. The scribes and Pharisees were largely responsible for this attitude. Jesus opposed it. He pointed out that inevitably it resulted in hypocrisy. Everything religious was done for show and for credit. He insistently denounced such conduct. He warned the people against hypocrisy in almsgiving (Matt

6. 2-4), in prayer (vv. 5-15), in fasting (vv. 16-18). He said that the conduct of unsafe public teachers must be tested—*"By their fruits ye shall know them"* (7. 15-23). When the Pharisees entered into conflict with him he did not decline the issue. He showed the hypocrisy of their casuistic reasonings (Mark 7. 1-13). He pronounced woes upon them for their selfishness and unethical legalism (Matt 23). That he could be stern, however, without personal ill feeling may be seen in the pathetic lament with which this terrible condemnation of the Pharisees is concluded (vv. 37-39).

Love is not incompatible with a burning indignation. When theological bitterness overcame humanity Jesus looked upon his opponents *"with anger, being grieved at the hardening of their heart"* (Mark 3. 5). When theological bitterness went to the point of seeing only evil in the very deeds of goodness he pointed out the awful danger of "an eternal sin," a perversion that would bring one into a state beyond hope of faith, or love, or pardon (Matt 12. 22-45; Mark 3. 22-30; Luke 11. 14-23, 29-32).

Even the teachings against the use of force are to be interpreted in harmony with the exercise of an ethical authority, such as that which impelled Jesus to dismiss the traffickers from the temple courts (Matt 21. 12f.; Mark 11. 15-18; Luke 19. 45-48; John 2. 13-22). Compliance with unfair demands is for the purpose of winning the aggressor by love, but this is not incompatible with a wise discretion when wicked men seek to take advantage of one's compliance. So Jesus would not allow his enemies to trick him into treasonable speech (Matt 22. 15-40; Mark 12. 13-34; Luke 20. 20-40). When he sent forth the disciples as "sheep in the midst of wolves," he immediately added another metaphor of counsel to be *"wise as serpents, and harmless as doves"* (Matt 10. 16).

Jesus's own aggressive righteousness is seen in the strange story of the healing of the demoniac (Mark 5. 1-20). Whatever may have been the cause of the loss of the swine, it seems clear that in Jesus's reckoning a man was worth more than many swine. That is dangerous doctrine, as so much of the doctrine of sacrificial love is. It does not bring peace but a sword. Jesus exhorted his followers to be true to their great task, even though families were divided and persecutions sustained (Matt 10. 34-39).

DIRECTIONS FOR STUDY

1. Is there any fundamental difference between the government under which Jesus lived and our modern democracy? What different application of the principles of Jesus would this involve from that which he himself made?
2. There are those who hold that the laws and government of modern society, inasmuch as they require police, law courts, etc., cannot be conducted in accordance with the principles of Jesus; they therefore decline to participate as citizens in the government. Is this attitude justifiable?
3. Read John 6. 1-15. Why did not Jesus allow the people to make him king? Could he not have been more effective if he had possessed political power? Does this mean that one cannot be a disciple of Jesus and at the same time hold political office? What is the difference between following Jesus and imitating him?
4. Why is the doctrine of nonresistance stated by itself an insufficient statement of the attitude of Jesus?
5. Consider the Juvenile Courts, the prison farms, the parole systems, the honor systems, the Mutual Welfare Leagues in several penitentiaries. How far are these in accordance with the brotherly treatment which Jesus prescribed, inasmuch as they still hold the prisoner in restraint?
6. Do the following programs violate the teaching of Jesus by substituting force for love?—the prohibition of the liquor traffic, the suppression of vice, compulsory education, taxation for the common good, compulsory service as witness or juror? What should be the attitude of the Christian on these matters?
7. Will the loyal disciple of Jesus suffer persecution to-day? Consider some respects in which this may be the price to be paid for the regeneration of modern society.
8. Is the opportunity of aggressive righteousness sufficient to

secure the development of those virile activities that war has produced in the past? In other words, can real Christianity be saved from softness?

9. Can war be conducted without hatred? What is the proper attitude of the Christian toward war?
10. Suppose the United States should abolish the army and navy, announcing that we should not resort to arms under any circumstances, would that fulfill Jesus's doctrine of the substitution of love for force? If not, what else would be necessary? What practical steps are possible in this direction?

CHAPTER XXXVI

THE INSTITUTIONS OF RELIGION

§ 1. THE TEST OF RELIGIOUS INSTITUTIONS

JESUS grew up in a certain religious environment. As we have seen, the Judaism of his day had a large ritualism that had been gradually developed, and to which accretions had come from many sources. It was elaborately institutionalized. At the same time it had elements of moral and spiritual power. His first religious awakening seems to have been in connection with the great festival of the Jewish Passover. His most solemn legacy to his disciples was spoken at the celebration of that same feast. The Jewish Scriptures were his constant inspiration, quotations from them coming naturally from his lips. The synagogue was the place of his early religious training, and continued to be dear to him as the place of worship and as an opportunity to teach (Luke 4. 16; Matt 4. 23).

Jesus believed that in the religion of Israel spiritual values had been revealed that were to be found nowhere else (John 4. 22). But he was very sure that spiritual religion must transcend the institutions of Judaism, and that ultimate religion was wholly outside of institutions, and was a direct spiritual relationship with God (vv. 21-24).

His test of a religious institution was pragmatic. He did not ask whether it was old, whether it was necessary for the creed, whether it had high ecclesiastical sanction. He did not even ask whether it was divine, for that would have been to beg the question. He asked whether it was religiously useful. The supreme test of a religious institution is expressed in his keen evaluation, *"The sabbath was made for man, and not man for the sabbath*" (Mark 2. 27). To say that the Sabbath was divinely ordained and, therefore, should be observed was to beg the question and was to set one immediately to the task of legal definition. To say that the Sabbath was divinely ordained for man's highest welfare and, therefore, should be used for his highest welfare, was to set one to a study of the social opportunities of this most valuable gift of time.

Jesus, therefore, found the test of all forms in the sincerity of their observance. Almsgiving, prayer, fasting are of no value in themselves. In so far as they are performed for the purpose of giving an appearance of religiousness they are positively harmful. They are of value when they are actually the expression of love, aspiration, contrition (Matt 6. 1-18).

The temple as the great central institution of Judaism was sacred to Jesus. He was grieved that the building, which the prophet had hoped was to be the house of prayer for all peoples, should have been turned into a place of sacrilegious traffic (Matt 21. 12f.; Mark 11. 15-17; Luke 19. 45f.). Yet he saw that the inevitable outcome of the Jewish attitude was conflict with Rome and the destruction of the temple (Matt 24. 1f.; Mark 13. 1f.; Luke 21. 5f.). But men could worship God without a temple (John 4. 21-24).

One religious institution Jesus definitely condemned because of its harmfulness. It was obscuring truth. It was leading the people into legalism. This was "the tradition of the elders." In the orthodox view the body of oral law had come down from Moses, side by side with the written law. It had the authority of his great name, but Jesus saw that it tended to obscure social obligation. It exalted the letter above the spirit, externals above essentials, ceremonialism above humanity. He swept it out of consideration (Matt 15. 1-20; Mark 7. 1-23). He set up his inevitable ethical test. The tradition of the elders did not make for truth, purity, honor, righteousness, love among men; therefore whatever it was, and whence-ever it came, it was not good.

§ 2. The New Wine in Fresh Wineskins

Jesus was not an iconoclast. He felt himself connected with the great religious life of the past. He believed that his life and teaching were in no wise contrary to what the prophets and the law had done for Israel, but, rather, an enlargement and completion of their work (Matt 5. 17-20). He founded his own faith on the Scriptures. He regarded himself as one with the prophets, and, indeed, called himself by that name (Matt 13. 57; Luke 13. 33).

But he held that all inherited custom is subservient to the needs of life. This came out most significantly in a discussion about fasting. Jesus had himself fasted in a time of profound moral struggle when the conditions seemed to require it; but he did not regard the traditional fasting as significant. He told the objectors that those who were sad should fast, not those who were rejoicing in a great gospel. Then he gave them the striking figure that new wine must be put into fresh wineskins (Matt 9. 17; Mark 2. 22; Luke 5. 37f.). He saw the inevitable break up of old forms as the new spirit sought fitting expression.

So Jesus plainly taught that the old law must be enlarged to meet the new ethical outlook. The *lex talionis* that seemed simple justice in the earlier days was not a rule for the kingdom of God (Matt 5. 38ff.). The elaborate distinction between the clean and unclean foods, which had held so important a place in Jewish custom, Jesus simply put aside as insignificant. With his keen ethical insight he said that a man was not defiled by what he ate, but by the evil that came out of his heart (Matt 15. 15-20; Mark 7. 17-23).

Jesus made the Sabbath a new day by laying emphasis on the deeds of love that should be performed (Matt 12. 1-14;

Mark 2. 23 to 3. 6; Luke 6. 1-11; 13. 10-16). Thus he carried over all the values of the sacred day and freed it from its burdens. He made the Old Testament a new book, freely criticizing its imperfect morality (Matt 5. 31f., 38; 19. 8; Mark 10. 5), but constantly drawing from it inspiration, and finding its supreme values in the teaching of the love of God and the love of man (Matt 22. 37-40). It was no longer necessary for expert scribes to give the interpretation of its noble words. Anyone could gain from the Scriptures what the Scriptures had for his need.

Holding all forms subservient to the spiritual life which they were to express, Jesus laid no emphasis upon any specific religious institution. He accepted the baptism of John because that striking ceremony was the means employed for expressing a desire to enter the new kingdom (Matt 3. 13-17; Mark 1. 9-11; Luke 3. 21f.). He seems to have continued John's baptismal ministry for a time (John 3. 22; 4. 1f.). After that there is no evidence that baptism was employed until the disciples made it the inaugural rite of the new church (Acts 2. 38). Jesus at the Last Supper used the bread and wine of the meal as one of his most impressive parables, telling the disciples that the broken bread was his broken body and the wine was the blood of the new covenant, poured out for them (Matt 26. 26-29; Mark 14. 22-25; Luke 22. 19f.). It was his last meal with them, and he bade them to remember the fellowship which had united them, and to think of him always as the Companion at their board. Their common meals were to be sacramental. Jesus was not so much instituting a ceremonial as he was asserting the reality of a fellowship which death could not destroy. Strangely enough, his simple act of kindly condescension at this same feast, the washing of the disciples' feet, intended as an example of service and a gentle rebuke of their contentions (John 13. 1-17), has been supposed by some to have been an authoritative institution. But, of course, it was the spirit, and not the act, that was important. Jesus did not overthrow one legalism in order to create another.

§ 3. The Religious Community and the Kingdom of God

Jesus did found a religious community. It had no organization. It had no constitution. Its terms of membership were willingness to do the will of God (Mark 3. 34; Luke 8. 21). It would have been difficult at any time to tell who were members of it. Jesus even went so far as to say, *"He that is not against us is for us"* (Mark 9. 40; Luke 9. 50). There was a very intimate community of the Master and the twelve apostles (Mark 3. 13-19; Luke 6. 12-16). A larger number followed him as his disciples (Mark 3. 13; Luke 6. 13-17; 10. 1-24). There were many godly women among the company (8. 1-3). An early tradition indicates that there were more than five hundred that regarded themselves as his followers (1 Cor 15. 6). Only a few of these people gave up their occupation. Most of them remained in their homes and continued in their business (Luke 10. 38-42; 19. 1-10; John 11. 1-3). There was no organization. They did not meet in societies. They had no common name. They had only the common feeling that Jesus had shown them the way of eternal life, the way to prepare for the kingdom of God (John 6. 6-8). They constituted, therefore, a more or less undefined body of people to whom Jesus could give his message.

It is fundamental to an understanding of the teaching of Jesus that the character of this religious community should be recognized. His teachings thus become intelligible. They were directed to those who had made the great decision to do the will of God. They were not offered as a program for an unregenerate society. They were offered as a challenge to those who were willing to make the great adventure of living as if the kingdom of God had come. Jesus expected that the number of these would increase as the mustard seed grows (Matt 13. 31f.). He looked for his ideals to permeate society as leaven changes the character of the flour (v. 33). He believed that the life that was thus lived would prove so attractive that men would eagerly desire it (vv. 44f.).

Naturally this religious community would take to itself organization. Jesus was not concerned with that. He was concerned with the wine of truth, not with the wineskins that might hold it. He was very sure that the old forms of social organization were inadequate to contain the revolutionizing doctrines of justice and love. He left others to provide the new wineskins, only he warned them that they must be flexible.

It was only natural that when the centripetal force of Jesus's personality was withdrawn the instinct of coherence should lead his disciples to group themselves more closely. The primitive church was the natural result. Of course it regarded itself as springing from Jesus. It carried over the sacred sign of baptism, which Jesus had accepted at the inauguration of his ministry. It kept alive its sense of fellowship with the Christ whom it worshiped by a frequent observance of the Feast of Remembrance.

Some organization became inevitable at once. This was naturally formed upon the model of the synagogue and of the Greek societies common at the time (James 2. 2). The officers were the *elders,* those same men of standing, wisdom, and maturity, whom we have found from the earliest times taking the leadership in every kind of organization (Acts 14. 23). Other officers were appointed as emergencies arose (6. 1-6; 1 and 2 Tim; Titus).

None of these things was established by Jesus. He seems to have been very little concerned with institutions. All of them naturally took their rise from the character of the apostolic group which had lived with Jesus. They were developed in the religious groups in which the principles of the kingdom were taught and practiced, as the fascinating story of the book of the Acts of the Apostles narrates. Why should not those groups become so large, inclusive, significant, that they should bring the whole world into their membership? This the church accepted as its commission (Matt 28. 18-20). How that splendid conception merged again into that of the church-state, how the teachings of Jesus became institutionalized, how the fresh wineskins grew old again, is the familiar history of the Christian Church. Jesus's own test of the value of religious institutions was forgotten, and they were regarded as being significant in themselves. The scribes and Pharisees often reappeared in the course of Christianity.

It would seem that Jesus is bringing again to our modern life the new wine of truth. Have we the forms and institutions in which it can be contained, or may it be that there are some things which we have come to value in themselves instead of testing them by the standard of their religious ministry to human need? Certainly, the truth will give us the freedom to keep all that is good bequeathed us by the past, but to retain nothing that fetters us and prevents us from expressing the spirit and the principles of Jesus.

DIRECTIONS FOR STUDY

1. Review the discussion of the oral law, pages 34f. and 170, and consider why Jesus regarded it as an institution harmful to religion.
2. Review the discussion of the Sabbath in Chapter XVI. How far did Jesus observe the Sabbath in accordance with the law? What was the ground of his free religious attitude toward the Sabbath?
3. Consider to what extent throughout his life Jesus was an orthodox Jew. Enumerate the instances in which he conformed to the practices of his people. Was this a mere outward compliance or did he find religious value in the observance? What was his general attitude toward a ceremonial that had been inherited from the past?
4. What is the proper attitude for us to take to-day toward the

ceremonies and institutions of religion that have been handed down to us?

5. Consider that Jesus drew continual inspiration from the Scriptures, although he did not regard them as binding his free thought and action. How can we gain most spiritual help from the Bible to-day?
6. Is it necessary to consider that Jesus actually intended to establish the kind of church to which we belong in order to gain religious benefit from the church? In what sense are we justified in calling it the Church of Christ?
7. What is the spiritual value of the Christian sacraments? Do they meet the test which Jesus applied to the ceremonies of his own time?
8. What ought to be the relation between the modern religious community and the idea of the kingdom of God? What are the social responsibilities of the church?
9. The Roman Church has laid emphasis upon its immutability, that it is always and everywhere the same. What is the value of immutability in religion?
10. Do the religious differences of our times relate more to the institutions of religion or to its inner meaning? If Jesus had intended to give specific directions for the establishment of new religious institutions, could he not easily have been more definite? Consider some points of difference among Christians which might have been averted by a few clear directions. What does the absence of these indicate?

CONCLUSION

CHAPTER XXXVII

THE SOCIAL TEACHINGS OF JESUS AND THE PROPHETS IN THE MODERN WORLD

§ 1. The Inadequacy of Literalism

If the social teachings of the prophets and of Jesus are to be regarded as definite directions which are to be obeyed in modern society, we are impressed at once by the large number of important subjects with which they do not deal. If a list of one hundred of the most vitally important problems of to-day were to be carefully made, it is doubtful whether any definite statements susceptible of *literal* application could be found in the entire Bible upon more than half a dozen of those problems. It is not by any means certain that a positive regulation could be found that would fully apply to a single one.

These are some of our most pressing questions: The rate of wages, the minimum wage, hours of labor, conditions of labor, the employment of women and children, the right of free contract, trades unionism, collective bargaining, the open or closed shop, the boycott, the strike, the lockout, profit-sharing, pensions, prison labor, immigration, direct and indirect taxation, tenure and taxation of land, the rights of inheritance, all the problems connected with the various theories of Socialism. Then there are woman suffrage and the entire question of feminism. There is the whole range of political questions even so fundamental as to what constitutes the best form of government, whether cities should be ruled by many elected officials or by commissions. There are the more definitely ethical questions of international character, involving peace and war, arbitration, the government of inferior peoples. Jesus and the prophets had absolutely nothing to say on any of these matters.

When we turn to problems more definitely religious the inadequacy of literalism equally appears. Should religion be taught in the public schools? If so, what religion should be taught? What methods should be employed? Should it be intrusted to the regular teachers, to the minister of the church, or to specially appointed teachers? How should Sunday be observed? Should the best ideals of the Hebrew sabbath be transferred to it? If so, what are the limits of proper activity on this day? Should people ride to church in public vehicles? Should the church have baseball games on Sunday afternoon? No literal directions on these problems are to be found in the prophets or the Gospels?

The expansion of the church in the last century has produced a maze of difficult problems of ecclesiastical and missionary policy. Should many denominations establish churches in a new frontier town? If a denomination regards itself as specifically commissioned to present important truth, is it justified in refraining from pressing forward, no matter what other churches may be already ministering to the people? How far may pagan customs be tolerated by Christianity—for example, if a husband of several wives become a Christian, shall he be obliged to put away all but one of them? Shall native churches formed among people of low intelligence be allowed self-government or shall they be kept under the superintendence of missionaries? Shall the church accept money from governments for the support of its religious education?

This large number of problems has been cited—and the list could have been greatly extended—in order to indicate the meagerness of the social teachings of Jesus and the prophets if they are to be regarded as definitive prescriptions calling simply for obedience. No wonder that many persons have turned away from these teachings in disappointment, finding in them so little that seemed to be of help in the pressing and difficult questions of modern life.

But not only is literalism inadequate, it is also misleading. There are, to be sure, certain teachings of the prophets and of Jesus which could be transferred bodily to modern conditions, but lifted out of their original social situations they become strangely unfitted to our life. Men have made sad errors in this process. The glorious promise of divine illumination in time of need has led to contempt for what was regarded as the pride of human learning; schools have therefore been abolished. The manifest fact that the state is not organized in strict accordance with the teachings of Jesus has led men to conclude that any participation in the duties of citizenship would involve disloyalty; they have therefore withdrawn from all political interest and effort. The biblical teachings have been employed to justify human slavery, and the manufacture, use, and sale of wines; and they are undoubtedly susceptible of such literal interpretation. Men have defended religious persecution from an urgent word of Jesus (Luke 14. 23). They have refused a woman divorce from a brutal husband, in obedience to what they supposed was his command. Churches have regarded themselves as derived from Christ and have excommunicated all others. The words and example of Jesus have been supposed to dignify mendicancy and to permit pauperism. No wonder that flippant men have said that anything could be proved from the Bible, and that earnest men have sometimes turned sadly away, convinced that the old meager Hebrew life had little to contribute to the great needs of to-day.

The words and deeds of Jesus and of the prophets give us very little to obey. But is obedience the prime need of a free spirit? They give us little to copy in slavish imitation. But is the mechanical reproduction of the acts of another the best means for the development of vigorous personality? We are not in need of directions but of inspiration. If we ever get the right motives, our own intelligence will determine the most valuable methods. We cannot transfer the Palestine of the prophets and of Jesus to the American continent, but we can acquire the social attitude of those who lived God's life among their fellow men.

A suggestive illustration may be found in our modern architecture. A superficial observer would find little in common between the sky line of New York from the harbor and the acropolis of Athens, little similarity between Michigan Avenue in Chicago and the Roman Forum. But, in fact, the stately architecture of the great structures which express the genius of our modern commercial accomplishment is directly inspired by the superb masterpieces of the ancient world. The careful student will find essential unity and genuine development where the casual observer will see only utter dissimilarity.

We cannot place Jesus and the prophets in a modern city and seek to follow their sandaled feet into our ways of duty. But we may go back and live with them in their social life; we may take the pains to understand their social situation; we may learn how they met the problems that confronted them; and in the process of understanding their social teachings to their day we shall find our motives purified, our eyes opened, our minds stirred with vital suggestions for our tasks.

§ 2. The Abiding Significance of Justice and Love

If we have been successful in our endeavor to reproduce in imagination the life of Israel, we have certainly discovered our kinship with those men of the old time. Amid far-reaching differences of social organization and tradition we have felt the same fundamental needs that they felt. The only hope for society is that men shall be just and loving one to another. Of course abstractly everyone will accept this proposition. It may seem to reduce our study to a commonplace. But when we understand the social teachings of Jesus and the prophets, justice and love cease to be abstractions and become definite contributions to the problems of ordinary life.

There is always danger that these noble social attitudes shall be identified with legality and charity and so be emasculated of their worth. Jesus and the prophets were not much concerned with legality. Conduct might easily be legal and unjust at the same time. It might even be just and illegal at the same time. Justice is no very simple matter. It is not to be settled by nice judicial decisions. The "square deal" is not to be determined by precedents. To the prophets every unfair and ungenerous advantage taken of another was injustice. That is why they denounced the taking of interest. That was really the basis of the humane provisions for the treatment of slaves and foreigners. Deuteronomy reminded the people that they themselves had been slaves and foreigners, and should therefore know how such must feel. So the Sabbath rest was a right which must be accorded to the toiler, and sharing good things with the alien was a right that he must receive. Many duties which no law could require are demanded by a fine sense of justice.

It is sometimes thought that Jesus did not speak of justice. But his Golden Rule was the finest of all definitions of justice. It lifts it entirely beyond legal quibble. The question is not what I must do and what the law requires, but what would seem to me to be fair if I were in the place of the other. It is a wonderful appeal to the social imagination, which is, after all, the basis of real justice. When we get that attitude we do not need specific directions. The whole problem of social justice is illuminated. We are not concerned with keeping within the law; we are not asking what the traffic will bear; we are not talking about a labor market, as if the price of men were regulated like the price of sheep; we do not form unions for the purpose of limiting the number of skilled workmen; we do not make might the standard of international obligation. The Golden Rule is a noble, generous justice, which has a magic power to simplify social problems, and bring people together in mutual accord. The study of the social teachings of Jesus and the prophets should make men's hearts burn within them in a passionate longing to make our social life equitable.

But even justice, great as it is, may be subsumed under the greater ideal of love. It is not correct to say that the prophets teach justice, while Jesus teaches love. The prophets constantly emphasize the love of neighbor, loving sympathy with the needy, the poor, the fatherless, and the widow, sometimes even with the foreigner. The development of legislation under the prophetic leadership showed an increasing humanitarianism. Their demand for justice was more emphatic because of the flagrant social evils that confronted them. But in the great summary of Mic 6. 8 love stands with justice as the supreme demand of God. Jesus spoke rather of love than of justice because he included a generous justice in his idea of love.

As justice does not mean legality, so love does not mean charity. The prophets never urged that contributions should be made to the victims of social injustice. While Jesus spoke much of giving to the poor, for that was the one means of social service available, he emphasized ever the personal relationship. The neighbor is not only to be fed; he is also to be loved. The parable of neighborliness shows personal service to the wounded traveler, not the mere giving of money. Jesus's idea of forgiveness was not merely charitable; it was generous, as that of the father to the prodigal. The kind of service that he sought for the least of men was the kind of service that one would give to his Lord. That the phrase "cold as charity" should ever have been possible shows how far conventional charity has traveled from the ideal of Jesus. We need ever to kindle our social service at the glowing altar of his love of men. He conceives of love in terms of the family. It is not a mere pity for poor unfortunates. It is an active, confident endeavor for persons who are to be aided in achieving their best.

There is another danger that justice and love will be misunderstood. They may be regarded as alternatives. From this danger, a very definite one in our time, the study of Jesus and the prophets may save us. How often men have seemed to think that God required of them to do justly *or* to love kindness. The social attitude of fairness is coming to be recognized among us. There is much talk of duty. There are men who are veritable apostles of justice. But there may be no love in it. There may be no gifts, no forgiveness, no kindness, no personal relation. We may offer to give men their dues, but we do not give them ourselves. We may pay good wages and all the rest, but it is a mere matter of business. The young ruler who came to Jesus had always done his duty. He had never learned the generosity of giving.

More easy, and perhaps more subtly dangerous, is the social attitude of generosity without justice. Men will give away whole fortunes, but will stand for their legal rights to the utmost. Great philanthropists are often vigorous opponents of social reform. Unscrupulous politicians are sometimes most generous men. Predatory institutions often give largely to charity. These are not necessarily hypocrites. Actuated by a genuine desire to do right, they choose the easier way of charity rather than the more difficult way of justice. But justice and love are complementary social attitudes. Justice democratizes love, saving it from becoming aristocratic and patronizing, which is its chief danger. Love humanizes justice, saving it from becoming grudgingly exact, which is its besetting fault.

Whenever we achieve in any adequate measure the social attitudes of justice and love, and seriously attack any social problem from such point of view, we find that we do not need specific directions from the Bible. The ideals of Jesus and the prophets come over and take their fitting shape in our modern situation. We know the truth and the truth makes us free.

§ 3. Jesus as the Ideally Socialized Personality

We are in the process of socialization. Such an institution as the family is sometimes socialized to a high degree. Each member lives for the good of the whole. Each regards the others as ends, not as means. Each identifies his own welfare with that of the group. The idea of exploitation is entirely absent. To the extent that this attitude obtains we recognize the true family. On the other hand, our business life is only partially socialized. Minor groups often seek their own advantage at the expense of other groups. The process of exploitation is carried on to a considerable extent. Employees and customers are often regarded entirely as means. Sometimes an individual utterly desocializes himself by putting up his own advantage against the welfare of all others. This is, of course, most clearly manifest in the criminal class.

The true socialization of the individual has taken place when, regarding himself as an end—that is, a being whose good is worthy to be sought—he regards all other persons also as ends, never using anyone simply as a means, and finds his own welfare in the welfare of every group to which in any wise he belongs, even the great human group in its entirety.

It is manifestly very difficult for one person to be socialized where others are not. The individual is likely to take the degree of socialization which his group has reached. He is also likely to achieve varying degrees of socialization according to the different groups to which he belongs. Thus within his family he may be one type of person, in the church group he may be somewhat different, in the business group very different, in the club group different again. It is quite possible to be a generous sacrificial family man, a domineering church member, a grasping man of business, and an easygoing social companion. Many other combinations are equally possible.

Socialization beyond the attainment of one's group is moral leadership. It is because men have been able thus to transcend the limits attained by their neighbors that moral progress has been made. But only in rare cases do individuals far transcend the socialization of their fellows. For example, it would be almost unthinkable among ourselves that a man should wish to pay a larger tax than the law requires, simply on the ground that he felt that he was not contributing his full share to the common good. It would scarcely be considered a worthy thing for a man to endeavor to win back to his home a wife who had been unfaithful.

The moral achievement of Jesus was that he exhibited the complete social attitude in all relationships. The love that seems to us so natural for our kin he actually felt toward all kinds of people. The sacrificial interest in another's welfare which seems to us the glory of the maternal love, Jesus felt for the people who were willing to crucify him (Matt 23. 37). The comradeship that we enjoy with our equals Jesus enjoyed with those who were considered outcasts (Matt 9. 10ff.). His Golden Rule is the perfect expression of socialization, for it sets the standard of one's own sense of personality as that by which one's attitude toward others is to be measured.

Jesus is often called the perfect Man. This must not be understood as an unearthly kind of absolute morality which separates him from human experience. We approach more readily an appreciation of his unique personality when we realize the simplicity of his moral achievement as that of normal social relations with all kinds of people on the basis of his own relationship with God and his estimate of God's relationship with men. To describe this achievement as simple is not to indicate that it is easy. It is, indeed, infinitely difficult. But there is nothing unhuman, unnatural about it.

It is the eminently human, natural, rational way to live. The socialized man is the normal man, the real human type, for he alone has the social imagination and sympathy that allow him to live to the full the human life in all its social possibilities. Thus Jesus is for us and for all generations the *norm.* Not that we shall imitate his acts, or even literally obey his words, but that we shall realize his attitude. We shall think of other men, feel toward them, act toward them, with the same sense of kinship and social reciprocity which he displayed.

It needs only a moment of imagination to realize what a marvelously efficient society we should have if we all had the spirit of Jesus. Family life, education, science, politics, the mastery of the physical world, the conquest of human ills would proceed with a most extraordinary vigor. The splendid faith of Jesus would be vindicated, "Seek ye first the kingdom of God and his righteousness, and all these things shall be added unto you."

§4. The Social Task of To-day

In the light of the social teachings of Jesus and the prophets our social task of to-day is four fold:

1. The social experience of the prophets and of Jesus was dependent upon their religious experience. The sense of the God of righteousness and love was the impelling power of all their efforts. It is for us to see that religion and social sympathy are never separated. It is our primary task so to present religion to ourselves, to our children, to all persons interested in religion that the social experience of Jesus shall be as impelling to them as his religious experience. The zeal for human welfare must become a passion. We must learn that he who loveth not man, whom he has seen, cannot love God, whom he has not seen. This is the social gospel. This is the task of religious education for adults as well as for children.

2. The social gospel, that God loves men and that men

ought to love God and to love one another, must be a propaganda. Men must be won in large numbers to desire to be partakers of the religious and social experience of Jesus. This is the good news of the Kingdom. Our social task is to let men know that they may actually live in the likeness of God through a spiritual companionship with him, and may express that likeness in social justice and love toward their fellows. This is the task of that larger and more significant evangelism which is so greatly needed to-day. It is the call to men to repent of their selfishness and ungodlikeness, for the kingdom of God is near and needs their help.

3. Our social task is a painstaking, continuous, scientific effort to understand the problems of modern society. Jesus and the prophets have not performed for us our scientific work. What wages ought to be paid, how industry ought to be organized, upon what tenure land shall be held—these and a thousand other questions are not susceptible of religious answer. They are scientific questions only to be understood by study, investigation, experiment. The fundamental prerequisite to such a study is a willingness to know the truth, a longing for justice and love to prevail—in a word, the social attitude of Jesus. Scientific social investigation, inspired by the spirit of Jesus, so that progressively we may learn how to live our modern life together, is the task of to-day.

4. As we discover from time to time opportunities of social amelioration, possibilities of improvement in industry, in education, in correction, in government, we must put these into operation just so far as may be possible in a society composed of persons of varying degrees of socialization. We cannot inaugurate the kingdom of God by amending the constitution. We have the practical problems of our complex, heterogeneous population. We must do the best thing that is possible. The public efforts of the whole community will never be equal to the social ideals

of the most highly socialized members of the community. Part of our social task is the exhibition of the patience of Jesus in securing the best results that we can with the men of limited vision with whom we must cooperate. It is an untiring effort to bring the community to the acceptance of better things. This is the work of practical philanthropy and reform.

APPENDIX

BOOKS FOR REFERENCE

The following list is intended to include only the most serviceable books to be used in connection with this study.

Josephus, Complete Works.

The Apocrypha, Revised Version.

Hastings's Dictionary of the Bible. Five volumes. Charles Scribner's Sons, New York.

J. E. McFadyen: Introduction to the Old Testament. New York, A. C. Armstrong & Son.

S. R. Driver: Introduction to the Literature of the Old Testament. New York, Charles Scribner's Sons.

B. W. Bacon: An Introduction to the New Testament. New York, The Macmillan Company.

James Moffatt: Introduction to the Literature of the New Testament. New York, Charles Scribner's Sons.

R. Kittel: History of the Hebrews. Two Volumes. London, Williams & Norgate.

H. P. Smith: Old Testament History. New York, Charles Scribner's Sons.

C. H. Cornill: The Rise of the People of Israel. Chicago, Open Court Publishing Company.

C. H. Cornill: History of the People of Israel. Chicago, Open Court Publishing Company.

C. F. Kent: A History of the Hebrew People. Two Volumes. A History of the Jewish People. New York, Charles Scribner's Sons.

J. S. Riggs: A History of the Jewish People. New York, Charles Scribner's Sons.

W. Robertson Smith: The Religion of the Semites. London, A. & C. Black.

George Adam Smith: The Historical Geography of the Holy Land. New York, A. C. Armstrong & Son.

R. H. Charles: Religious Development between the Old and New Testaments. New York, Henry Holt & Co.

Shailer Mathews: The History of New Testament Times in Palestine. New York, The Macmillan Company.

Stevens and Burton: A Harmony of the Gospels. New York, Charles Scribner's Sons.

Alfred Edersheim: The Life and Times of Jesus the Messiah. London, Longmans, Green & Co.

Emil Schürer: A History of the Jewish People in the Time of Jesus Christ. Five Volumes. New York, Charles Scribner's Sons.

G. H. Gilbert: Jesus. New York, The Macmillan Company.

C. H. Cornill: The Culture of Ancient Israel. Chicago, Open Court Publishing Company.

Edward Day: The Social Life of the Hebrews. New York, Charles Scribner's Sons.

G. M. Mackie: Bible Manners and Customs. New York, Fleming H. Revell Company.

H. B. Tristram: Eastern Customs in Bible Lands. New York, Thomas Whitaker.

Alfred Edersheim: Sketches of Jewish Social Life. London, Religious Tract Society.

S. Angus: The Environment of Early Christianity. New York, Charles Scribner's Sons.

H. Clay Trumbull: The Blood Covenant. Philadelphia, John D. Wattles.

H. Clay Trumbull: Studies in Oriental Social Life. Philadelphia, John D. Wattles.

W. Robertson Smith: The Prophets of Israel. New York, D. Appleton & Co.

G. G. Findlay: The Books of the Prophets. Three Volumes. London, Robert Culley.

C. H. Cornill: The Prophets of Israel. Chicago, Open Court Publishing Company.

L. W. Batten: The Hebrew Prophet. New York, The Macmillan Company.

J. M. Powis Smith: The Prophet and his Problems. New York, Charles Scribner's Sons.

W. T. Davison: The Praises of Israel. London, Charles H. Kelly.

W. T. Davison: The Wisdom Literature of the Old Testament. London, Charles H. Kelly.

H. G. Mitchell: The Ethics of the Old Testament. The University of Chicago Press.

H. H. Wendt: The Teaching of Jesus. Two Volumes. New York, Charles Scribner's Sons.

George B. Stevens: The Teaching of Jesus. New York, The Macmillan Company.

H. C. King: The Ethics of Jesus. New York, The Macmillan Company.

Shailer Mathews: The Social Teachings of Jesus. New York, The Macmillan Company.
W. N. Clarke: The Ideal of Jesus. New York, Charles Scribner's Sons.
A. B. Bruce: The Kingdom of God. New York, Charles Scribner's Sons.
F. G. Peabody: Jesus Christ and the Social Question. New York, The Macmillan Company.
F. G. Peabody: Jesus Christ and Christian Character. New York, The Macmillan Company.
Samuel G. Smith: Religion in the Making. New York, The Macmillan Company.